P9-CDV-617

The Color of Our Future

Also by Farai Chideya

Don't Believe the Hype:
Fighting Cultural Misinformation About African Americans

The
Color
of Our
Future

Farai
Chideya

NEW HANOVER COUNTY
PUBLIC LIBRARY
201 CHESTNUT STREET
WILMINGTON, N. C. 28401

William Morrow and Company, Inc.
New York

Copyright © 1999 by Farai Chideya

All rights reserved. No part of this book may be reproduced
or utilized in any form or by any means, electronic or
mechanical, including photocopying, recording, or by any information
storage or retrieval system, without permission in writing from
the Publisher. Inquiries should be addressed to
Permissions Department, William Morrow and Company, Inc.,
1350 Avenue of the Americas,
New York, N.Y. 10019.

It is the policy of William Morrow and Company, Inc., and its
imprints and affiliates, recognizing the importance of
preserving what has been written, to print the books we publish
on acid-free paper, and we exert our best efforts to that end.

Library of Congress Cataloging-in-Publication Data has been
applied for.

ISBN 0-688-16530-3

Printed in the United States of America

First Edition

1 2 3 4 5 6 7 8 9 10

BOOK DESIGN BY JENNIFER ANN DADDIO

www.williammorrow.com

TO THE NEXT GENERATION:

Shed the prejudices of the past
while sharing history's lessons.
Forge the America of tomorrow, today.

Acknowledgments

Thank you to everyone who has helped me. This book has taken me over three years to complete, and countless people have helped me sort through this complex topic.

First of all, thank you to all of my interview subjects. Without your openness and honesty, this book could never have happened.

A toast to Claire Wachtel (my editor) and Charles Flowers, who helped rescue this book when I was ready to give up. Kudos to my agents Charlotte Sheedy and Neeti Madan. And thanks to Leigh Haber, who originally bought the book.

Now to the people who sustain me always: friends and family. The greatest thanks to my mother, Cynthia Chideya (I keep trying to get her to write her own book!); my sister, Sekai Chideya; my grandmother, Mary Stokes; and everyone else in my U.S. family who keep me centered. My father, Lucas Chideya, is quite a character, and he no doubt has contributed to my character. To all of my family from Zimbabwe, especially Uncle Israel and Munyaradzi.

Big ups to all of my friends across the United States and throughout my life: Polly, Cindy, Julie, Deidre, and everyone from school in Baltimore . . . Pam and all of my friends from college . . . and to all of my friends in New York, across the country, and across the oceans. (That includes John, Marcelle, Justin, Marcus, Susan, Hewitt, Paula, Winifred, and Tavis. Some of you are mentioned in the first chapter, and I'm only going to get into trouble if I try to name you all.)

To my mentors, especially Mark Starr. To my past and present colleagues at *Newsweek*, MTV, CNN, *Vibe*, *Time*, and ABC. I have learned and continue to learn so much from you. Special thanks to Kate O'Brian, Diane Sawyer, Michelle Genece, Caitlin Nobile, Nelli Kheyfets, Sherry Berman, Marney Hochman, Jen Gonnerman, Rob Kenner, Walter Isaacson, and Gail Evans and everyone in the CNN political unit.

To all of my research assistants. There have been too many to mention but they include Nicole Childers, Anthony Duignan-Cabrera, Dalton Jones, Joceleyn Boryczka, Darcel Rockett, Ericka Blount, and Laura DeNey.

To all of the people I admire who have reached out to me, including Jonathan Kozol, Aretha Franklin, Maxine Waters, and Walter Moseley.

To "study breaks," especially the WELL and any kind of music that makes you shake your groove thang!

To City Year, Do Something, Wasatch, the East Harlem Tutorial Program, Habitat for Humanity, and all the other groups trying to make a difference.

And to you—thanks for reading!

Contents

III. The Political as Personal

IV. Predictions and Prescriptions

I

The New Face of Race

ONE

Race Right Now

America is a chameleon. A land populated by hundreds of Indian tribes became home to European settlers seeking religious freedom and economic opportunity. As the number of those settlers grew, the Native American population shrank—plagued by new diseases and pushed by the immigrants to ever-smaller plots of land. The European immigrants reinvented themselves as a nation, calling themselves Americans, and setting themselves and their country apart from their European forebears. These European Americans introduced yet another population to this land: the Africans who came—not all, but nearly so—as slaves.

When America was formally founded in 1776, it was already a multiracial nation, though few at the time would ever have thought to call it that. America is fundamentally different from most other cultures. For centuries, Europe had its nation-tribes: the Germans, the French, the Celts. So did Africa and Asia, where today's societies have grown out of ones that have existed for millennia. America was not homegrown but born out of the arrival of different peoples on an already-populated continent. The interactions between English and French settlers, blacks and whites, whites and Native Americans made America what it is today. We can't understand America without first understanding it as a cross section of cultures.

Over time, the blood of many whites, blacks, and Native Americans mingled. And the Mexicans who settled the West and Southwest had already formed their own mixture as well, Spanish and Indian blending into mestizos. As America took control of Mexican lands in California, Texas, and the Southwest, the nation became even more diverse. The thousands of Chinese immigrants who came to the United States in the mid-1800s to build the transcontinental railroad eventually settled in West Coast cities like San Francisco, though Chinese immigration was later curtailed by law. And on the East Coast, the turn of the century saw a great wave of European immigration, itself quite diverse: Jewish, Greek, Russian, Polish, Irish, Italian.

Trying to encapsulate America's history is probably foolish, and always controversial. But in order to understand where we are today, we have to try to find some common understanding of the past. America's "founding fathers" may have been white, but this nation never was populated or built by just one race. It's more critical than ever that we remember this, given the massive transformation our society is about to undergo.

America the chameleon is changing colors once again. Today, thanks to demographics, we can gaze into our future—one far different from our racial past. According to the U.S. Bureau of the Census, we're entering a century in which race in America will be turned upside down. By the middle of that century, whites will be a minority, and minorities will be in the majority.

A "Majority-Minority" America

In 1950, America was nearly 85 percent non-Hispanic white.[1] Today, this nation is 73 percent non-Hispanic white, 12 percent black, 11 percent Hispanic, 3 percent Asian, and 1 percent Native American.[2] (To put it another way, we're about three-quarters white and one-quarter minority.) But America's racial composition is changing more rapidly than ever. The number of immigrants in America is the largest in any post–World War II period. Nearly one-tenth of the U.S. population is foreign born.[3] Asian Americans, the fastest-growing group in America, have begun to come politically of age in California and the Pacific Northwest (where a Chinese American is governor of Washington State).[4] And the Census Bureau projects that the number of Latino Americans will surpass blacks as the largest nonwhite group by 2005.[5]

There's a much larger change looming for America. Around the year 2050, whites will become a minority.[6] This is uncharted territory for this country, and this demographic change will affect everything. Alliances between the races are bound to shift. Political and social power will be reapportioned. Our neighborhoods, our schools and workplaces, even racial categories themselves will be altered. Any massive social change is bound to bring uncertainty, even fear. But the worst crisis we face today is not in our cities or neighborhoods, but in our minds. We have grown up with a fixed idea of what and who America is, and how race relations in this nation work. We live by two assumptions: that race is a black and white issue, and that America is a white society. Neither has ever been strictly true, and today these ideas are rapidly becoming obsolete.

Our idea of "Americanness" has always been linked with "whiteness," from tales of the Pilgrims forward. We still see the equation of white/American every day in movies and on television (where shows like *Mad About You*, set in majority-minority New York, have no nonwhite main characters). We witness it in the making of social policy. (The U.S. Senate is only 4 percent nonwhite—though over 20 percent of the country is.)[7] We make casual assumptions about who belongs in this society and who is an outsider. (Just ask the countless American-born Asians and Latinos who've been complimented on how well they speak English.)

"Whiteness" would not exist, of course, without something against which to define itself. That thing is "blackness." Slavery was the forging crucible of American racial identity, setting up the black-white dichotomy from which we have never broken free. The landmarks of American history are intimately intertwined with these racial conflicts—the Civil War, Jim Crow, the Civil Rights movement. But today, even as America becomes more diverse, the media still depicts the world largely in black and white. The dramas and sitcoms we watch are so segregated that the top ten shows in black households and the top ten shows in white households barely overlap.[8] Or examine the news media. The three-year-long coverage of the O. J. Simpson trials portrayed a nation riven by the black/white color line. And when *Nightline* did a first-rate series on race, it still didn't cover the true range of diversity but "America in Black and White." Race is almost always framed as bipolar—the children of slaves versus the children of slaveowners—even when the issues impact Asians, Latinos, and Native Americans as well. School segregation, job integration—they're covered in black and white. Political rivalries, dating trends, income inequalities—they're covered as two-sided dilemmas as well. For all the time we spend talking about black and white, the only thing we can agree on is that we disagree. Affirmative action: equal opportunity or reverse racism? Afrocentrism: black pride or hatred of whites? The entire race debate becomes nothing more than a shouting match, a sort of *McLaughlin Group* gone awry.

Everyone gets exposed to media images of race. Americans who have never met an immigrant from China or Mexico will doubtless have seen their images on the nightly news and formed an opinion about immigration from those images. Kids who have never met an African American will learn about slavery in school, listen to rap or R & B, and read an article on welfare reform or the NBA. It's only human nature to put together those pieces and try to synthesize an idea of what it means to be black. The media and pop culture have such a tremendous power in our society because we use them to tell us what the rest of the society is like, and how we should react to it. The problem is that, too often, the picture we're getting is out of kilter.

If you're not black and not white, you're not very likely to be seen. According to a study by the Center for Media and Public Affairs, the proportion of Latino characters on prime-time television actually dropped from 3 percent in the 1950s to 1 percent in the 1980s, even as the Latino population rapidly grew.[9] Asian Americans are even harder to find in entertainment, in the news, or on the national agenda, and Native Americans rarer still. How we perceive race, and how it's depicted in print and on television, has less to do with demographic reality than our mind-set. In the basest and most stereotypic terms, white Americans are considered "true" Americans; black Americans are considered inferior Americans; Asians and Latinos are too often considered foreigners; and Native Americans are rarely thought of at all.

America can't move into the future if we as a society don't acknowledge who we are. But I can't chastise people for buying into the vision of a black and white America—after all, that's where I grew up.

Jews, Grits, Blacks, and Niggers

Race is probably the most tangible and subjective force in our lives, dependent not on biology as we'd like to claim, but on our perceptions of color, class, age, and place. My first perceptions of race were formed in Baltimore, Maryland. When I grew up, and where I grew up, there were three basic races of people: black, white, and Jewish. I attended Baltimore City Public Schools from the mid-seventies through the mid-eighties, or, to demarcate it the way my politically aware family might, roughly from the start of President Carter's term through the end of President Reagan's.

Like many cities with a majority-black population, Baltimore had a school system that was *really* black. Lots of white parents sent their kids to private schools, or at least made sure they got into majority-white public ones. I started first grade at Mordecai Gist Elementary, three blocks from my house. Like the residents of our Forest Park neighborhood, a working- and middle-class area with shingled single-family homes, the student body was all black. Forest Park used to be mostly Jewish—filmmaker Barry Levinson, singer Mama Cass and novelist Leon Uris all attended the high school named for the tree-lined nabe. But by the time my family moved in in 1975, the Jewish families were all gone.

For second through sixth grades, I went to the Gifted and Talented Education (GATE) program at Harford Heights Elementary School. Harford Heights was deep in the 'hood, a hulking gray brick edifice that housed nearly three thousand students, most of them black. But GATE, a magnet program that bused in talented students from around the city, was an oasis of racial diversity. At that time I was very, very dimly aware of the differences between Jewish students and the other whites. (For International Day, when students brought in food from other cultures, we got to eat a lot of latkes.) We even had two Mexican American brothers in GATE, a rarity not repeated the rest of my school years.

By junior high (at Falstaff Middle School) and especially during high school, the black/white/Jewish distinctions were accepted as common knowledge. Western High, another magnet school, is one of only two all-girl public high schools left in the nation. Our student body, once all-white, was just over half black. It would have had even fewer white students had the school not had such a good reputation. Though it claimed to wrap itself in a mantle of general excellence, the school used tracking to separate kids it deemed high achievers from the rest of the lot. "A" course kids got to take the really challenging classes like calculus and AP English, and virtually all of the Jewish students at the school attended the "A" course. They dressed preppy or artsy and lived in the wealthier neighborhoods. Some of their moms and dads were professors at Johns Hopkins, and several of the students drove their own cars instead of taking the bus. My friends and I used to call them the Cross Keys Girls, because even though we were supposed to have a closed campus, they mysteriously got to sneak out and go have lunch at the nearby ritzy shopping center Cross Keys.

The real "white" students, as we saw them, were Christian and mostly working class. They wore hard-rock T-shirts and faded corduroys, had bilevel haircuts with fringed Farrah Fawcett wings. Our unkind name for them was "grits." Most of the white students had a classic "Bawlamer" accent, a city-specific twanginess rooted in Appalachia. (I won't attempt to fully explain the Bawlamer accent, but rent an early John Waters movie for a full demonstration.) Most of the black students, if they had an accent at all, had a slight Southern drawl and possibly Ebonics-afied grammar shaping their speech.

I'll always remember a conversation I had freshman year with a girl in my class. Donna was a pretty, doe-eyed girl who looked the way *Friends* star Courtney Cox did back when she got to run up on stage in Bruce Springsteen's video. One day in homeroom we all started talking about race. Donna said her grandfather had been telling her about black people—more precisely, the difference between "black people" and "niggers." Needless to say, I joined several of my classmates in vociferously protesting "nigger" as a valid racial category. I calmly explained that the word "nigger" was a slur with no parallel in other racial groups, not even "white trash." "Nigger" is the all-American trump card, the nuclear bomb of racial epithets. It's slavery and Jim Crow, spit on your face and all the stories your grandpa ever told you. (Perhaps that's one reason why young blacks have seized on the term so fiercely. The only way they can dissipate the bomb's power is to hug it tightly to their chest and implode.)

I told Donna that rather than calling someone a "nigger," she should just chalk them up as a lazy, violent, or hostile black person, the same way we'd talk about a lazy, violent, or hostile white person. (Of course at the same time I was speaking with such enlightenment, I was thinking, "Grit! Grit!!!!")

Donna was genuinely sweet, one of the girls who bridged the black/ white clumping that typified even our open-minded homeroom. Our little debate didn't produce any lasting tensions. I didn't even think about it until three years later, when we were signing each other's yearbooks. I wrote a quick one liner about "staying cool" in hers, while Donna wrote a long passage thanking me for teaching her about race and changing her ideas and opinions. When I read what she'd written, I felt both proud and schmucky (for underestimating her sensitivity).

Perhaps because we were in the majority, Western's black students, who stuck together at least as much as the Jewish girls and "grits" did, had no one stereotype. Black girls could be preppy, athletic, or rough. They could belong to the Fashionettes (yes, that was an official club) or even a tough, stylish lesbian clique called the Pony Girls. Artsy, nerdy misfits like myself were a relative rarity among the black students. To top it off, my two best friends were Cindy, the daughter of Chinese immigrants who ran a restaurant downtown; and Polly, the child of white activists, who had an adopted black-biracial sister. Our clique, if you could call it that, was probably the most unusual in the school.

I didn't fit any of the typical stereotypes, either racial or class-based. I grew up intellectually, but not financially, privileged. My father, a Zimbabwean immigrant, met my mother in graduate school at Syracuse University. They married in my mother's hometown of Baltimore; spent two years in Zambia, where my mother was a newspaper reporter; and then, after I was born, settled into a middle-class lifestyle in New York City. My dad worked for AT&T. My mother freelanced a bit, concentrating on raising me and my younger sister. I went to a private kindergarten on the East Side and played in Central Park. When I was six, my family moved to Baltimore, my parents divorced, and my mom got a job as a medical technologist. I challenge any MBA to make a salary stretch as far as hers did: a mortgage on a four-bedroom house and upkeep of a rickety, beloved Volkswagen Beetle we occasionally had to push to get started; clothes that were often handmade or used; and, where others would splurge on new wardrobes, tuition to academic summer camps.

I find it hard to judge whether my childhood was circumscribed by race and class, or partially freed from it. My mother, who'd grown up akin to the way I did—without much money but with lots of books—

went off to college and then to Morocco with the Peace Corps before meeting my father. As I grew, she constantly broadened the world for me with books, history, and stories of her own life. But while her efforts to keep me on course academically worked admirably, her efforts to broaden my understanding of race and culture could only go so far. I was a lower-middle-income girl growing up in a virtually all black neighborhood, and to me, Baltimore—and the world as I knew it—was split between black, Jewish, and white.

Race Is How (and Where) We See It

I'm the first to admit my perceptions of race then—and my perceptions of race now—were and are subjective. Yes, my high school perceptions were based in fact: blacks, Christian working-class whites and Jewish Americans each make up huge chunks of Baltimore's population. But once I moved away from Baltimore to go to college at Harvard, I began to realize that everyday racial categories are our own constructions.

When I showed up at Harvard, I went from a city that is majority-black to one where blacks are less than 20 percent of the population, and some still get called "nigger" to their face. (I did, just once, and that was more than enough for me.) Boston's Irish Americans are as strong a subcategory of "white" as Baltimore's Jewish community, their racial status shaped by residential isolation and poverty in much the way that black identity is. But even though I got to see Boston's neighborhoods, I spent most of my time on campus in Cambridge. I bonded immediately with my funky-fresh freshman roommate Pam Ling—later known to teens and twentysomethings worldwide as "that girl on MTV's *The Real World*" (San Francisco cast). We stayed roommates for all four years, and senior year ended up in a rooming group we jokingly called the U.N. There was Mirka (Puerto Rican), Lucy (white, from a wealthy family and raised partially in England), Lena (white, from working-class Pensacola, Florida), Pam (Chinese American), and me. In high school, I thought that having a diverse group of friends was just happenstance. But in college I started thinking, okay, maybe this time it isn't a fluke. Maybe being friends with people of different races is part of the way I choose to live.

Right after college I moved to New York, where I live today. Two of my close friends and former roommates, Elaine Chen and Tanya Selvaratnam, are Chinese American and Sri Lankan–born American, respectively. Others are black biracial, including my friends Isolde Brielmaier and Danzy Senna, who has written a novel on the subject. (Isolde also happens to be half African, like several of my friends. Some, like Isolde, are biracial; others are, like myself, half African and half black American.) And then there are my Caribbean-born black friends, and my white friends (Jewish and gentile, haute WASP and working class), and the many, many folks who are black Americans, just like me.

I know I'm the exception to the rule. Most of us live and work in a multiracial America, but we socialize with "our own," whether that means segregating by race or class or both. The fact of the matter is, most of us hate being minorities of any kind, and we retreat to a place where people *are* like us and (we presume) *will* like us. Being with "our own" isn't in and of itself a bad impulse. I couldn't imagine life without a black family, culture, and community. That is who raised me; that is who I think about first in the racial debates; that is who continues to support me most enthusiastically in my life and my career.

But my mother (who would take me and my sister, for example, to the Greek festival to go folk dancing) taught me that it's important to cross the culture barrier as well. I've gone to the South Asian festival of lights, the Deepavali, with my friend Tanya, and I've gone to Kwaanza celebrations in Harlem. I'm probably one of the few black women in the universe who's seen both the thrash metal band Slayer and, later, the rapper Snoop Doggy Dogg in concert. I've spoken at the National Association of Black Journalists convention, and also at the National Lesbian and Gay Journalists Association convention. It's not that I don't get flustered when I go "out-of-group." There are always potential misunderstandings and pitfalls. But to me, there's no better way to lead life than to try to see the fullness and the richness of many people's existence.

I go to brunches, dinners, and house parties where whites are absent or in the distinct minority. And of course—more frequently than I'd like—I find myself in a room where I'm the only person darker than a "flesh"-colored crayon. It's happened at holiday parties, rock concerts, conferences, and confabs of political analysts. I find it impossible to be in one of these situations without pondering the political subtext. Right now it's all the rage to talk about black "self-segregation"—the tendency of blacks, especially on college campuses, to hang together because they're supposedly anti-integration and antiwhite. But it's funny how the issue doesn't come up when I'm the only black person at a gathering. (Even if you chalk the divide up to socioeconomics, I'm hardly the only Ivy-educated, gainfully employed, media-savvy black person who could be invited to an event. I wonder if there's a quota where one is enough?) I suppose it would be downright impolite for me to carry around a sign saying, WHO'S SELF-SEGREGATING NOW?

The only way I can survive the race debates without becoming embattled or embittered is to try to truly understand the nation we live in. First, I tried to tackle the issue of black-white relations. I started working for *Newsweek* when I was nineteen years old, as a college intern in Boston. The bureau chief, a guy named Mark Starr whom I feel lucky to still count as a friend, took me under his wing and nurtured a real love for journalism. I started working at *Newsweek* full-time two weeks after my college graduation. That's where I learned the ropes and decided this was the career I wanted to pursue. But I also learned that the "objective" world of journalism was inevitably shaped by the (understandably human) biases of journalists. My coworkers asked me enough times what black America was like (or, worse, *told* me what black America was like) that I decided it would be in my best interest to definitively find out.

My first book, *Don't Believe the Hype*, paired media stereotypes of blacks with research and Census Bureau statistics shattering those stereotypes. On the one hand, a comprehensive study shows that 60 percent of network news about African Americans is negative in tone—depicting welfare dependency, criminals, and crime victims.[10] On the other, government statistics (hardly known for being favorable to blacks) show that blacks and whites have equal rates of drug use; blacks have a higher rate of receiving welfare but whites are the largest group on the rolls; and whites who live in socioeconomically isolated areas (white ghettos like Boston's "Southie") have the same crime rates as comparable blacks.[11] With *Don't Believe the Hype,* I was able to take my intuition that the media was stereotyping black America and mark it down as hard fact. (Yet one story I constantly hear from people my age is that when they read parts of the book to their parents, their parents react with disbelief. They tell their children that the statistics on blacks I've found just *can't* be true. Racism *can't* still be a big factor in American life, and, well, aren't the tables now turned against whites? If what I said *was* true, then my friends' parents would have to reevaluate how comfortable they've been with their own passive role in America's racial dramas.)

Now, over the past couple of years, I've been rethinking race from a multiethnic perspective. I've been trying to understand how close (or far) my personal perceptions are to some larger reality. I don't discount the fact that I'm the kind of person who chooses to cross culture barriers, or that I'm living in New York, one of the most ethnically mixed cities in the world. But I do know that my experience of race has broadened from a purely black and white view to one that encompasses more knowledge of Asians, Latinos, and others, both native- and foreign-born.

The Color of the Millennium

Our notions of race depend heavily on our age, our generation. When I decided to write about America's racial future, the first question was how to approach a topic this huge. I didn't want to write just a statistical analysis of race, nor did I want to do a memoir, relating racial issues purely from my own experiences. I wanted to combine a bit of both approaches with what I found the most compelling: real life stories of

Americans who epitomize the changes we're going through. Even that was far too big a canvas, so I decided to focus in on one group: America's young adults.

The future will be created by the Millennium Generation, today's fifteen- to twenty-five-year-olds. They are the most racially mixed generation this nation has ever seen—the face of the new America. As a group, they are 60 percent more likely to be nonwhite than their parent and grandparent generations, those Americans baby boom–aged and older. No less than one-third of young Americans aged fifteen to twenty-five are black, Latino, Asian, or Native American.[12] While the older generations largely rely on the media to provide them with images of a multiethnic America, this generation is already living in it. The teens and twentysomethings of the Millennium Generation are the true experts on the future of race, because they're re-creating America's racial identity every single day.

The members of the Millennium Generation I interviewed for this book defy the easy racial stereotypes, as I found when I chose people to interview for this book. Take an issue as heated as illegal immigration— and the life of an Oakland teen named Diana. Serious and thoughtful, with hopes of going on to college, this Mexican immigrant has lived most of her life in California. She's more familiar with American culture (not to mention more articulate in English) than most teens. But she doesn't have a green card, and her chances of pursuing her college dreams seem slim. Her dad has a green card and two of her four siblings are U.S. citizens because they were born in the United States. Diana was born in Mexico. So, even though she came to the U.S. at the age of two, Diana will have a nearly impossible time getting citizenship unless she finds the money to hire an immigration lawyer to fight her case. It would be easy to think of Diana as some kind of anomaly, but she's not. Countless undocumented immigrants have spent the majority of their lives in this country. And in California alone, there are over a million residents who belong to families of mixed immigration status.

Another flashpoint is the battle over affirmative action. Berkeley student LaShunda Prescott could be portrayed as a case of affirmative action gone awry, a black student admitted to a school she wasn't ready for. An engineering student, LaShunda dropped out of Berkeley twice before graduating. But during that time she looked out for a drug-addicted sister, took care of one of the sister's children, and dealt with the death of one family member and the shooting of another. In context, her circuitous route through college is not a failure but a triumph.

LaShunda's schoolmate Steve Mohebi shows another side of the new racial dilemmas. The vice president of the Berkeley College Republicans, he defends, even promotes, recruiting in fraternities where "minorities are not welcome." What's new is not the sentiment, but the fact that Steve himself isn't even white. Nor is he black. He's Middle Eastern, a Persian immigrant.

The lives of people like Diana, LaShunda, and Steve are compass points on a map of America's complex social terrain. If we want to understand where America is headed, we've got to take a look at where this generation is today—and how they differ from the generations of the past.

The Generational Race Divide

For me, getting to know this generation—telling their stories and exploring their lives—is the ultimate assignment. It contains elements of everything I've been driven to cover as a reporter—politics, racial issues, youth, future trends. I started working for *Newsweek* magazine full-time just before I turned twenty-one. Since then I've worked for MTV News, CNN, *Vibe* magazine and ABC News. I've never done just the "race beat," but at every one of these very different institutions, I've managed to devote some of my time to covering America's greatest obsession.

I'm fascinated by race and ethnicity in America, the clash between old and new, nativeness and foreignness. At heart, I'm a collector of tales, the facts and trends that tell us who we are and what America is. Scouring newspapers and magazines, watching glossy network television programs and grubby public access shows, and talking to my friends and walking the nation's streets, I search out clues on American identity. Everything is fair game: politics, pop music, food, schools, hairstyles. Each snippet of information—from a Supreme Court decision on affirmative action to a dance craze like the macarena—is as bright and enticing as fruit dangling from a tree. As a reporter for ABC News and a writer for magazines, I hunt for the fruits that are ready to pick: the timely news stories. If there's a racial incident or a court case, it's easy for me to get my editors committed to a story. But sometimes the most interesting information about who we are has nothing to do with violence or lawsuits. A feature on bangra music (a fusion of Hindi songs and American pop and rap) would reveal a lot about the growth of the Indian and South Asian communities in America today. But that story may not seem compelling enough to sell to a wide audience. An article on how Tiger Woods exemplifies mixed-race identity, by contrast, has been done many times.

Some of the best stories about race in America are about America's youth as well. And the young Americans I have interviewed illustrate a fault line in the race debates that most of us don't even think about: a massive generation gap. On the one hand, America is led by baby boomers and people from the generations that came before them. These movers and shakers in government and industry came of age before and during the Civil Rights era, while America was dealing with (and reeling from) the struggles of blacks to gain legal equality with whites. But Americans in their teens and twenties see firsthand evidence in their own schools and neighborhoods that America is becoming less white and more racially mixed. America's pop culture today is infinitely more likely to show blacks as well as whites (though other races often remain unseen). The billion-dollar hip-hop industry, produced by blacks but driven by sales to young fans of all races, is one indicator of the cultural shift. Even more significant, 80 percent of teens have a close friend of another race.[13]

That's not to say that everyone in this generation lives a cookie-cutter version of life in an ethnically diverse America. Quite the contrary: how (and how much) we each experience diversity varies widely, and it depends on everything from geography to income. But there is a fundamental difference between this generation and the ones which came before. Until laws were revised in 1965, the United States accepted few immigrants besides Europeans. In most of the country, especially the East and Midwest, the vision of America as a black and white country largely held true. Today, especially for Americans younger than my twenty-nine years, the issue of race can no longer be described as a dichotomy. In many cases, "race" alone doesn't do justice to the issue; ethnicity and socioeconomics are just as important in the new America. There are more and more American kids who look like one "race" (say, Asian) but whose "ethnicity" is something entirely different (like the many Asian Latinos raised in Latin America). How does their history, their identity fit into the American agenda? My own life is a small example. Racially, I'm black. Ethnically, I'm half African (Shona, to be exact), though I was raised in America and identify as black American. Socioeconomically, I was raised as middle-*class*, even though we didn't have a lot of money. Anytime we reduce someone to just a race, we miss out on all these complexities.

It's difficult to define race, let alone quantify it. In many ways, it is a figment of our collective imaginations more than a biological phenomenon. For the purposes of this book, I treat black, white, Native American, Asian, and Latino as races. The U.S. Census doesn't. Its categories include black, white, Native American, and Asian/Pacific Island. The Census Bureau classifies Latinos/Hispanics as an ethnicity, not a race. The Merriam-Webster dictionary defines an ethnicity simply as an "ethnic quality or affiliation," and defines an "ethnic" person as "a member of a minority group who retains the customs, language, or social views of the group."[14] Latinos are definitely an ethnicity, and can be of any race. But Latinos are treated as a race in most sociopolitical contexts (for example, when describing the constituency of a politician or describing a mixed marriage between a Latina and a white man). Black

Americans, on the other hand, have been seen as a race almost without ethnicity. Most black Americans are the descendants of slaves, who were forced to discard their language and their customs here in the United States. But as more blacks immigrate to America from around the world, ethnicity is becoming a factor along with race.

Living in New York City, I see glimpses of the future of race every day. Here, the black community is no longer one but many. A child with brown skin and kinky hair may speak American-accented English—or Spanish, or Senegalese French, or Haitian Creole, or English with a Caribbean lilt. A man speaking fluent Spanish to his children on the subway one moment may switch to fluent, American-accented English the next. At a chic downtown club, a female DJ spins bangra for a multiracial crowd. That's a taste of young New York's diversity, but here, like other places, whites are often the most self-segregated. New York's public school system is disproportionately black, Latino, and Asian, while many white parents send their kids to private schools. This city of eight million people includes many racially and socioeconomically discrete neighborhoods. Some, like Chinatown, seem to welcome visits by outsiders; others, like Bensonhurst, have been the site of vicious racial incidents. Of course, New York is unique in how many cultures it encompasses. But the reality about race is this: every day America's heartland looks more and more like New York and Los Angeles, not the other way around.

I mean this literally, of course—there are more and more nonwhites in virtually every region and area of the country. But I'm also talking about the way ethnic culture permeates even the smallest, whitest towns. Consider another town I visit in the book. Delphi, Indiana, is a farming and industrial community of two thousand residents, almost all of them white. But most of the local teens listen to rap music as well as—sometimes instead of—rock and country. They spend countless afternoons watching hip, black kids on MTV and in sitcoms. They have the same albums, clothes, and shoes that inner-city kids do. And they're hungry for more. Says eighteen-year-old B. J. Bushnell, who moved to

Delphi from Los Angeles: "It bothers me—but it's kind of hilarious—that some people will report at school that they saw a black person over the weekend. . . . They'll come up to me and say"—he feigns excitement—" 'They dress just like they do on TV!' " You can't help but laugh, nervously, at the idea of white kids getting a buzz over seeing a real, live black person—but it shows how "minority" culture has shifted from the sidelines to the center. Today, rap music regularly tops the pop charts, and 60 percent of rap album sales are to whites.[15] Even in the heartland, American culture *is* multiracial culture.

After the Old, Before the New

Young Americans today aren't just on one side of a generation gap. They ARE a generation gap, the core of a massive transition. America has been a majority-white nation obsessed with black and white issues. And America is becoming a majority-minority nation with a multiracial and multicultural population. The problem is that, in some ways, we're neither here nor there. We haven't left the first model behind, nor fully embraced the second.

A moment emblematic of the tensions between the black-white and multiethnic views of America occurred in 1997, when President Bill Clinton convened a seven-member advisory board on race relations. One of the members, Korean-American attorney Angela Oh, announced that she thought the board shouldn't waste too much time analyzing slavery and race relations via "the black-white paradigm." "We need to go beyond that, because the world is about much more than that," she said. "We can't undo this part of our heritage. But what we can affect is where we are headed." Oh is in her early forties and grew up in Los Angeles, a multiracial city with strong ties to Asia, Mexico, and Latin America. She became a spokesperson for Korean shopkeepers looted after the Rodney King verdict, and serves on the Los Angeles human rights commission. Even though she's a baby boomer, she grew up in one of the nation's most multiethnic enclaves, and thinks along those lines.[16]

But esteemed African-American historian John Hope Franklin, professor emeritus at Duke University, responded sharply to Oh's request: "This country cut its eye teeth on black-white relations. Without knowledge of the past, we cannot wisely chart our course for the future." Franklin was born in Oklahoma in 1915. Unlike Oh, he's seen Jim Crow and the Civil Rights movement firsthand.[17]

Of course, Franklin and Oh are both right. No one can deny that slavery created both racial income inequalities and the American concept of "blackness" (including the stereotypes of intellectual inferiority) that exist to this day. But we can't think that studying black and white relations alone will give us the keys to a better future—that future will come in many colors, not in monochrome. However, we can't forget the economic opportunities between blacks and whites during this time of transition. Many blacks and whites fear (with some justification) that in a multiracial America, blacks will simply be pushed to the bottom of a bigger barrel. It doesn't help matters that America's nonwhite groups have so much trouble learning to cooperate. In cities as far flung as New York, Washington, Houston, Chicago, Los Angeles, and Oakland, there have been tensions between Latinos and blacks, or blacks and Asians, or all three groups at once. In Houston and Oakland, blacks and Latinos battled for control of the school systems; in Los Angeles and New York, blacks and Asians warred over who should profit from shops in the 'hood. But Mexican Americans have joined blacks as scapegoats of the affirmative action wars, and Asians have joined the ranks of those most targeted for hate crimes. While all of these groups are battling each other, they're ignoring one important fact: they're all the common enemy of people who think that one day soon, America will become too nonwhite.

What We See Is What We Fear

The very idea that America will become majority-minority scares the hell out of some people. That's why we find ourselves not only at a point of incredible change, but of incredible fear. The nineties have seen a full-scale backlash against immigrants and nonwhites, both in word and in deed. As the visibility of nonwhites has been rising, hate crimes have too—with attacks on increasingly visible Asian Americans rising the fastest. We're still holding on to the old prejudices: a study by the National Opinion Research Center found that the majority of whites still believe blacks to be inferior (with smaller numbers holding the same views of Southern whites and Hispanics).[18] But the biggest backlash has been in America's policy arena. In 1997, the U.S. Congress passed and President Bill Clinton signed restrictions not just on illegal but *legal* immigrants.[19] The debate over affirmative action has turned ugly, with opponents like University of Texas law professor Lino Graglia stating that "blacks and Mexican Americans are not academically competitive with whites" because of "a culture that seems not to encourage achievement." (He later added: "I don't know that it's good for whites to be with the lower classes. I'm afraid it may actually have deleterious effects on their views because they will see people from situations of economic deprivation usually behave less attractively.")[20] Even the basic tenets of the Civil Rights movement are still controversial. Take Supreme Court Justice Antonin Scalia's response when asked by a law professor how he would have ruled on the *Brown v. Board of Education* case, which ended legal school segregation. Scalia pondered for a moment—then said he might well have decided in favor of the segregated school system.[21]

On the positive side, America's minorities have never been more visible than they are today. They are the athletes and entertainers filling the nation's sports arenas and movie screens, the public officials pushing new policy proposals; they appear in commercials for everything from Tide detergent to, yes, Texaco gasoline. A black, Latino, or Asian-American person is probably part of the local news team that greets you in the morning, then recaps the world's day for you at night. Talk-show host/actress/producer/business mogul Oprah Winfrey is one of the best-liked and highest-paid people in America. On the negative side, compared to the statistics about who commits crimes, the evening news gives us far too many images of bad guys who are black or brown. (Whites are the majority of Americans, and the majority of violent criminals. But too often, the nightly news is filled with back-to-back images of black and Latino perpetrators.)[22]

Images of minorities—frequently negative images—are everywhere. That leads us to the politics of race. We don't have a problem with minorities, right? At least not as long as they're looking for equality. But maybe things have gone too far. Maybe now there's a new racial scapegoat—the white Americans being forced into a shabby, second-class minority status.

The message that America has "gone too far" toward embracing minorities is being shouted out from the lecterns at Washington think tanks and neighborhood bar stools alike. The 1994 national elections, which swept in a right-wing Republican Congress for the first time in forty years, were widely seen as rising from the populace, the revenge of the "angry white male." (A year earlier, a *Newsweek* cover story on "White Male Paranoia" quoted a retired marketing executive saying, by example, "The white male is the most persecuted person in the United States.")[23] And conservative Washington think tanks have funded a slew of books promoting the idea that America is under dire threat from racial diversity. In his book *The End of Racism,* Dinesh D'Souza calls for nothing less radical than overturning the Civil Rights Act.[24] And the book *Alien Nation,* penned by a British immigrant, details how nonwhite immigration is supposedly destroying America.[25]

The biggest-selling race book of the decade was *The Bell Curve,* which not only polarized the perception of race in America but had a tremendous influence over public policy. (Not incidentally, the conservative Bradley Foundation gave coauthor Charles Murray a nearly million-dollar grant to do his research.)[26] Conservatives like former Speaker of the House Newt Gingrich blamed the "Great Society" programs for the decline of the inner city and American culture alike.

And don't even bring up the word "multiculturalism" without expecting a political debate. Some young Americans think of multiculturalism as a commonsense approach to America's diversity. Others find it a smarmy, let's-sing-"Kumbaya" way of dealing with racial issues. But virtually none find it worthy of the vitriol expended by opponents. For example, a syndicated piece by *U.S. News and World Report* columnist John Leo ran with the overwrought headline "A Generation Worse Than Skinheads." Its thesis: young college students are hypnotized by multiculturalism to the point where they lack all morality. Or, as he writes, "In the new multicultural canon, human sacrifice is hard to condemn, because the Aztecs practiced it."[27]

Multiculturalism has become the new evil "ism" many Americans feel compelled to fight. (Racism—the original foe—is something we too often try to ignore.) The underlying message of these various attacks on multiculturalism is the same: a fiery, almost hysterical warning of impending doom for America's institutions and culture. Why the vehemence, the fin de siècle venom of the attacks on "minority rights"? Perhaps it's because we're so used to viewing race as conflict. We assume an increasingly nonwhite America can only mean bigger and nastier battles over equality. Or perhaps it's a question of *appearance*, with the increasing visibility of nonwhites giving rise to fear. Compare today to the '50s and '60s, when nonwhites were not seen or heard on mainstream television and radio. Then consider Disney's 1997 version of the Cinderella story for its Sunday night television show. The cast was exuberantly multicultural—the Queen, King, and Prince were played by black, white, and Filipino actors respectively. Cinderella herself was played by black actress and pop star Brandy Norwood. All of the bit parts and extras were filled by actors of every race—almost to the point that skin color became an element of the decor.

The images in *Cinderella* may exaggerate America's current racial mix, but it's hardly part of a plot to destroy American culture. Yet to some, the increasing visibility of minorities presents a threat—a vision of a nation where power is being wrested from (deserving) whites and given to (undeserving) nonwhites. The subtext is easy to read: whites represent American culture at its purest; nonwhites, either a bastardization of our culture (as with American-born blacks) or a foreign "invasion."

But there's a big difference between visibility and power. The halls of power in America look much like they did half a century ago, before Martin Luther King, Jr., marched to Selma. Ninety-five percent of corporate management—the presidents, vice presidents, and CEOs who run America—are white males.[28] Or as *Newsweek*'s article put it: "White males make up just 39.2 percent of the population, yet they account for 82.5 percent of the Forbes 400 (folks worth at least $265 million), 77 percent of Congress, 92 percent of state governors, 70 percent of tenured college faculty, almost 90 percent of daily-newspaper editors, 77 percent of TV news directors."[29] The image of a hostile takeover of America by nonwhite guerrilla forces is patently a lie.

What remains a sad truth is the racial divide in resources and opportunity. Here are just a few statistics from the Census Bureau and other agencies:

- Higher Education: In 1995, 24 percent of whites, 13 percent of blacks, 14 percent of Hispanics, and 9 percent of Native Americans aged twenty-five and older had received a college degree. The figure was 38 percent for Asian/Pacific Islanders, the highest of any racial or ethnic group. That's still an improvement for both blacks and whites over the figures for 1980, when 18 percent of whites and 8 percent of blacks over the age of twenty-five had completed four years or more of college.

- Employment: For decades, the black unemployment rate has been approximately twice that of whites. In 1995, the unemployment rate was 3.3 percent for whites, 6.6 percent for blacks, 5.1 percent for Hispanics, and 3.2 percent for Asian Americans.

- Income: Forty percent of white families earn $50,000 per year or more, versus 21 percent of black families, and 46 percent of

Asian/Pacific Islander families (which tend more often to be extended families and include more employed workers).[30]

- Life Expectancy and Infant Mortality: Black life expectancy is sixty-nine years, while white life expectancy is seventy-six years. Likewise, the black infant mortality rate is 16.8 deaths for each one thousand births, more than double the rate for white infants.[31] Yet in the military, where families have equal access to health care, the infant mortality rate is virtually equal among races.

Recent polls indicate that most Americans know little about the profound differences separating the income, health and educational opportunities of Americans of different races. This makes a big difference in how we think of racial issues. Polls show that Americans who believe that blacks and whites have equal incomes and opportunities are much less likely to support programs to end racial discrepancies.[32] Too many of us try to wish away the problem of race instead of confronting it. Instead of attacking the problems of race, we seem intent on attacking nonwhite races, including those members of the next generation who belong to minority ethnic groups.

Stereotyping a Generation

How do these attacks affect young Americans, and why have they now become so fierce? It's no coincidence that today's racial backlash coincides with the rise of this new multiethnic generation. It's as if America has decided to eat its young now that it knows they are not just white but black and brown. This generation's unprecedented racial demographics mark them as unique, as well as a target. Right-wing rhetoric and government action attempt to isolate and divide them: first, from previous, overwhelmingly white generations, and second, against themselves—white against black, Latino, and Asian. The media uses too many racially charged stereotypes to describe the next generation, but these labels say less about their lives than our need to pigeonhole them.

Consider the terms "slacker" and "Generation X," the latter coined from the Douglas Coupland novel of the same title. One of the earliest articles on Generation X, in 1991, described them as: "invisible . . . the Lost Generation . . . the in-betweens . . . [possessing] no intellectual pride or content."[33] There was a nugget of economic truth behind the slacker myth. The early nineties were some of the worst years for college graduates to find work. But today the term is virtually meaningless. On the other hand, a new stereotype holds all too much coded meaning. The late nineties brought a focus on youth criminals, dubbed the "superpredators" by a Princeton professor.[34] No matter that FBI statistics reveal America's fear of youth is overstated, that the proportion of murders (and all crimes) committed by teens actually dropped in the past decade. This image of a dark-skinned menace to society has become an integral part of how we view the next generation. As Nell Bernstein, the editor of the daring San Francisco teen newspaper *YO!* wrote: "While the [Generation X] twentysomethings were represented as if they were almost entirely white, their younger siblings have mysteriously become predominantly black and Latino."

Middle-class blacks and Latinos aren't immune to being stereotyped, either. They're described as the coddled affirmative-action babies destroying young white Americans' chances at advancement. *The Bell Curve* even tries to excuse antiblack sentiment on campus, stating: "Racial clashes on campuses began to surface in the early 1980s and apparently have been growing since then, with the bulk of the difficulties between whites and blacks. A plausible explanation is that whites resent blacks, who are in fact getting a large edge in the admissions process and often in scholarship assistance, and many of whom, as whites look around their own campus and others, 'don't belong there' academically."[35]

Yet the 1998 book *The Shape of the River* by William G. Bowen and Derek Bok, the former presidents of Princeton and Harvard, respectively, documents that affirmative action benefited not only blacks but whites as well. Black students who attended the most selective schools in this massive study were even more likely to graduate and to get high-paying jobs than black students with similar test scores who attended less competitive schools. The authors also argue that affirmative action benefits whites by giving them a hands-on experience of integration.[36] But white Americans receive more direct benefits of affirmative action as well. A study of admissions at the public universities in Washington State found that white students made up three-quarters of "special admissions," which take into account race, income, and socioeconomic factors.[37] It was exactly this type of "special admissions" that anti-affirmative-action forces attacked, and dismantled, in Washington's and California's state-run colleges.

Despite evidence to the contrary, youth are still stereotyped as lost, white slackers, psychopathically violent urban youth, and affirmative-action babies. One reason the stereotypes persist is because we see so little in-depth coverage of young adults. One study found that eighteen-to twenty-three-year-olds were virtually absent from most news coverage except in sports and crime stories.[38] The lack of coverage of important issues affecting young Americans makes it clear that we can't rely on traditional sources to accurately portray the next generation. We have to go to the source—young Americans themselves.

Redefining America

The backlash against racial diversity is an attempt to keep America fixed in time—demographically, socially, and culturally. This way of defining diversity as something frivolous at best, dangerous at worst, also represents an attempt to keep young Americans from making their mark on society. Conservative critic Robert Bork, for example, not only vehemently argues against young adults' multiculturalism, but also writes: "Every new generation constitutes a wave of savages who must be civilized by their families, schools, and churches. An exceptionally large generation can swamp the institutions responsible for teaching traditions and standards."[39] From his perspective, today's youth should blindly give themselves over to older visions of American society rather than presuming to think for themselves.

Yet it is precisely the transformative power of youth that has shaped America throughout its history. Our society has been propelled by the desire of each new generation to reinvent our laws, our economy, our culture. It was true from the colonial era to the baby boom generation. We know how much the 'boomers, 72 million strong, changed American life. They popularized rock 'n' roll, began enthusiastically popping The Pill, and provided both the manpower to fight and the outrage to end the war in Vietnam. Now look at what's next. The young multiethnic generation coming of age today is the cusp of the "baby boomlet," estimated at 79 million people. They're already starting to change the social values of our society. As an article in *American Demographics* put it, this is "the first generation to accept mixed races, 'nontraditional' families, and gender-bending sex roles as mainstream."[40]

A look at the issue of multiracial identity shows how this generation is helping to reshape social policy as well. There are few concepts more entrenched in this nation than the notion of distinct racial categories. By U.S. law codified during slavery days, anyone with "one drop" of black blood was considered black. It's not just an ancient concept, either. As recently as 1986, the Supreme Court ruled that a Louisiana woman who was 3/32 black was legally black.[41] But over the course of the past two decades, mixed-race Americans and their parents have made ever stronger appeals to be recognized as multiracial.

In October 1997, after a heated debate between traditional civil rights groups and ones representing mixed-race individuals, the U.S. Census weighed in. For Census 2000, Americans may mark themselves as several races—black, white, and Native American, for example. But they may *not* mark themselves as multiracial.[42] This issue hit the national radar screen because there are more mixed-race Americans than ever—most of them young. And it should come as no surprise that the most high-profile person to speak out during the Census debate was a member of the next generation: a twenty-one-year-old golfer named Tiger Woods. While he was growing up, Woods invented a word, "Cablinasian," to sum up his Caucasian, black, Indian, and Asian heritage. (His mother is Thai and his father is black with white and Indian blood.) But Woods's statements continue to cause controversy. To put it bluntly, Woods looks black. Though he's of mixed heritage, most people continue to classify him as a "black golfer"—and many African Americans felt aggravated that he chose not to identify himself as such. Whatever you feel about his choice, Woods and other young mixed-race Americans symbolize the unique place of this generation—taking issues that we've debated for centuries and pushing them to the next level. They form a bridge between one understanding of race and another, the old America and the new.

Of course, none of us knows exactly what this new America will look like, or how it will function. The increasing number of mixed-race Americans could develop a new racial category, or they could choose to group themselves among the ones that exist now. Growing communities of South Asians and Middle Easterners, who span the spectrum of skin color, may end up assimilating largely into white America, or find commonalties with black America, or neither. In some cities where blacks and Latinos share neighborhoods and socioeconomic statuses, they get along (and intermarry); in many others, they're rivals. And of course, the way white Americans act and react to these changes will shape much of the debate. With California's Proposition 187, whites and Mexican Americans found themselves on opposite sides of the immigration debate. In 1998, California voters dismantled bilingual immigration. And in 1996, another California referendum, Proposition 209, ended affirmative action in the state. Despite a handful of black, Asian, and Latino spokespeople, the bulk of affirmative-action opponents are white. But in 1997, the white mayor of Houston, Bob Lanier, defended affirmative action and successfully helped push for the election of the city's first black mayor, Lee Brown. These days, there are no givens in the race game, no unshakeable alliances or unchangeable opinions. The one thing that we can all do to help understand where we're headed is to get a sense of how other Americans are living their lives.

With no one racial reality in America, we are left to interpret the national debates through our personal experiences. We're "placed" in a racial context on at least three levels: geographically, socioeconomically, and by personal choice. Geographically, race is regional. In the Northeast and Southeast, race tends to run on a black-white axis. In the Southwest, it's often Anglo-Mexican American. In parts of the Rockies, it's white-Indian. And in California, it tends to be a four- or five-way free-for-all. Socioeconomically, whether people live in cities, suburbs, or rural areas (and how rich or poor those areas are) greatly affects their experiences with race. The tensions are often more overt in poorer areas, more hidden (though not necessarily nonexistent) in richer neighborhoods. And finally, as we enter the twenty-first century, race is increasingly a matter of "placing" yourself in a context, choosing your own place in the racial hierarchy.

Through a Reporter's Eyes

When it comes to media's portrayals of race, we're missing the hottest story of our time. What we're missing is the future of race today, the clear, unmistakable signs that America is in the midst of a massive change. We're missing the story because we think we know what race is about and we've heard all the bad news before—tensions between blacks and whites, immigration run amok, white fears of reverse discrimination. We're so mired in one way of thinking that we can't see the future that lies right in front of our eyes.

My approach to reporting this national story is hardly unique, but it is controversial. Usually a reporter is forced to choose one perspective on a subject—insider or outsider, a member of the group being examined or a dispassionate observer of it. I see myself differently, as a passionate observer who hopes to bring a reporter's eye to a story I care deeply about. I've tried to marry the analytical and the personal, the hard facts about American life and the emotional realities of how we see race today. In the second section of the book, I gather different perspectives on what "race" means to different Americans and how it affects their lives. Because race is so dependent on place, I decided to crisscross the country to get different images of American life. Hanging out in Delphi, Indiana—going to the Dairy Queen, high school graduation parties, meeting people's families—gave me one view of American life. Spending time with mixed-race twentysomethings in fast-paced Los Angeles gave me another. In the third part of the book, I focus on what happens when teens and young adults are drawn into larger controversies like the end of affirmative action at Berkeley or life on the border in El Paso, Texas.

In some ways, I needed to go no further than my own hometown to see evidence of these changes. These days, on my frequent trips back to Baltimore I see East Indian, Latino, Asian, and Arab families strolling through the local mall. When I rushed to the mall more than a decade ago to buy back-to-school clothes, all of the faces were black or white. America is changing—city by city, school by school, neighborhood by neighborhood.

I see the political as personal as well. During the 1996 presidential campaign season, I was a political commentator for CNN. One night, at a gathering with other young political analysts, I had a conversation with an editor of the conservative *National Review*. Halfway through dinner, the editor started talking about race. Wasn't it obvious that blacks now have an unfair advantage in the job market—and that includes the media business? "Well, only five percent of newspaper reporters are black, and only two percent of magazine editors are black, so I don't see where you're coming from," I replied. Where he was coming from, he said, was the clear evidence that affirmative action had created a nation ruled by reverse discrimination. We now lived in a country where talented white men didn't have a chance against blacks competing for the same slots. "Hmmm," I said. "That must be why when I was at *Newsweek*, only five of the one hundred reporters there were black." The editor shot me a look of half-admiring exasperation. "You're very good with the numbers.

But how can it be that what you believe is so at odds with the lives people are leading today?"

"Well," I said, "It depends on whose lives you examine."

The truth is this: the "truth" depends on whose lives you examine. Most of the time, especially on important and controversial issues like race, we get the most input from older middle- and upper-class white guys. It's not that their input isn't important, but there's a lot more to this nation. The lives of nonwhites aren't usually examined with the same rigor or fairness as those of whites. And today, the lives of the next generation aren't being examined nearly often enough or well enough. Maybe that's because this generation doesn't offer us easy answers, only more questions. Are they more tolerant than previous generations? Many of them. Are they absorbing the rancor of the racial debates and turning against each other? Some. Are they leading us down roads we've never taken before? Definitely.

If we understand that how we see race depends on the lives we examine, it's also worth taking a look at who's doing the examining. Most books on race are written by whites, about blacks and whites. Many are written by blacks, also about blacks and whites. Where's the rest of the picture? Even though my interest in race comes directly out of my perspective as an African American, I realize it serves us no better than it does whites to ignore the growth of other communities. Blacks have become a kind of "everyminority"—highly visible, often attacked, occasionally rewarded for our high profile. Asians, Latinos, and Native Americans have the opposite problem; they don't register as often on the national radar. Young Americans of all races—and especially those who are neither black nor white—are the most ignored of all.

This generation—not just white but black, Latino, Asian, and Native American; not just native born but immigrant—is both the inheritor and the architect of American culture. Today's young adults are paying the price for being different, growing up in an era where the diversity they represent is feared. We can only hope that they will chart a better course for race relations than Americans have in the past, that they will help lead us away from our centuries-long battles. If they do forge a new American unity, it will be because they've learned to work within the multiethnic nation we inhabit, rather than denying or decrying its very existence. Will they learn to work together? Will they yield to or rebel against the wishes of the generations before them? And how will their vision of American life reshape our culture? No one can answer these questions but this generation itself.

II

Race Is Place

It's nearly impossible to make a blanket
statement about "the state of race relations."
How can you lump together the tensions between whites and Native Americans in the
West with the snared and shifting ethnic politics of a megalopolis like Los Angeles? How
can you talk about "the state of Black America" or "the state of Latino America" when
the differences within each ethnic group are
as profound as the differences between them?
We talk of national indicators, national problems, and national solutions to the racial divide, but first and foremost racial issues are
local.

"Other":
The Future of
Mixed-Race Identity

New York City
Los Angeles, California
Johannesburg, South Africa

What makes a person black? Skin color? Well, there are lots of light-skinned blacks (some blue-eyed and blond-haired) who are fairer than dark-skinned whites. What makes a person Asian? Eye shape? My sister's almond-shaped eyes come from Africa, not Asia. What about genetics? Of course family origin and genes shape who and what we are—but according to top scientists like Stephen Jay Gould, there is no such thing as a person who is "genetically black" or "genetically white." (Even though there are clear visual ways we distinguish race, there are more genetic differences within each racial group than between, say, a randomly chosen black and white person.)[1] The conundrum of how we classify people becomes even more complicated for Americans whose heritage includes more than one race.

In America, the issue of multiracial identity hit the headlines full-force in 1997. Tiger Woods, the telegenic twenty-one-year-old who rocketed to the top of the pro golf circuit, gathering tens of millions of dollars in corporate endorsements along the way, shocked many people when he went on television and said he wasn't black. Such a claim, made on the *Oprah Winfrey Show* no less, proved inspiring to some and alienating to others. After all, by American racial standards, Woods clearly "looks black." Yet his mother is from Thailand; his father, also a golfer, is black, but has Chinese, white, and Native American blood. Woods told Winfrey that when he was growing up, he invented a word, "Cablinasian," that reflected all of his heritage. But for better or worse, people don't see all of his heritage when they look at his face in photos or on the television screen. When Woods won the prestigious Masters Cup that same month—the first time a "black" person had done so—African Americans cheered. Fellow golfer Fuzzy Zoeller didn't. With a look of disgust on his face, he turned to the cameras and admonished the "little boy" not to serve fried chicken and collard greens at the Masters dinner next year. (After a national outcry, Zoeller apologized and said he was only joking.) Significantly, the racial slur was directed only at the most visible part of Woods's heritage. Zoeller didn't admonish him not to serve Pad Thai.

The taboo against black-white sex, marriage, and childbearing is an integral part of race in America. Though times have certainly changed, our biases about miscegenation haven't disappeared yet. More and more young Americans will have to confront America's prejudice about race mixing; the number of multiracial children quadrupled between 1970 and 1990.[2]

Make no mistake: race mixing is nothing new. By some estimates, 80 percent of African Americans have at least some white blood, and a quarter have some Native American blood."[3] Nothing demonstrates that fact more clearly than a story that made front-page headlines in November 1998: evidence that Thomas Jefferson had fathered at least one black child. Like other American "founding fathers," Jefferson was a slave-owner. Yet he, more than many, shaped the language by declaring America a land where "all men are created equal." From today's viewpoint, Jefferson's rhetoric about equality certainly clashes with owning slaves. But some historians argued there was a more fundamental hypocrisy in his life: that among the slaves he owned were his own mistress, a woman named Sally Hemings, and their children together. For years, most historians and Jefferson descendants denied that he could have fathered Hemings's children. But in 1998, genetic tests proved conclusively that Jefferson had fathered at least one child with Hemings, a son named Eston Hemings Jefferson. In an odd twist, Sally Hemings was not only biracial but the half sister (through her slave-owning white father) of Jefferson's own wife.[4]

What happened in the Jefferson family is just a high-profile example of the way most black Americans became mixed with white blood: through sexual unions—sometimes consensual, often forced—between white male slaveowners and black female slaves. In the South, the myth of the black male sexual predator emboldened and justified the actions of groups like the Klan. The myth is an old one: Shakespeare's Iago calls Othello a "black ram . . . tupping [the] white ewe." But the white ram and the black ewe largely produced the color spectrum within black America and set the stage for today's battles over what constitutes black and mixed-race identity.

What is new in America's racial classifications is the trend toward identifying as multiracial. In the past, America defined anyone with "one drop" of black blood as black. And it became a point of pride in the black community for even those who could "pass" for white to proudly proclaim their black identity. It shouldn't come as a surprise, then, that most young mixed-race blacks still identify as black. But more and more are identifying as multiracial, and a few (depending on skin color as well as upbringing) as white. The issue is far broader than just a black and white one. Today's young adults include black-Asian individuals like Woods, Asian Hispanics, white Native Americans, and every other possible combination.

How to classify people of mixed race has become a huge political headache for the Census Bureau. In 1990, nearly 10 million Americans marked the "Other, Not Specified" category on that year's census.[5] Some are multiracial; others are Latinos who don't want to check a race in addition to "Hispanic origin." (The Census Bureau considers Latinos an ethnicity, not a race.)[6] Throughout the nineties, multiracial Americans and their parents started petitioning for new categories on school and job forms. They won local victories, pushing some cities and states to add a "multiracial" option for, say, school enrollment forms. But in 1997, the issue went national, as the U.S. Census Bureau debated what to put on its Census 2000 forms. The nation's top magazines and television shows were filled with stories on multiracial identity. And finally, near the end of the year, the Census Bureau handed down its decision. Americans can check more than one box under race—for example, "white" and "Asian"—but there won't be one box reading "multiracial." In some ways it's a small gesture, but it's also the biggest change in how we look at race in centuries.

From this nation's earliest years, Americans who were part black—even a tiny part—were considered legally black. Mixed-race blacks used to go by labels like "mulatto," "quadroon," and "octoroon," but their second-class legal status remained the same. It's also been a cultural tradition within the black community that anyone with mixed blood must firmly claim their blackness; anything less has been seen as trying to "pass." Now, both the legal and cultural traditions are changing. More Americans than ever are claiming their multiracial heritages. How we deal with the "other"—folks who don't fit the typical racial categories—is one of the most compelling issues in America today.

A Battle over Laws, and Attitudes

For most of America's history, racial categories have been used to segregate and to deny opportunity. For the past two decades, part of the government has sought to flip that equation. In 1977, the Federal government's Directive No. 15 instructed the Census Bureau to collect racial data for civil rights purposes. Antidiscrimination programs ranging from the Voting Rights Act to school desegregation to affirmative action needed a way to track the racial progress.[7] Twenty years after Directive

15 was instituted, the Census debated creating a mixed-race category, and new dividing lines were drawn. Black and Latino civil rights groups including the NAACP and The National Council of La Raza argued that a new "multiracial" classification would make antidiscrimination enforcement more difficult. Think of it this way: most Americans will still look at a mixed-race black person and think of them "black." That means most employers, police officers, or apartment owners will see them as "black," and act accordingly, whether that means treating them fairly or discriminating against them. If these Americans are counted as multiracial, it could be harder to track any discrimination. On the other hand, a federal lawsuit filed by one mother of biracial children argues that not allowing people to mark themselves as mixed is its own form of discrimination. The group she belongs to, Project RACE, has already gotten seven states including Ohio and Florida to create mixed-race categories.[8] But marking yourself as "mixed" doesn't indicate if you're black and white, or Asian and Latino, or five or six ethnicities at once. The decision by the U.S. Census Bureau to allow people to mark more than one category is either a stroke of genius or a cop-out, but it doesn't give either side exactly what it wants.

What happens when people *are* given the chance to pick "multiracial"? When the Census Bureau ran a test in 1995, the only group that lost a significant number of people to the new category was Asians. A bigger problem may be the arbitrary nature of racial categories themselves. The one time I remember filling out the census was in 1990, just as I was about to graduate from college. My roommate Mirka, who's Puerto Rican, was highly aggravated that she was supposed to mark a race in addition to "Hispanic origin," which is considered an ethnicity. "I'm not white," she said. "I'm not anything else. I'm just Hispanic." I, of course, simply checked black. But like most black Americans, I have evidence that I am technically "biracial." My father is from Zimbabwe and ethnically fully African, while my mother, whose family is from Baltimore, is no doubt part white. My mother has light skin and hazel eyes, same as my grandfather did, while my aunts and uncles run the gamut of skin color. One of my great-great-grandparents is listed on immigration records as a "mulatto" who landed on U.S. shores in 1827 on a ship that sailed from Scotland. One genealogist told me that means he was probably the child of a Scottish slaver in the West Indies. I must admit I occasionally joke about showing up at "the Loch" (wherever it is) and shocking my Scottish relatives. But no matter what their skin color or hair texture, most African Americans who have two black parents will check only one box on the census.

Political battles seem tame compared to ordinary human interactions. Earl Carr knows that better than most. I met the sophomore at the College of William and Mary when he was lending a hand at a conference for minority high school students. Most of the college students helping run the conference were black; one of the organizers was Asian American. Earl is both, or neither. He grew up on Roosevelt Island, a middle-class neighborhood in New York City. On the weekends, he'd play soccer with an amateur team made up mostly of Africans. His mom, whom he lives with, is ethnically Chinese, but she's a native Spanish speaker who grew up in Panama. His dad, whose family he goes to visit often, is a Jamaican ambassador who's often posted in Asia. A soft-spoken, devout Christian, Earl looks like a Chinese American with wavy hair and a tan, but most of his friends are black.

One day we meet in New York and walk around Chinatown. Earl's taking Chinese at school, and he tries out a few phrases on a local shopkeeper. "You're not Chinese!" the shopkeeper says. Earl looks crushed. He hates the term "other" to describe multiracial identity ("It's like you're some kind of extraterrestrial alien!"), but he wants to claim all of his heritage. At William and Mary, he's almost certainly the only student who belongs to the Chinese, the black, *and* the Caribbean student associations. He sings in a gospel choir, and he tries to make sure his Chinese friends show up to hear him sing.

New York City was a good place for him to grow up multiracial. He even dated a girl in high school who was also part Jamaican and part Chinese. But he just has to look one generation back to see how hard it was for his mom to break the color barrier. In his grandparents' opinion, "It was appalling for my mom to even have the *thought* of marrying a black man." They cut her off for nearly two decades, and Earl has never met them. He dreams of going to visit them one day, in the hopes that their apparent change of heart is real. Just as his mom battled the prejudice that was directed against her because of whom she chose to marry, Earl sees himself in a struggle to claim all of the parts of his heritage— and to act as a human bridge between the different communities he calls his own.

America's Multiracial Mecca

The region of the country that has the highest number of multiracial Americans is clear across the country from Earl Carr's New York. According to the Census Bureau, that distinction goes to Southern California, a place full of contradictions. There's the seductive sparkle of Hollywood juxtaposed with the blank, vacant storefronts of South Central. It's a multiracial mecca, with residents who've moved to California from all over the world. It's also a place where the freeways neatly segregate neighborhoods and residents. And the biggest news events emanating from L.A. this decade have been of violent racial division—the O. J. Simpson murder trial and the Simi Valley trial over Rodney King that led to the L.A. riots. I decided to take a look at the new frontier of multiracial identity by looking at the lives of three young people in Los Angeles. Nicole Brown grew up in the burgeoning multiracial movement; Maceo Senna grew up in a city polarized between black and white, but has found a completely different set of rules in Southern California; and L.A. native Camille Maston finds that even in America's most multiracial city, it's hard to transcend the traditional racial divisions.

A Daughter of the Multiracial Movement

Fifteen-year-old Nicole Brown is a thoroughly L.A. teen. She goes to one of the city's top prep schools, Harvard Westlake, and heads off to a prestigious music camp in the summer. She's the daughter of a black father and a white mother, but she's also a daughter of the multiracial movement. From the time she was an infant, Nicole's parents taught her to see herself as multiracial, and they've been fighting to get others to see her and others like her that way too. Nicole's mother, Nancy Brown, a psychotherapist, helps run a group called MASC (Multiracial Americans of Southern California). MASC and groups like it provide a support network for multiracial kids and their families, families which were once (and sometimes still are) ostracized. But for Nicole, that kind of support has always been a given. "When I was little I would go to MASC meetings on Friday nights. Now I think I take it for granted," she says. But she admits, "I see a lot of people my age who really need it," especially teens who've been taught that they should identify only as black. "I identify as mixed," Nicole says, which doesn't mean she denies her black heritage. She belongs to the black cultural awareness group at school and hangs out with friends both black and white. But Nicole sees herself and her friends as part of a bigger moment in history. "I think this generation has definitely made America a different America. It's Asian, it's Latino. It's everything," she says.

Of course, Nicole is the first to admit that her perspective is a privileged one. She lives not only at a time when multiracial identity is becoming more widely accepted but in a city where she's not a rarity or an oddity. Not everyone is used to seeing multiracial people. She went on a YMCA bus trip through small towns in Wyoming and other states. "It was really weird," she says. "People looked at us. We went to Denny's and everyone in there was white. We were all hanging outside of Pizza Hut and they called the police on us. It's so different in other places; it's not as diverse as here. I feel lucky."

"The Tragic Mulatto Is a Thing of the Past"

Nicole's mother, Nancy, also feels "positive" about the way things are going, even though she admits that the battle to create a new category has been tough. She was president of MASC until 1994, and in 1996 this group and dozens of others staged a multiracial march on Washington. Groups like MASC have been fighting legal battles over everything from the proposed census category to rules on transracial adoptions. But they've also been trying to achieve something more basic: raising their kids to be psychologically secure. "With this new generation of multiracial people we've been birthing and raising . . . what we're seeing is healthy happy people with good self-esteem," she says. "The union between their parents is celebrated, they're told they're okay, and if someone has a problem, that's THEIR problem. We're raising a whole crop of children with a different mindset. The tragic mulatto is a thing of the past."

The "tragic mulatto" of which Nancy Brown speaks is a true American icon, immortalized in hit books and movies of the past like *Imitation of Life*. They usually involved a mulatta passing for white, being discovered, and meeting a tragic end—abandoned by both blacks and whites. The "tragic mulatto" may be an icon of the past, but America's obsession with the color line is as old as the nation itself and as recent as yesterday's headlines. In 1986, the Supreme Court refused to review the case of a Louisiana woman who wanted to be legally declared white, but who'd been declared black because her great-great-great-great-grandmother was a slave.[9] (She wanted to marry a white man whose family didn't accept her.) Brown calls the way we think about race, "the one drop rule, an antiquated system. It's the way the power structure chose to keep the races separate." The rule saying that anyone with "one drop" of black blood is black made it easier for white slaveowners to hold on to any of their human "property." A significant number of slaves were more "white" than "black." Homer Plessy, the slave in the 1896 Supreme

Court ruling *Plessy v. Ferguson*, which codified the "separate but equal" doctrine, was only one-eighth black.[10]

Now Nancy Brown worries that the rule of the slaveowner has become the rule of the descendants of slaves. Like the traditional Civil Rights groups, many African Americans have opposed creating a mixed-race category. They feel that mixed-race blacks want to dissociate themselves from any racial stigma. "We are always accused of trying to disclaim the person of color within us," says Nancy Brown. "I say us—I'm Caucasian—but I identify so much. [Blacks] have had to fight hard to be where they are. They feel something is being taken."

"I Feel So Mixed All the Time"

Many mixed-race blacks are raised to identify only as black precisely because their parents worry they'll end up denying their heritage. "Blackness," in the face of racial mixing, can be seen as a political choice, a way of identifying with a group some people try to "pass" to get out of.

Maceo Senna, who also lives in L.A., grew up in a family acutely aware of the politics of race. Named for jazz great Maceo Parker, the twenty-three-year-old has light brown skin, close cropped hair that would be wavy were it longer, and a roman nose. In a nation obsessed by putting people into racial categories, the lanky artist is hard to type. But our presumptions about race are always based on the options we're familiar with. (For example, many New Yorkers can distinguish—or, just as important in the game of race, *think* they can distinguish—Puerto Ricans and Dominicans. Most other Americans probably don't have a good idea what either Puerto Ricans *or* Dominicans look like.) In Los Angeles, where Latin Americans from different nations have joined Mexican immigrants, many people assume Maceo is Latino. "It's really frustrating, you know, I really physically don't fit into any kind of category," he says. "And also mentally, I don't associate myself with any racial characteristics because I feel so mixed all the time. To me race is just such a burden that we're still carrying around, such a primitive idea even though there are political reasons for it."

Every member of Maceo's family looks different. His mother, Fanny Howe, is a well-known poet from a Boston Brahmin family; his father, a writer named Carl Senna, is the son of a black Louisiana woman and a Mexican prizefighter. Maceo's oldest sister Ann Lucien, whom most Americans view on sight as black or black biracial, is a law student at Oxford University. She's just had her first child, a daughter, with her British husband, who's ethnically Pakistani. I'm close friends with Maceo's other sister, Danzy, who's often mistaken for white. She and I met while we were both working for *Newsweek* magazine. Danzy's first novel, *Caucasia,* published to critical acclaim in 1998, is a piercing look at mixed-race identity. (In an amusing family aside, her parents fought with doctors at the hospital where she was born so they could write "Brown" under the racial category on her birth certificate.)

Maceo had to be aware of race from the moment he was old enough to comprehend the world around him. In 1974, whites in working-class South Boston rioted when black kids were bused to neighborhood schools. The neighborhood where his family lived, Jamaica Plain or "JP," wasn't nearly as segregated as Southie, but it wasn't an oasis from the tensions which rocked the city, either. Says Maceo of his childhood: "(*a*) It was right after the sixties, and (*b*) It was Boston, OK. Boston's crazy. And (*c*) Here I was one of three kids who all kinda looked like they came from a different family, at least from the outside. So we were all really, really aware and our parents always told us that we were mixed but we always knew that there was some sort of political reason to say 'black.' That came at a very young age, and we all took that on without even questioning it." He feels a strong sense of black political consciousness but he is reluctant to slap one label on himself or demand that other biracial blacks do the same. "I can't tell anyone what they want to call themselves," he says.

Maceo's older sisters went to public schools, where they often had to deal with the issues of race head-on (some students called Ann Lucien, who has curly hair, a "nigger," though they didn't usually verbally attack Danzy, whose hair is straight). Maceo went to private schools, where the racism was less obvious. From second to eighth grade he attended a local private school, "predominately white and, you know, really preppy and really Waspy. And it was strange though because by the time I was in like, fifth grade there was total break dancing and graffiti . . . that was the thing at that point." The fact that black culture was "in" made him a hot social commodity. He and another black kid wound up "being the biggest break-dancers in the school. . . . It was a pretty liberal school and it was suddenly at a point where all these cultural symbols that were associated with being black and Latino were suddenly really cool. . . . But I started to wonder why is it that I have to sort of choose one or the other [racial identity], live up to one or the other."

The pattern of having to live up to—or defy—the racial expectations of others continued through high school at Andover and college at UCLA, where he studied painting. In high school and college, he wanted to try to meld together his separate groups of black and white friends, something which never quite worked. Now he's given up. "I don't even want to anymore. It's like I'm just a common link, you know, between random people. So I just have to deal with them as an individual, and not as a clique. . . . But it's crazy," he shrugs. He holds a day job at a juice bar while continuing to work on his art and hanging out with his girlfriend, who's also multiracial, a mix of white and Latino.

His review of the racial dynamics of Los Angeles is mixed. Because L.A. is a cross section of black, white, Asian, and Latino (with the latter two groups particularly prominent), mixed-race individuals are no rarity, something Maceo appreciates. But he adds, "By the same token I've never been in a place where I also felt more threatened as a black and Hispanic person." Because he looks Hispanic, he says, "I've been pulled over [by the police] for doing nothing. . . . I play it really safe. I stay calm. I don't move my hands more than I have to. But it always upsets me." He chalks up to two things the fact that he's usually not harassed too much when he's pulled over: that his driver's license reveals that he lives in a "nice" (read: mostly white) neighborhood, and his skin color. "The fact of the matter is that in those type of situations I'm so lucky that I'm in a lighter-skinned group. . . . God, it's totally disgusting," he says, shaking his head. "It's so visual. . . . I mean, just because of the way that I look I can just be arrested at any time of the day. And that's just a really bad feeling, [that] totally promotes all kind of this paranoia and really negative feelings toward U.S. society.

"L.A. is sort of like a testing ground," he says. "Sort of like, OK, this is how things are going to be everywhere soon, you know? . . . Just the balance of people here makes you feel more tolerated." He also sees a generational difference in how he's allowed to construct his identity. During his grandparents' generation, "I would have been passing," he says. Then, during the time his parents were coming of age, the Civil Rights era, "that would have been the beginning of someone like me having a black consciousness," he says. Today, Maceo thinks he benefits from "having a more complex way of looking at identity. And it needs to get better still, because it's still too binary, too black and white."

"Two Completely Separate Worlds"

While Maceo Senna sees America evolving away from a black and white view of race, Camille Maston feels that that's all there is. The twenty-year-old graduating senior at UCLA grew up in "two completely separate worlds," one black, one white. Until she was in fifth grade, she lived with her Africa-American mother in the working-class Mid-Wilshire district. For two years after that, her mother alternated custody weekly with her wealthy white father, who has a three-story house nestled in the Hollywood hills. At the time, she attended a public magnet school, and depending on whose house she was staying in, "I would just get on a different bus." Finally, in seventh grade, her father recommended—demanded, Camille implies—that she come live with him. He sent her to a wealthy, virtually all-white private school.

"It was evil," Camille says bluntly. Seventh grade "was the most hellish year of my life," as she felt racially and culturally dislocated. "How can I say I'm black? I'm going home to my white father, I'm going to my white school, I'm going to my white family to celebrate Passover. How can I say I'm white? I can't," she recalls. "I'm an outcast at my school. I have, like, no friends.

"I think my life would have been happier, I think my life would have been a lot easier, if I had been allowed to be around black people when I was younger," she continues. When she left her mother's house for her father's, everything, large or small, changed: her hair, her family, her speech. "With my father, the black vernacular was just ignorant. It was some low-down, dirty, low class . . ." she trails off. "When I went to live with him, I was hating him because I couldn't say one sentence without him repeating it back to me." And when she left her mother's house, she ran into a BIG problem: her huge mass of curly hair. "When I look at my pictures, I look completely horrible!" she says. "My hair, my hair! My hair has always been a problem. It's not black, it's not white. I can't use Pantene and I can't use Afro Sheen." The final straw was the difference in how her white and black families expressed their emotions. At her mother's house, she says, "I was used to people picking me up, and all my cousins around me so I could barely breathe. There was so much love. When I came here, it was like," she pauses for the anticlimax, "a kiss on the cheek. They don't mean to be snooty. That's really how they express their love. It's a really different way of expressing it."

"Everything Is Race to Me"

Today Camille is a pretty, round-cheeked woman with curly hair she cut short after high school. She's about the color of actress Halle Berry. She says she was "pushed up a bit too far" by some blacks "because I have quote unquote 'good hair . . .' It's just like this comment I got the other day from a white guy: 'You're not really black.' He was trying to say that because I don't have black features altogether, I'm a little bit higher, I'm a little more superior, I'm a little more pushed up on that hierarchy." If she were in New York, most people might think she was Puerto Rican. In fact, she laughs, "I remember one time I saw a Puerto Rican. And I was like, are you biracial? And he was like, are you Puerto Rican? And we were both disappointed. It was very funny actually." But despite the fact that she's constantly asked "what are you?" by people who can't quite peg her ethnicity, Camille firmly asserts that she's black. If anything, her experiences growing up in two different worlds have solidified her belief that race will forever be polarized. "Maybe because I'm biracial, race is a huge part of my life. Everything is race to me," she says. "I'm biracial but there's no room for that—I'm black. There's no room for any of the mixture and the combination. It's like, the available narratives that are there for black women are the ones that I'm seeing. They're the only ones that I have to try to say something."

Her final thoughts on the subject seem shocking. "I don't agree with interracial relationships in some ways," she says. "People think it's funny, people think it's a contradiction. [But] one match seems to happen in such high frequency: black men and white women. It does not seem like love. It docs not seem like two people happening to meet each other. There are too many other things going on." Like many other black women, Camille suspects that the black men who date white women are looking to their love life for some kind of recognition from white society. They're looking to "trade up" from black women—doubly stigmatized by race and sex—to the white women who they couldn't have whistled at without being lynched in the twenties or forties or fifties. Black women who date white men are also accused of "trading up," and whites who date blacks are accused of fetishizing the exotic or looking for a sexual thrill. For many couples the stereotype is terribly unfair, but in a society which tells us race shapes how attractive and successful and desirable we are, we can't expect everyone to be immune to the stereotypes about race and sex.

Camille herself lives with her boyfriend, a black man nine years her senior. They began dating five years ago, and both of her parents accept the relationship. But they don't accept her opposition to interracial relationships. "Both of my parents are like, 'How can you say something like that?' " she says. "To me, they both seem to be having this pattern in these relationships. . . . There seems to me, when there's a pattern like that, there's some kind of ulterior motives going on. So when there's ulterior motives going on, I'm against interracial relationships."

The experiences of Nicole, Maceo, and Camille, all young multiracial Americans living at the cultural crossroads of Los Angeles, couldn't be more different. For Nicole, being part of a multiracial community gives her a level of comfort with her identity; for Camille, switching between black and white worlds causes constant tension; and for Maceo, his own political awareness helps him deal with America's efforts to racially pigeonhole people. What Nicole and Maceo have in common is that both of their parents talked to them explicitly about their mixed racial heritage. Nicole's mother has urged her from the beginning to be proud of being multiracial. Maceo's family taught him to be proud of his mixed background as well, but with a more overt political emphasis on the black community. It's Camille, who was shuttled back and forth between two totally separate racial worlds—and who feels her white father urged her to reject the black world—who has the least desire to claim a "mixed" heritage. It shouldn't come as a surprise that parents' attitudes toward their children's mixed heritage plays a huge role in whether that heritage is seen as a blessing or a curse.

We Americans are hardly the only ones grappling with how to classify racial identity. When I visited South Africa in 1997, I found that mixed-race teens have an entirely different political history, and attitude.

Postcard from South Africa

Like many of the teens at the Chris J. Botha school near Johannesburg, Charlene Franse has taffy-colored skin and curly brown hair. She's multiracial, or "Coloured." But the sixteen-year-old, decked out in a typical public school uniform, feels that the category has now outlived its usefulness. When the repressive apartheid system ended in 1995, South African activists and politicians talked about building a "nonracial" country by abolishing the racial categories that were once so brutally enforced. So when I tell Charlene that America is considering creating its own mixed-race category, she gives me a look of genuine horror and cries, "That would be primitive!" Even more shocking to a teen who's seen racial categories enforced by the state is that multiracial Americans like Tiger Woods are the ones leading the crusade for recognition of their heritage.

While mixed-race American teens are rebelling against the legacy of the "one drop rule"—which denied them mixed status—Coloured South African teens are trying to escape the stigma of their own mixed category. For 300 years, white Afrikaners categorized mixed-race Coloureds separately from blacks. Under apartheid, blacks, who comprise 70 percent of South Africans, were restricted to living on just 13 percent of the nation's land.[11] Whites make up less than 20 percent of South Africans (compared to over 70 percent of Americans); and Coloureds comprise 10 percent of South Africans, far more than the 2 percent of people in the United States who call themselves mixed.[12]

South Africa's leaders used Coloureds as a buffer between blacks and whites—giving them limited access to political and economic power—and inspiring the ire of blacks. A "Group Areas Act" legislated that blacks, whites, Coloureds, and Asians (people of Indian descent) each had to live in their own strictly segregated areas. An "Immorality Act" forbade interracial sex and a "Mixed Marriages Act" banned interracial marriage.[13] During apartheid, Coloureds were sandwiched in status between whites and blacks. Today, in a nation ruled politically by blacks and economically by whites, many Coloured South Africans feel their new place on the totem pole is squarely at the bottom. In 1994, Coloureds voted overwhelmingly for the National Party, the architects of apartheid. In early 1997, frustrated by their loss of power, activists rioted in a Coloured neighborhood or "township" near the school where Charlene Franse goes.

When I go to South Africa, Deshun Deysel gives me a tour of the area where the riots occurred. She's a poised and attractive twenty-six-year-old who in 1996 went from being a teacher to being the first black woman to attempt Mt. Everest. "Black" is just one way she defines herself. Even though she's the color of, say, actor Denzel Washington, she's racially categorized as Coloured.

"During apartheid we weren't white enough. Now we aren't black enough," Deshun says, repeating a phrase on the lips of many Coloureds these days. Some blacks berate her for not speaking Zulu and some Coloureds scorn her for not being light enough, but she's equally happy to answer to either label. Her friend Beverley Braam, a light-skinned and wavy-haired teacher who was classified as Coloured under apartheid, only accepts one racial category. "I'm black," she says firmly. "Why is it important for America to start a mixed-race group? That's my question."

When it comes to mixed-race identity, another similarity becomes clear: both nations defined progress as the road not taken. In America, where mixed-race individuals were forced to be Native American, black, Latino, or Asian, a "multiracial" option seems to reflect the true breadth of American diversity. In South Africa, where rigid labeling was the norm, many young Coloureds think it's safer to avoid all labels, period. Charlene Franse's schoolmates at the Botha school are unified in their belief that creating more racial categories is a bad idea. Sixteen-year-old Natalie Whener says that "too many fights break out" because of racial classifications. To her, more classifications would mean more fights. "I don't think they should start it," she says of Americans. Adds Brigitta Beck, seventeen: "In South Africa, we are trying not to categorize people according to races. We are all just going to be known as South Africans, not as Coloureds, blacks, whatever. So I don't think Americans should do it."

New Labels, New Frontiers

The only thing that's clear from examining the lives of the teens in America and South Africa is how much racial identity is shaped by circumstance. Everything from skin color to family attitudes to national politics helps shape how we interpret who we are. For now, Americans like Earl, Nicole, Maceo, and Camille aren't allowed to mark themselves on government forms as multiracial. But it's becoming clear that America will have to adjust to the increasing number of people who claim two or more races as their own. Figuring out what labels to use is only a tiny part of the problem. (Just ask the young Coloured South Africans.) Even advocates of a "multiracial" category realize that the issues of community and equality far transcend the language we use to describe each other. No new label alone will be able to eliminate the inconsistencies of race, or free us from prejudices we've battled in America for centuries.

THREE

Back to Antebellum: An Interracial Couple in the Old South

Thomasville, Georgia

God's country is what you see when you drive down Highway 319, an unprepossessing two-lane stretch that leads from Tallahassee, Florida, to Thomasville, Georgia. The heat in southern Georgia is molten liquid, not the dry heat of the Southwest or the mere mugginess of the Northeast. Clothes stick to your back on the walk from the car to the market. House pets, if outside, lie in the shade. People cease to move except in vehicles. But the green, endless variants of green, is everywhere, deep and rich with summer's rain and sun. The sky, to a city dweller, is remarkable first for simply being visible, but most for being a robin's-egg blue suffused with marshmallow-fluff clouds.

The land is beautiful but not easy. Farming, which was once the major industry of the area, has yielded its primacy to low-paying jobs in construction, nursing home care and at the local kitty litter and meatpacking plants. The average household income in Thomas County is just twenty-two thousand dollars a year, and over a quarter of residents live below the poverty level. Thomasville, the county's main city, is home to eighteen thousand people. Fifty-two percent are black; 46 percent are white.

By many accounts, the two races mix as little as humanly possible. Thomasville's shady, select streets are filled with stately colonials, while nearby plantations, monuments to the antebellum South, are a minor tourist attraction. But the side roads of Thomasville are different. There's the local housing project, a residence motel known for the drug dealing and drivebys most often associated with big inner cities, and trailer parks with gravel roads rutted by hurricanes.

Even if money doesn't come easy, it would be tempting to think that other intangibles would, qualities like the feelings of rootedness you get living in a small town where few people move out and even fewer move in. Maybe Thomasville had that, once. But it was shattered on March 27, 1996, when the *Atlanta Constitution* printed the story that a local all-white Baptist church had threatened to disinter the body of a mixed-raced black infant. That baby—baby Whitney, named after her parents' favorite singer—died from a birth defect before she was a day old. Her mother's family, who were members of Barnett's Creek Baptist Church, decided to bury the child next to the grave of her great-grandfather. The funeral went without incident, but days later the deacons and pastor of the church offered the family seventy-five dollars to remove the body of the child. Their reasoning: she was a "half-breed" who didn't belong in an all-white cemetery. The family declined the paltry payment and went to the media instead, redoubling the already furious national debate over how well we accept interracial relationships and the children who come from them.

Interracial Hate

Like everybody else, I read the newspaper accounts with disgust. For a church in the 1990s to consider unearthing a body because of its race seemed unthinkable. But I also read the stories with a sense of eagerness, the buzz a reporter feels when she's on to a good story. On the one hand, America's come a long way. Until 1967, interracial marriages were illegal in some states. But today, 2.2 percent—or 1.2 million—of America's marriages are interracial, a figure that has been rising every year. (The different cultural identities of young mixed-race Americans is covered in chapter 2.) There are many parts of the country where nobody bats an eye if a black man and a white woman walk together hand in hand. But there's another side of the story as well: all of the neighborhoods where interracial relationships are still utterly taboo. Some are towns like Thomasville, places steeped in the history and culture of the Old South, places where race is and always has been black and white. Black men were lynched as recently as the fifties for daring to so much as wink at a white woman, and it was wise in many towns for blacks to be off the streets by sunset. Some think that's prudent even today.

Baby Whitney's parents may have heard of the New South—a place of opportunity and racial equanimity—but they've never lived in it. When Whitney was born, Bubba Johnson was twenty-five and out of work, an unskilled laborer who'd grown up in the housing projects of Thomasville and Ft. Lauderdale, Florida. Jaime Johnson was eighteen, a high-school dropout whose mother and stepfather worked at the local meat-processing plant. Bubba and Jaime met at a local pool hall, a place they were later thrown out of for daring to flout local racial taboos. Bubba has ebony skin, a trim, muscled body, and the impassive gaze of a Yoruba sculpture. Jaime is a plump woman with wary eyes and a pallid complexion. One of the first things they tell me about when I meet them is how common racial incidents were in their everyday life. "It was right by the drugstore in Thomasville," Jaime remembers. "A guy with a child and his wife in the car yelled, 'Nigger loving whore!' out the window. And he turned the car around, and he come into the parking lot. And he rolled down the window, and he was reaching for a gun in his glove compartment." When Bubba and Jaime ran into the store, the driver pulled away. "The bad thing about it," Jaime says, resigned, "was that there was a baby in that car. And he was teaching that child, you know, to hate people."

Hating people, especially in so obvious and crude a way, is supposed to be unacceptable in today's America. And yet it happens often enough that we can't deny it or forget it. Statistics gathered by the Klanwatch organization show that interracial couples are often a target. In 1992, interracial couples in a slew of states from Indiana to Pennsylvania to Wisconsin found crosses burned on their lawns. In 1993, a black man was killed in St. Louis, Missouri, for dating a white woman. In 1994, members of interracial couples were beaten in states including Indiana, New York, and Virginia. In 1995, three members of a neo-Nazi skinhead group were indicted for firebombing an interracial couple's home in Mississipi the year before. And in 1996, the St. Louis home of yet another couple burned after a Molotov cocktail was thrown through their window.[1]

To me, investigating what I see as a clear hate crime against Bubba and Jaime is an extension of work I did interviewing young women in the hate movement. The hater and the hated are two parts of the same vicious cycle. When I was reporting on hate groups, I met a few Klanspeople face-to-face, but I did most of my interviews over the phone for obvious reasons. One woman I will never forget is Beth, who at the time was a twenty-two-year-old studying to be a midwife in Washington State. She was so many things that we think white supremacists are not: from a wealthy family and raised in an urbane Southern California setting, well educated and blue blooded. Her family is even listed in the Social Register. She broke the gender barrier in the hate movement, becoming the first woman to lead a major faction of the skinheads, the young footsoldiers of the hate movement. Yet in many ways, Beth fit the mold of the "typical" hate group participant. She feels her family is dysfunctional, and she feels disenfranchised from American society. So Beth adopted the skinhead movement as her family.

While attending the prestigious Art Institute of Chicago, Beth joined the American Front, a group whose leader was later convicted for bombing a NAACP office and gay bar in Washington State. Before she was nineteen, Beth had become the American Front's codirector. The American Front and other skinhead groups use youth-friendly recruiting tactics, including telephone hot lines, websites, and, perhaps most important, a thriving hate-rock music scene with underground hit bands preaching race war. Beth even met her husband at the Aryan Youth Conference Games, where they won in the men's and women's divisions of the hammer toss. "Our prize," she says, "was getting to light the ceremonial swastika together that night." What did she learn from the hate movement and, in turn, preach? "Jewish people fabricated tales of Nazi gas chambers to get a free ride, a ticket to pull on people's heartstrings." And blacks? "Whites are stronger and more intelligent," she says. When skinheads do commit hate crimes, she claims blacks have provoked them. "Being white and being proud, we're backed into a corner," she says.

The scariest thing I realized while researching the hate movement was not the depth of their hate but the depth of our national loyalty to outmoded stereotypes. Groups like the American Front couldn't exist without the more subtle prejudice that permeates American society. Most of the people I interviewed for my article were raised by parents who taught them taboos against interracial marriage and friendships, perhaps not realizing how profound an impact those warnings would have. The everyday verbal venting of racial prejudices helps embolden the few renegades who act on their worst instincts.

Acting on the Hate

Bubba and Jaime happen to live in a place where racial tensions bubble close to the surface. Hate crimes can take place anywhere, but how often they happen has a lot to do with a community's values and taboos. In America's biggest cities, interracial dating is common, even hip. When Whitney Elaine Johnson died that March, the most famous interracial couple in America was Orenthal James and Nicole Brown Simpson, the latter brutally deceased. The fact that they were an interracial couple added to their allure when both were alive and the lurid attraction of the case once Nicole Brown Simpson was dead. Their lives couldn't have been more different than Bubba and Jaime's. The Simpsons lived in

Southern California, a place the Census Bureau projects has the largest numbers of multiracial children. The Simpsons also lived lives of glamour and privilege; if anyone had a problem with their relationship (and doubtless some still did), it was probably whispered behind their backs rather than thrown up in their faces. Bubba and Jaime—broke, living hand-to-mouth with relatives—had no such socioeconomic cushion.

In fact, it soon became clear to me that Bubba and Jaime's poverty put them in a position where they could never escape the racial problems they faced, no matter how hard they tried. They ended up fleeing from city to city, sometimes supported by their families and sometimes rejected by them, hoping for a stable life one moment and then seeing those hopes dashed the next. Ultimately the story of what happened to Bubba, Jaime, and their families—and to my perceptions of their situation over time—is more than an inside look at the depths of the racial divide. It's at least a three-pronged tale: of how deeply ingrained the old prejudices run, of how we as a society react when we learn a racial incident has occurred, and of how the dual forces of race and poverty arc the surest way to tear a family apart. I started learning how precarious their lives were as soon as my plane landed.

Journey to Thomasville

A muggy June Saturday three months after Whitney Elaine Johnson was buried, I stagger off the airplane and into the Tampa airport, woozy from having gotten just three hours of sleep the night before. After I make my way through the rental car line, I punch in my calling card number and dial up Sylvia Leverett, Whitney's maternal grandmother. Sylvia had done the brunt of the media interviews after baby Whitney's death, decrying with righteous fire how her granddaughter was treated. She was the one who gave me the news that Bubba and Jaime had fled to the Tampa area—staying first with Jaime's sister and then, when she kicked them out, with a friend. I'd called and spoken to them a couple times, but for the past two days, they hadn't returned my phone calls.

Her voice raspy from cigarettes, Sylvia tells me she's got bad news. Jaime and Bubba moved to Ft. Lauderdale two days ago. "They went to stay with Bubba's dad. Things weren't working out. Jaime said to tell you she's real sorry."

With those simple words, my plan for this trip falls apart. The whole point of me flying into Tampa was to interview Bubba and Jaime. I whip out my battered road atlas. Ft. Lauderdale is right above Miami, at the bottom right of the printed page; currently, I'm in Tampa, the middle; Sylvia Leverett is at the top, just north of the Florida-Georgia state line. I'd already planned on driving the five hours northwest to Thomasville and spending the night before crashing services at Barnett's Creek Baptist Church, the nexis of this crisis. Now I was faced with trying to hit two locations catercorner across the entire state of Florida in three days. I call the new number Sylvia gave me for Bubba and Jaime and arrange to fly into Miami airport and interview them in Ft. Lauderdale on Monday.

The new plan in place, I pick up my rental car—a less-than-inconspicuous red Grand Am—and hit I-75 north. The closer I get to the Georgia state line, the more signs I see for thin-shelled pecans, ripe peaches, homemade preserves, all the bounty of the South. But the sign that finally makes me pull over is one for a Russell Stover factory outlet. I ship some home to my mom and grab a tin to give as a token to Sylvia and her husband.

I cut across Route 84 from Valdosta and drive into Thomasville. But what to do now that I'm here? I don't have anything planned until to-morrow, so I decide to poke around the town, at least until it's dark. (Call it Northern paranoia.) The city, such as it is, is modest. The town center is pretty enough, with a colonial-style hall and a visitor's bureau that is already shuttered. There are two or three streets of businesses, and a mini-mart at the first intersection in town. The town's even sup-posed to be crowded this weekend. I'm staying in Tallahassee because two local hotels told me there's a big reunion taking up all the rooms. But no one seems to be on the streets. There's a couple of black kids walking, two or three cars in the mini-mart parking lot, and a few others driving the streets but that's it.

I test out the directions Sylvia Leverett has given me for reaching Barnett's Creek Baptist and keep going in circles. Is the bridge I'm crossing the bridge she told me about? Doesn't seem to get me anywhere but a residential neighborhood. On my third pass through the same streets, a black boy of about twelve smiles and waves at me. He's sitting on the stoop of a small, run-down convenience store with a girl a little younger than him. A woman with a Jheri Curl (though stylistically outlawed in the Northeast, you can still find the goopy hairdos in parts of Southern California, Chicago, and the South) stands in the doorway. I make a U-turn in the middle of the empty road, park the car and say hi. The woman nods when I tell her I'm looking for Barnett's Creek. She's heard all about what happened there, but (of course) has never been. Her store is remarkable for being almost empty, not just of customers, which it is, but also of food. The shelves of the dimly lit shop contain spare, discrete piles: one brand of flour, one brand of cornmeal, one brand of coffee. What she does have is chili dogs and chili Polishes (the second bigger than the first, with what ought to be an illegal number of calories and dripping fat). I rationalize that because I haven't eaten since breakfast and it's near dinnertime, I can order one of each. I scarf them down while leaning over the counter, as she scours the phone book and even calls a friend to try to get me where I'm going.

The shopkeeper ultimately doesn't have a clue how to get me to the church, but as the sun begins to dip behind the trees she tells me a bit about herself, her children, and her own childhood. She grew up in a rural area closer to Atlanta than Thomasville, a place where the father of her closest childhood friend eventually forebade them to speak, because he and his daughter were white. It was a place where the police enforced the law on whites and the Klan enforced their own on blacks. What happened to Bubba and Jaime here is unusual, she says; most of the time, blacks and whites just avoid each other. The city doesn't have much to offer anyone of any color, she adds, but at least the chances of a young black man getting hooked in with a gang are lower here than in the big city. "My sister moved up to Atlanta," she says. "Now her son is mixed up with drugs. I guess I'll stay here," she adds without much enthusiasm, "at least until my son is grown."

The Country Church

After spending the night at a nondescript hotel in Tallahassee, I wake up bright and early, pick up some batteries and cassette tapes at Wal-Mart, and take 319 back into Thomasville. The trees form a canopy over the road and the asphalt is dappled with sunlight from above. Family fruit stands sit by the roadside, selling more of those fresh Georgia peaches, the size of a heavyweight boxer's fist. My family, though rooted not in the Deep South but in Maryland and Virginia, imbued me with a love of the land. In our modest-sized backyard, my mother grew and still grows peaches, corn, tomatoes, berries, melons, peppers, herbs. The heat and humidity in Baltimore sometimes approach the suffocating blanket of hot air here. I almost feel like I'm home.

Last night I'd spoken to Sylvia again; I did have the wrong bridge. Today I get it right. It's half an hour before services are scheduled to start and I drive down a twisting road off 319 to Barnett's Creek Baptist Church. It's beautiful and simple, modestly sized. The main building is storybook perfect, with three-tiered eaves and a small spire. Quite appropriately, I think to myself, the church is all white.

There's no parking lot, just a wide expanse of lawn with space for cars on the right side and a small graveyard on the left. The space where Whitney Johnson is buried, right next to her grandfather, is one of the closest graves to the church. The family has no money for a headstone so her resting place is still unmarked.

I'd tried calling Pastor Leon VanLandingham to set up an interview over the phone; his wife bluntly declined on his behalf, refusing to even take my name. I figured I'd show up and try to talk to him anyway, though I wasn't sure he'd let me. VanLandingham had thrown Dennis

McCafferty, an *Atlanta Constitution* reporter who graciously gave me some background on the story, out of the church. When I told my friends before I left New York that I intended on crashing services at the all-white church, they reacted with unvarying horror. And while I put on a game face for their behalf, I was downright nervous about making my debut in white small-town society.

Torn between sneaking in before the 11 A.M. service started and dashing in at the last moment, I sit in my car, the air conditioner on, playing an alternative rock station at low volume to reassure myself I'm not really that far from civilization. At 10:40, I try tugging on the doors to the church, none too aggressively. They don't open. I run back to the car. At 10:43, a man with a big belly in a gray suit pulls up in a white Chevy truck and parks it on the open lawn by the cemetery. From his entitled swagger—which Sylvia Leverett described as his defining feature—I think it might be the Deacon Logan Lewis, the man who masterminded the plan to move Whitney's body and admitted to the *Atlanta Constitution* he had called her a "half-breed." By 10:47, even the car's air-conditioning can't mask the sweltering heat. Parishioners begin arriving, pushing open the door rather than pulling it as I did. My gutlessness is so ludicrous I have to laugh at myself.

I leave my notebook in the car. I feel that it's somehow inappropriate for me to bring my scribbling into the hall, and besides, it's a sure way to get myself kicked out. The church inside is as simple and clean as it is from the outside. The pews are three across, and less than twenty from back to front. The deacons of the church, a neat array of gray-haired white men, sit in the row closest to the altar. I sit down and almost wedge myself into the far right seat of the last pew on the right, feeling more comfortable closer to the doors. Families filter in slowly. All of them are white, of course, but that's about the only similarity. Some are dressed quite plainly, in plaid shirts and slacks; others wear nice Sunday dresses. Some are elderly, some have small children. Some come in large family groups, others come alone. Sylvia's husband describes Barnett's Creek as a "country church," one where you don't have to put on airs to attend.

I think about the people I'm sitting among—individuals who still choose to attend this church even though they know the deacons ordered a dead child dug up and moved, people who have been the focus of national scrutiny and outrage. Are these abject, hard-core racists? Or are they passive (though hardly innocent) bystanders to actions that they did not commission and do not condone? Before the services start, an elderly white woman comes over and introduces herself. I introduce myself by name only—no description of purpose, no state or town of origin. Simply by my opening my mouth it's clear, however, that I'm a Northern Negro—Not From Around Here. Perhaps I didn't even have to open my mouth. I'm wearing an appropriately long (calf-length) navy print dress with a black jacket, but my hair is in elaborate "silky dread" braids that I haven't seen anywhere in the South. And, most obviously, if I'm black and have chosen to attend Barnett's Creek, I'm definitely Not From Around.

"Would a Bunch of Racists Do That?"

Pastor Leon VanLandingham, who delivers the sermon, is a tall, well-proportioned man who many no doubt consider handsome. His hair is a thick curly gray, not unlike William Jefferson Clinton's. After services are over I head outside and hover near VanLandingham, waiting for the right opportunity to question him alone. I would love to question the parishoners, but that could nix my chances with the pastor. Several women come up, curious and friendly. One moved here from New Jersey. I won't be with them long enough to judge their characters, but these are real people, not racist caricatures. Of course they want to know who I really am, but the question remains unasked, and unanswered.

After most of the parishioners drift away I corner VanLandingham, telling him humbly that I am a reporter. There are many ways of approaching an interview subject, and I sense this is a man who would welcome the chance to rehabilitate his tarnished reputation. He pauses for a moment, dramatically, on the stairs of the church, before replying.

"This is the result of a few malcontents, and I'm very angry with them, I'm angry with the press," he says. I ask him directly if he offered the family money to move Whitney Elaine Johnson, and he replies—very clearly—"No,we didn't. Look over there. That child is buried right there in the plot that I gave to her great-grandfather, I donated the land, it's so conspicuous, it's right over there.

"There was never any meeting to determine about moving the child," the pastor continues. "There was just a meeting to discuss a problem with the nursing home [that prepared the child's body]." Was the problem that the nursing home didn't tell you the child was black? Did that make you uncomfortable? "No, it didn't make any of us uncomfortable, I think it made the family more uncomfortable. Look, this church has been here for a hundred and forty years. We've never had any racial problems. You heard what we were discussing in church today. We're going to go help rebuild some the churches in Alabama that were burned, the black churches in Alabama. You look around here, and our church needs some rebuilding itself." I tell him the church looks pretty nice to me. "We need to add on," VanLandingham says. "We could be using that money ourselves, but we want to help people in the black churches. Would a bunch of racists do that?"

I've asked the direct questions and gotten denials or nonanswers, so I thank Pastor VanLandingham for his time. "These doors are open; come back any time," he says, closing by inviting me to come to his brand-new restaurant. He used to work with children doing social services, he says, but he quit. "It's always been my dream," he says, "to own a restaurant."

Blue Glass Figurines and the Confederate Flag

"His dream?" Sylvia Leverett snorts, a cigarette in her hand. "He was working with the D.A.R.E. program," which provides anti-drug-abuse programs to schoolchildren. "And naturally he's working with every type of children, OK. And if he makes these type of statements, they don't want him." In other words, she claims, he was fired. "And the thing of it is," Sylvia continues, incredulous, "he lost his job, and he wanted Bill and I to feel sorry for him!"

I'm sitting in the trailer of Sylvia and William (Bill) Leverett, a pristine home nearly the size of a small suburban ranch-style house. I've delivered my gift of Russell Stover candies and settled down on a couch next to Sylvia. Their trailer park is a large circular drive off of a dead-end street. The drive, which has a pond in the center and trailers just off to either side, is rutted and pitted from the relentless Southern storms. Most of the vehicles that circle it are homes of last resort. One is nothing more than an aluminum vacation trailer, its windows boarded up due to frequent hurricanes. (Even the Leverett's shiny new trailer has one window out.) One home, near the entrance, has a nice built-on deck, but most are bereft of add-ons—with the notable exception of the trailer to the side of the Leverett's, which flies a Confederate flag.

Then again, Bill and Sylvia used to fly the flag, all the way until the battle over Whitney's legacy heated up. A local television reporter came out to their trailer and told Bill he might want to consider taking it down before the interview. "Until she told me," he says in an improbably matter-of-fact way, "we didn't know what it meant to some people." Six months ago, Bill and Sylvia probably couldn't have conceived of being the center of an antiracism crusade. But then again, as Sylvia puts it, "They disrespected my granddaughter."

Her voice is tight with anger, but Sylvia's home is so pleasant it seems as if it ought to be transported to a less depressing locale. The outside gleams, and once you step inside, everything, absolutely everything, is blue. There's an immaculate, midtoned blue carpet, a blue sofa, and La-Z-Boy chair. The curtains are blue, as are many of the decorative items and tchotchkes hanging from and lining the walls. Sylvia collects china and glassware, little figurines of Mandarins dressed in blue and tiny clear glass sculptures of deer and such. Bill, who looks the way the Marlboro Man might if he chose to wear a tracksuit on Sundays, sits chain-smoking in the recliner. Sylvia, forty-one, a plain woman with outsize tinted glasses, radiates the strain she's been through and is still under. Like her husband of nine years, she smokes, and she lights up again and again as she tells me about what the family's been through.

Baby Whitney's birth and death was a tragedy even before Barnett's Creek got involved. "We only had five days," Sylvia says of the time between finding out that her granddaughter had no skull, and the day she was born and died. Long before Jaime's due date, doctors should have discovered that the child she was carrying had a brain, and a face, and a scalp—and even hair covering her head—but no skull to protect her once she was born. Jaime had been having pains, Sylvia says, pains her doctor pooh-poohed. Finally, they performed an ultrasound. They sat, and waited, and waited, and sat. They waited so long they knew even before anyone told them that and knew from how long the doctor was taking that something was terribly wrong. Jaime was ordered to go the next morning to a bigger hospital in Tallahassee.

"Well, needless to say nobody got any sleep that night, so we were running on nerve," Sylvia says. "The doctor told us there was no way she could survive. Number one she couldn't be delivered vaginally because of the skull not being there, and number two that she would never survive outside of Jamie's body, OK. So we dealt with that. He wanted us to go to Augusta because they have a fantastic hospital in Augusta and they thought maybe they could take either sheep, baby sheep bones, or something like that and build her a skull, 'cause they didn't really know what they were dealing with until she was actually delivered. Well we gathered, pooled, all our money together, like I said, we're not rich people by far, but we pooled all our money together." Sylvia, Bubba, Jaime, and her sister Kathy, on no sleep and with little money, set off by bus. It took them nineteen and a half hours to get there. And then, adds Sylvia. "We were only there thirty minutes when they told us there was nothing they could do. We had to turn around."

She shows me a picture of Whitney—beautiful, brown, healthy-looking. Then she shows me a clipping of the obituary: "March 22, 1996. Services for Whitney Elaine Johnson, died March 18." Finally she shows me a crucial letter—an apology signed by the church's deacons and by Pastor VanLandingham, the man who just denied anyone had asked to have baby Whitney moved. It reads:

Barnett's Creek Baptist Church
Ochlocknee, GA

We, the members of the Board of Deacons of Barnett's Creek Baptist Church regret the frustrations and anxieties brought on by the actions of the body in requesting permission from the family to remove the body of little Whitney Elaine Johnson from the Church cemetery. With the presentation of this letter we respectfully extend our apologies to the entire family and ask that this matter be laid to rest on this date, March 30, 1996.
As much as is possible, this grave with all the others in the cemetery will be protected from desecration.

Sincerely,

The signatures of the six deacons and VanLandingham follow. This letter is the most concrete bit of evidence supporting Jaime Wireman and the Leveretts.

Sylvia says three deacons dropped this letter at her mother's home and quickly departed. "That's how brave they were," Sylvia says.

She and Bill first got a hint something was percolating from her mother, who told her Deacon Logan Lewis was going to call. "When my mom called she said, 'It's probably they're going to offer to pay for the funeral. You know they offered to pay for your daddy's,'" Sylvia recalls. Instead, he asked that Whitney's body be moved, calling the child a "half-breed" and saying she had no place in a "one hundred percent white" cemetery.

According to information from a sympathetic deacon, say the Leveretts, this is what happened leading up to Lewis's call: First, he convened a meeting of the board of six deacons, expressing a desire to move Whitney's body because she was black. "He told them to go home and pray about it. They would come back that night, and they would make their decision," Sylvia says. "They went in there. Three deacons voted for it; three deacons voted against it. When they left, the three deacons that voted against it in their mind thought that was the end of it, OK?" She pauses to take a drag from her cigarette. "Logan Lewis comes in behind their back, gets with the other two that besides himself, and decides to call me."

When the family refused to move Whitney, Logan came back with an offer of seventy-five dollars to pay to disinter the child. When he pressed the issue, Sylvia and Bill contacted the media, who swooped in from across the country to cover the story. In an interview with the *Christian Index of Georgia*, Pastor VanLandingham charged the nursing home that prepared the body with "deception" for not revealing Whitney was biracial. But the Leveretts say he knew exactly what the situation was. The Wednesday after Whitney's death, Bill and Bubba met VanLandingham to measure the space available to bury the baby in the church lot. "At the time, Bill said, 'This is the baby's father. He and I are going to be pallbearers . . .' But then later in order to try to cover his tracks, with the deacons see, [VanLandingham] said he thought Bubba was a grave digger.' "

At one point, the Leveretts say, Logan Lewis wanted a letter of apology from *them* for what he saw as smearing the good name of the church. But during a fiery forty-five-minute meeting between Bill, Sylvia, Pastor VanLandingham, and Deacon Lewis, monitored and taped by a Tallahassee television reporter, the tables were turned. Lewis, says Sylvia, "kept rattling on about this that and the other and I looked him dead in the eye and said, 'I want you to say what you are apologizing for.' And he just kind of hemmed and hawed, and I said, 'What are you apologizing for?' And he said, 'Well, because I wanted your granddaughter to be moved because she was half black.' I said, 'What did you call her? . . . You called her a half-breed.' " Lewis denied it, while VanLandingham simply said, "A lot of things are said in anger." Eventually, both offered a vague apology generally, but never mentioned the racial slur.

Says Sylvia, fire in her eyes, the lit cigarette forgotten for a moment and burning closer to her trembling fingers: "Bill's really the one that said, 'You know as Christians, we need to try to put an end to this.' OK, but that was the hardest thing I have ever done, was to talk back in that room with the two men that disgraced my granddaughter in such a way and to be able to sit across the table and not knock the living hell out of them."

A Fresh Start, or a Dead End?

By this time, I feel as if I have a better picture of what must have happened in Thomasville—the naked racism of Deacon Lewis, abetted by the cowardice of Pastor VanLandingham. But Bubba and Jaime remain two-dimensional figures. I set out to meet them in Ft. Lauderdale, first flying from Tallahassee to Miami, then driving north on I-95, which stretches from Miami on its southern tip to Maine (and finally Canada) in the north. Ft. Lauderdale is one of America's spring break capitals, a place where fit, tanned coeds play beach volleyball and frolic in the waves. But the Sunrise Boulevard exit doesn't let you off at the beach. It lets you off next to Sunnyland Park, a community segregated by race, income, and urban planning. There, a series of narrow, alley-like streets crosshatch each other but don't, save a couple of exceptions, enter or exit onto the main boulevard. It's as if the city couldn't bear the thought of allowing the housing project's black residents easy egress from their maze.

These aren't Chicago-style high-rise projects; instead, they are short, ludicrously short in fact. The tiny green bungalows, stenciled with the words NO LOITERING, NO TRESPASSING, don't look much more than ten feet tall. Each one contains a cramped two-bedroom home, a place where the oppressive South Florida heat ricochets off of the smudged white interior walls.

One of these homes belongs, as much as they belong to anyone besides the government, to Dorothy Smith, Bubba's aunt. Bubba's father, who left his mother when he was seven, is now the minister of a nearby storefront church. I navigate the maze and park my car next to a bungalow that looks like all the others; Dorothy, a pleasant, heavyset woman, greets me at the door. Jaime and Bubba emerge slowly, warily, as if they haven't yet gotten their bearings in this new town. We make awkward introductions. Later, they explain to me that it's not just the shock of finally leaving Thomasville that disorients them. It's fear. They know they are a burden in this overcrowded abode, extra mouths to feed in a household that can't feed enough. And if that burden gets too great, they will be asked to leave. They've experienced rejection before—living in, and being kicked out of, not only Bill and Sylvia Leverett's home, but Bubba's mother's and Jaime's grandmother's as well. They've lived in a run-down residence motel in a drug-infested neighborhood; and for five months, they even made a home of a beat-up car.

We sit talking about the lives in Thomasville at a beachfront café to which I've driven them. There's barely enough room to breathe in Dorothy's house, and they relax visibly once we leave. Bubba is trim and muscular, with a molasses-thick Southern accent and hair cropped short to show its tight waves. Once she warms up, Jaime is outgoing and does most of the talking. Jaime turned nineteen just days ago. She and Bubba have been in Ft. Lauderdale less than a week, and both are alert to everything within the horizon—the palm trees, the sand, even the salt air. Both are wearing nondescript shorts and T-shirts, and both use the unearned honorific "Miss Farai" when speaking to me, no matter how hard I try to dissuade them from doing so.

"I can't even tell you all of the feelings I get out of what happened," Jaime begins. "I mean, I just . . . Sometimes I could be sitting here laughing, and just bust out crying, you know—it bothers me that bad." First of all, being part of an interracial couple in Thomasville was enough to drive her to tears. "I'm gonna tell you, it's just about as bad as the whites used to treat the blacks back in the days. It is just that bad. Because if people could have it the way they wanted to, they would hang us." That seems like awfully dramatic language. Then again, the white supremacist bestseller *The Turner Diaries,* a tract designed to incite a "race war" (and alleged to have provided a blueprint for the bomb used to destroy the Oklahoma City federal building), includes a scene in which white women who've committed the sin of "race mixing" are hung from lampposts.

Bubba and Jaime are veterans of America's real-life race wars. By their own description, their daily lives in Thomasville were nothing less than sheer hell. "The police in Thomasville, they hated me and Bubba," Jaime says, launching into a seemingly endless litany of run-ins with the cops, with Bubba being sprayed with pepper gas one time and being told, "Look here, boy, you better take your ass in the house before I take your ass in jail," on another. Once, says Jaime, five cops surrounded Bubba, claimed they had a warrant for his arrest, and slammed his head onto a cruiser so hard that his nose bled. Jaime had learned police procedure from her mother, who used to be a desk-duty cop. And when Jaime asked to see the warrant for Bubba's arrest, they claimed they'd made a mistake and drove off. "They always thought he was selling drugs. And I don't see how he can be," she adds with rueful humor. "A person that sells drugs has money, right?"

Not that Bubba and Jaime are saints. Bubba was once arrested for hitting a woman he was seeing at the time. And when she was eighteen, Jaime spent twenty days in jail for disturbing the peace at a party. The couple have a lot more in common than skirmishes with the law. Both of their mothers and fathers split up. Jaime barely knew her father, a man who she believes to have fourteen children scattered around the country and who Sylvia tells me was a drug addict. Jaime also says she was physically and sexually abused by a relative when she was in elementary school, "until he turned his life over to God." Bubba's father split when he was seven; after that Bubba and his mom moved to Thomasville. Neither Bubba nor Jaime have any marketable job skills. Bubba has a diploma from Thomasville High but has only really worked as a laborer. Jaime dropped out of school in tenth grade, and was working full-time at Hardee's by the time she was fifteen.

When Jaime worked at Hardee's she was dating another black guy, something that nixed her employment prospects. "The boss lady, which is a white woman, pulled me off to the side when she found out I was dating one of the guys who worked there, a black guy," Jaime says. "And these were her exact words: 'How can you stand to date a nigger?' "

"And I looked at her and I said, 'Look here, that's none of your business. You need to tend your business and stop tending everybody else's.' Not so long after that, she started cutting my hours back to one day a week, to where I had to quit. And I worked there almost two years."

By the time Jaime started going out with Bubba, she had learned enough to try to hide their relationship. One time, the two of them applied for jobs at the same plant separately, and were both hired. But when the supervisor saw them sitting together at lunch, he fired them without cause, Bubba and Jaime say. Then when they went to the local office of the Department of Labor to see about filing a discrimination claim, they maintain they were discouraged from filing a complaint. I ask Bubba and Jaime who they'd spoken to at the labor office. Bubba just sighs. "I don't even know. That's been so long ago. I mean, when things like that happen, you try not to remember, you know?"

Jaime remains defiant about her relationship, but pessimistic that the racism she faces will ever end. "Most mixed couples that I know, they're scared to be walking down the street holding hands. Scared they're gonna get shot. Me, I'm not. If I have something that I believe in and I'm proud of, then I'm gonna show off what I have," she says. But "because the old people teach the young people," prejudice "will never disappear until people really stand up for themselves," she says. "And I guarantee, you can talk to any mixed couple in the South, and every one of 'em will tell you they never had it easy."

I ask her why she thinks some Thomasville residents have been so hateful. "I believe that a lot of white people sit back and think, they see us and they think, how can she stand to be with him? I wonder what it would be like to be with him. You know? Like, how is it different? What would it be like? They're too scared to do it, because they know society don't accept it. And because we're doing it, they're like, 'Oh my God, they don't look like they're ashamed of anything.' "

I point out that they have nothing to be ashamed of. "I'm not," she says. "I'm not. You know, it's like this big old stink about the gay people and all. I'm like this—do what you wanna do, you know? As long as you don't hurt me or my family, that's fine. Who am I to tell them what's right or wrong? I'm not the person to tell them what's wrong."

What's been most hurtful is that the group of people telling them their relationship was utterly wrong included members of their own families. Jaime's grandmother, who still attends Barnett's Creek, might've been the most blunt. "Called him a nigger. Called me a nigger lover. That hurt me bad," Jaime says. And she adds that her mother and step-father just began to accept their relationship. "They knew Bubba for his color, and not for who he was. Now, I feel they've changed.

"See, this past Christmas," she continues, "I had called. And I talked to my mama, and I said, 'Mama, can Bubba come over? He has nowhere to go for Christmas.' And Mom said, 'It's fine with me. You have to ask your dad.' Well, he told me no. And he hurt my feelings so bad, I cried and cried. And I kept asking him, I was begging him. I said, 'Daddy, just talk to him and see what he's like.'

"He said, 'No, no, that's against my religion, I can't do that.' So I went and spent Christmas with Bubba's aunts.

"My dad told me he would accept the baby and love the baby, but that he just wouldn't accept Bubba, because he was black. And I looked at him one day and I said, 'How can that be a reason?' And he said, ''Cause God don't want it that way.' I said, 'Well, God don't want a lot of things the way they are, but they happen. If it is a mistake, I'm the one that's got to pay for it, not you.'

"I cried and cried and cried. And I prayed and I prayed. I said, 'God, that's all I want. Just to let them get to know him as a person, and not as a color.'

"Well, my wish finally came true.

"After we found out what was going on [at Barnett's Creek], my dad said, 'Go get Bubba.' And I said, 'What?' And he said, 'Go get Bubba.' I said, 'And what?' 'And bring him here.' I said, 'Are you sure?' He said, 'Yeah, I'm sure. I'm tired of going through what we're going through. Bring him here.'"

Jaime laughs, remembering. "I went to get Bubba and he was like, 'Are you sure he ain't gonna try to kill me?'"

Sylvia and Bill Leverett tell me the same story, marveling that Bubba actually feared for his life. For the first time the family was unified, if only by mutual pain.

A Flawed Racial Morality Play

This would be a great place to leave the story of baby Whitney—on an up note of racial enlightenment—except that (a) it's not that simple and (b) it doesn't end here. It does offer a chance to examine the American mentality in dealing with race in general and hate crimes specifically. Bill and Sylvia Leverett didn't have to think about their own racial biases until the racism of Thomasville hit home in their own lives. That kind of myopia—avoiding any deep examination of our own racial beliefs— runs deep in our society. A study by the National Opinion Research Center found that most whites still believe blacks to be inferior—less intelligent, less patriotic, and lazier. It's ironic, though no less unacceptable, that Southern whites are often pegged with the same labels.[2] But though we cling to racial stereotypes, study after study shows that whites (though not blacks) believe that racism is no longer a significant social issue. When we hear media reports on a racial incident, we often perform a very complicated set of mental gymnastics. First we accept the incident, then we isolate it. We admit that, for example, the deacons at Barnett's Creek could ask for Whitney to be unearthed—but we immediately reassure ourselves that such incidents are unbelievably rare, and perpetrated by a bunch of lunatics to boot. We don't want to think that perhaps this is just one of the few times the perpetrators were exposed, or that the people who perpetrated the act might not be lunatics but flawed people similar to us.

The fact that racial incidents still seem shocking and rare testifies to our ability to maintain a thin veneer of civility, even though that civility masks deeper and more complicated emotions. Because we want so desperately to think that racism is all but vanquished, we ignore many incidents, then focus intense scrutiny on the ones that catch our attention. Bubba, Jaime, Bill, and Sylvia were besieged by media attention at a time when they were barely able to mourn. They were turned into public victims, a status that puts a huge strain on everything they do and everything they are. Because race is a measure of America's values, racial incidents become morality plays. We demand "perfect" victims to exemplify the moral high ground. But reality is not nearly so neat. There are rarely such things as perfect victims, and Bubba and Jaime are no exception. After most of the reporters stopped following them, their story continued—less about racial victimization than the instability of their daily lives.

From Victimized to Demonized

On July 15, Jaime and Bubba go to the local Wal-Mart with one of Bubba's cousins. Jaime and Bubba's cousin start browsing through the store together. All of a sudden, according to Jaime, they're surrounded by police officers; the cousin tries to make a break for it. He's stolen a fistful of expensive sunglasses, and a store clerk alerted the authorities. Although she says she knew nothing about Bubba's cousin's plans, Jaime is arrested and sent to the Broward County Jail.

Bubba, who has no money and no idea how to get Jaime out, lingers by his aunt's telephone waiting to accept his girlfriend's collect calls. Because he's demanding too much—too much telephone time, too much food, too much space—Aunt Dorothy asks Bubba to leave. (Later Bubba tells me she was also given an ultimatum by the housing project because having nonresidents living in her apartment is against the rules.)

Bubba leaves town with just enough money to get him back to Thomasville by bus. Jaime, a woman who has never lived more than a few minutes from her family, is left all alone in the infamous Broward County Jail. Broward is so overcrowded that prisoners routinely sleep on the floor. This summer, one male prisoner nearly died when he was bitten by fire ants, to which he was allergic, while sleeping under a stairwell. Valerie Young, a mentally ill prisoner who became violent after being placed among the general population rather than in solitary, was overdosed with Thorazine and found dead eight hours later. "It's real bad here, Miss Farai," Jaime says, over and over, as she calls me from the prison pay phone.

This is how she describes her jail cell: "It reminds me of a cave. There's seven rooms and a shower. Each room has two girls, fourteen girls total. There are four on the floor in one cell, in the dayroom. When I come in here, I slept on the floor for five days. When you come in here you're not likely to get a blanket before a couple days. You're likely to get a pillow in a week." Worst of all, for two weeks Jaime thought she might be pregnant; then she found out the prison's urine test was wrong. "I want to go back to Thomasville," she whispers. "I have had nothing but bad luck since I left Thomasville."

Our relationship changes over the month and a half Jaime's in jail. No longer does she view me as just another reporter trying to get a quick hit off of her family's pain. She begins to call me, incessantly, and rely on me to be conduit between her and the outside world. Her mother, both for financial and emotional reasons, doesn't always take Jaime's phone calls.

"She says it's Bubba's fault," Jaime says to me one day on the phone, crying, after having called collect, the only way she can. "She said she won't accept any more of my calls unless I break up with him." For a while, Jaime pretends to have forsaken Bubba, just to have regular contact with her family, but eventually her mother's comments are too much and they fight openly. It's while Jaime's in jail that she learns her mother has had a serious accident at the meat-processing plant where she works. She falls on a spill of some sort, breaking her leg and wrist and severing the nerves in her arm. Not only is the injury devastating, but Bill tells Jaime the plant refuses to pay Sylvia workers' comp. The fact that her mother is broke and disabled—and that her stepfather has to support the family, nurse his wife to health, and fight for her disability payments alone—only whipsaws Jaime more violently between guilt and defiance when she tries to decide how to respond to Bill and Sylvia's demands that she leave Bubba.

I don't feel comfortable offering Jaime advice, but I do take an active role in finding out the status of her legal case. I end up calling the head of the Broward County Public Defenders' Office and asking him why a woman without a history of violent crime is being held for weeks on end without bail, without even being arraigned for the crime she supposedly committed. The top defender, Howard Finklestein, promises to see what he can do. First, he gets a judge to reduce the bail from seventy-five hundred to twenty-five hundred dollars, which means Jaime only has to post two hundred and fifty dollars to a bail bondsman to go free. But she and Bubba can't get even that together. Then Finklestein interviews the lead suspect in the shoplifting case, who admits—even though it incriminates him—that he committed the crime alone, and that he thought being with a white woman would give him some cover. Prosecutors still refuse to drop the charges, but hint that they may plead down to a misdemeanor rather than a felony.

Jaime tells her mother that she ought to be out soon. Sylvia, a former police officer, tells Jaime she thinks she can get her a job as a security guard when she comes home. But then the media—which first wrapped Jaime in the mantle of perfect victimization—picks up on the shoplifting story. On September 14, the *Atlanta Journal and Constitution* runs a piece about Jaime's arrest under the headline NEW STATE, MORE TROUBLE. In Thomasville the local newspaper and television station follow suit, the latter running a story on Jaime saying she was "in trouble again." It's as if they blame Jaime and her family for disturbing Thomasville's tranquillity by challenging the racism of Barnett's Creek, rather than blaming the deacons and the church itself. Stung by shame and embarrassment over the negative coverage, Sylvia again cuts Jaime off from contact.

The media attention has always been a double-edged sword, and just as quickly as it seems to have hurt Jaime, it helps her again. Over the next week, Finkelstein makes a circuit of local radio shows to talk about the case. A series of strangers—most of them the parents of interracial children, and sympathetic to Jaime's plight—then put up money for her bail. Even though Finkelstein now has a security video that shows Jaime wasn't involved in the shoplifting, Jaime agrees to plead guilty to a misdemeanor instead of waiting for a trial. It's far better than the felony conviction she could have received, one that would have marred job applications and personal records for decades to come, but it's still a mark against her she doesn't deserve.

A Hardscrabble Life

There's nowhere for her to go but back to Bubba's Aunt Dorothy's house. She hands over all of the money well-wishers have given her to buy the family food in exchange for her board. By mid-October, Jaime scrapes together enough money for a bus ticket back to Thomasville. She and Bubba cobble together a hodgepodge life. After being kicked out of Bubba's mother's house, they stay with friends when they can—sleeping on their porches when the hospitality runs thin. Bubba is working on temporary assignment loading trucks at All Dry, the cat litter factory, but he won't be paid for another two weeks. Jaime is looking for work cleaning homes, raking leaves, whatever. They got a referral to a local shelter, but it doesn't help much since the shelter's full. They're eating from food stamp money, which only does them so much good since they don't have a place to stay. "What good are food stamps if you don't got no stove to cook the food on?" Bubba says. "You only can go so long snacking on potato chips and so on."

In early December, Jaime calls. "We got married this morning, Miss Farai," she says happily. "A reporter from the paper asked us why we would want to spend the last thirty dollars we have getting married. We told him we're in love and the Lord will provide." But a mere eight days before Christmas, Jaime calls me from her mother's house, sobbing. "Bubba busted me in the lip, the nose, choked me in the throat. He's sitting in jail right now and I know he's going to do a lot of time. We just got married. I gotta see about filing for divorce.

"He hit me a couple times before—before I got pregnant, before I got married. He drinks real bad," she says. "When he drinks he gets violent. He's been good for a long time. Now he gets home from work and gets drunk and then there's really no reasoning with him."

Now the tables are turned. Bubba is the enemy, Sylvia, whose health has gotten even poorer, is an ally. "My mom has always been here for me. When I call her, she's there. I thought maybe me getting married and showing him I truly love him would sway him to the right thing," Jaime says of Bubba. "But he's getting worse. We've only been married three weeks and look what happened."

The next week, Jaime calls again, from a pay phone, with Bubba on the line. "We're back together, Miss Farai," Jaime says. "I'm going to try to do this program that pays you to go to school. Bubba is getting counseling to control himself." Put Bubba on the line, I demand. I ask him if he's serious about the counseling. He mumbles a few sheepish assurances.

Never Inconspicuous

If Bubba and Jaime's lives are a morality play, it is one with many victimizers—including the couple themselves. Stories about the racism that lurked in Thomasville thrust Jaime and Bubba briefly into the spotlight. Now that spotlight has receded, but the incident will continue to define their entire lives. They cannot buy a loaf of bread or look for an apartment without people knowing what happened to them—and, more important—speculating about what kinds of people they are. Their relationships with their parents, already strained by poverty and race, have become even more complicated. They epitomize America's past, and America's future. Every day there are more interracial couples like Jaime and Bubba. But as a symbol of the irrational power of race to inspire hate, they epitomize what we as a nation desperately hope to leave behind.

Young Americans in particular find themselves barraged with mixed messages about interracial dating. Some parents try to imbue them with the notion that interracial relationships are wrong; but pop culture tells them that it's cool. "Gen X" advertisements for Levi's Wide Legged jeans, soda, and dance music compilations show groups of interracial friends and lovers chillin', dining, bumping, and grinding. Popular teen shows like *Head of the Class* and network made-for-TV movies feature young interracial couples as well as same-race ones. And now, dropping a long-held interdiction, even dating shows like MTV's wildly popular *Singled Out* don't let race get in the way of a hot rendezvous. On MTV's show (which at one time featured cartoonish sex symbol Jenny McCarthy), young singles pick their mates based on answers to quirky questions. As in *The Dating Game,* they don't get to see the contestants until the competition's complete. Black women have ended up with white men, Asian men with white women. Such a racial free-for-all obviously pushed the buttons of a guy from Pompano, Florida, whose letter I got while working for MTV News from 1994 to 1995. Shortly after *Singled Out* hit the airwaves, he faxed in a handwritten missive (with a couple of typos), which reads in full:

Does 'Singled Out' have an agenda? Is it miscegenation? It would seem so. When you have a black date and 80 percent (more or lesss) of the contestants are white the end result is obvious. Perhaps you feel 'Singled Out' is just a show and the 'dates' are frivilous, but what kind of an example are you setting for society. Hence, the question—Do you have an agenda? Is it miscegenation? Shouldn't you tell the audience about it at the beginning of every show? Why do you have a hostess (the very goofy Jenny McCarthy) bleaching her hair so she can appear to be blonde when the show features miscegenation? Shouldn't her hair be in dreadlocks, or cornrows, or how about a nice bleached-out blonde afro? Gosh, maybe her implants would leak at the thought of it. To avoid embarassment do you query contestants to make sure thy don't have an aversion to miscegenation?

Note: copies of this letter are being sent to MTV, Sumner Redstone at Viacom, and your advertisers.

Most people wouldn't be so blunt about their feelings, but these kinds of sentiments bubble just below the surface of our everyday interactions. And while Bubba and Jaime's story may be extreme, it's also illustrative of what happens in communities where the racial orthodoxy is challenged. A white church deciding to exhume a black child in 1996 is clearly at the outer limits of the American experience. But sometimes we have to know our limits in order to figure out who we are—a society with a long way yet to go in dealing with intimacy between the races.

A Happy Ending?

Bubba and Jaime have a long way to go, too, but by the summer of 1997 their lives had improved considerably. Both were working full-time, she at the local Dairy Queen. They've bought a used eight hundred dollar car that runs "real good," she says. They're still sharing a room in a boarding house, but they hope to find a new place to live soon. Today is good—but then again, there's always the uncertainty of tomorrow.

I think back to what they told me in Ft. Lauderdale, words that sum up where they've been and no doubt what lies ahead.

"We've been through a lot together," Jaime says. "I mean a *lot*."

"And still going through it," Bubba adds.

Jaime finishes: "Probably go through it 'til the day we die."

FOUR

Hip-hop in the Heartland: MTV as Cultural Common Denominator

Delphi, Indiana

October 2, 1996

Dear *Vibe:*

I'm a seventeen-year-old white male living in a small rural area called Delphi. It's located in Indiana about an hour and a half from Indianapolis, the center of the decent music. In my area I have two choices of music to listen to: the same old Alanis Morrisette, Hootie, grunge stuff (it's cool sometimes but not every station!!!) or my choice the oldies. The oldies station out here often plays the classic stuff like the Temptations, Al Green, the Spinners, and they even once played "Can't Get Enough of Your Love, Babe." I wish that out here they would have an R & B station and also mix in some funk. . . . But I guess I'll just have to settle for my own CDs until someone in this area decides to do something different, but maybe that person will be me!!!!. . . . (OutKast is the Shit)

Sincerely,

B. J.

I pulled B. J.'s letter from a pile I'd culled out of the letters department at *Vibe,* a hip-hop and urban issues magazine that I write for. *Vibe*'s offices are in the heart of Manhattan, a cacophony of color and sound. The walls are filled by posters of R & B and rap artists; desks are stacked high with CDs and promotional gear; the hallways are clogged with back issues and clothes ready for fashion shoots. The magazine's editors rub elbows daily with the royalty of the rap music world like Sean "Puffy" Combs—a privilege their readers lust for; a modern-day teen dream. *Vibe* has over 2 million readers, young adults of all races. Many live in America's cities. I wasn't interested in them. The reason I sorted through the letters pile was specifically to find someone like B. J.: a white hip-hop fan from a rural, all-white town.

I presumed that kids in all-white towns don't spend a heck of a lot of time thinking about race, and that the issue doesn't impact their lives on a daily basis. But how and when *does* it come up? What happens to your perceptions of blacks and Asians and Latinos when there are practically none around? Is the fear of the unknown just as powerful as the fear of the known? Or do the lives of other races, unseen, seem mysterious and enticing? Even when everybody in your town has the same skin color, you're going to form an opinion about other races. The media and pop culture help shape those opinions.

Even the most isolated teenager will experience racial diversity vicariously: through the music they listen to, the television shows they watch, the clothes they wear, and what they think is cool. Race is about a lot more than weighty social issues like hate crimes and desegregation. It's about dope rhymes and fly beats, macking the hotties (for the uninitiated, that means looking hard for a date) and having a good time. Culture has always been one of the frontiers of racial change, especially for teens and young adults. Rock 'n' roll was originally a way for white kids in the 1950s to plug into a (sexy, taboo) black culture. Today, rap music has that distinction.

The ways that culture is disseminated today are more rapid and pervasive than ever. Via the miracle of satellite and cable, a kid on a farm in a town of five hundred can watch rappers Master P and the slain Tupac Shakur on TV. Via the miracle of malls and mail order, he can dress exactly like them. And if he's "wired," he might even get a chance to do an e-mail chat with one of his heroes, or build his own fan website. Today's young Americans live and breathe America's racially mixed popular culture, even if the city or town where they live is utterly homogeneous. And just as it did in the early days of rock 'n' roll, race has a lot to do with what's hot. Some teens uncharitably call white kids who are into hip-hop "wiggers"—white niggers. When I called B. J. on the phone, one of the first things he told me was how much he hated the term.

Before I went to Delphi, I had the local chamber of commerce mail me some info. Delphi has roughly twenty-five hundred residents; the surrounding county has just under nineteen thousand. Of that nineteen thousand, just twenty-five are black. Overall, the area where B. J. lives is 99 percent white.[1]

KKK Day

Delphi is about an hour's drive away from another 99 percent white town, Morocco, Indiana. In 1993, Morocco became the nexis of an ugly culture clash over the "dangers" of importing black culture into the heartland. A few teen girls at North Newton High School decided it would be cool to wear hip-hop-inspired outfits to school. What they found cool, their classmates found threatening. Some yelled epithets and allegedly assaulted them; a teacher kicked one girl out of class when she refused to remove a headband. And a few students even organized a "KKK Day" just in case the girls hadn't gotten the point. (Indiana, incidentally, is where the KKK was founded.) Of course the sponsors of the KKK Day were white. But so were all of the girls who wore hip-hop gear to school.

The tension became so bad that a state police officer warned an

Associated Press photographer to "watch out for gun blasts." The incident was seized on by national media outlets ranging from the *New York Times* to the *Montel Williams Show*. Most of the time you expect an incident like this to flare up and fade away. But a year later, the situation was apparently just as severe—and half a dozen of the wiggers had dropped out of school because of harassment.[2] Some of the girls befriended black students from other cities, but, according to news reports, they were ostracized by most of the teens in their hometown.

The wigger debate isn't over yet. In 1997 a Buffalo, New York, newspaper reported perhaps a bit too soberly that: "Four Kenmore West High School students who are members of a clique known as 'wiggers' were arrested Wednesday on charges stemming from the beating last week . . . of Andrew Harding, a member of the group known as 'freaks . . .' The incident, which stunned parents and police alike, occurred about 3 P.M. across the street from the school. . . . 'Wiggers' are devoted to 'gangsta rap' and prefer the low-slung baggy pants and baseball caps worn backwards that characterize some inner-city gangs. 'Freaks' favor alternative rock and more punk-like hair and clothing."[3] But just as that newspaper clip portrays wiggers as violent, out of control teens, another—with the same suspiciously serious air—anoints them the bearers of good racial tidings and great joy. "Are wiggers a good thing?" the *Chicago Tribune* asked. "Appreciating someone else's culture is good. An increased level of interest among whites in what makes some African Americans groove can only be helpful to improved race relations. . . . They've proven that popular style can be created by a few, appreciated by many and owned by none. They've also had the decency to give the creators their due."[4] As Montel Williams might say, "Wiggers: Sinners or saints? You decide."

The Road to Delphi

You get to Delphi from Indianapolis (what B. J. calls "the center of the decent music") by going north on I-65, then northeast on Highway 25, a two-lane road devoid of streetlights and dotted only occasionally with traffic signals. The town is crisscrossed by railroad tracks that bring high-priced tennis shoes and compact discs into Indiana and ship the corn and hog products out. It's a place where "wrong side of the tracks" has literal as well as metaphorical meaning, and where drivers are too-regularly hit by trains while trying to hurry and cross them.

B. J. tells me his house is easy to find: go past the Dairy Queen and the Hardee's, cross the railroad tracks, make a right at the streetlight and another one near the Marathon gas station. This is a real, albeit small, town, where the Main Street shops have apartments over them and the houses are comfortably near each other. It's the kind of place where you can still get a vanilla Coke (OK, a vanilla Pepsi) at the "DQ," or Dairy Queen. The town has only a handful of traffic signals, and absolutely no place cool, the local teens later tell me, for them to hang out. Still, I find my first sight of Delphi comforting on one level.

I love big cities, but I've always wondered what it would be like to live in a small town. My Mom did when she was young. She and her friends in the black town of Turners Station belonged to the 4-H club, not some city kiddy group. And every now and then, she talks about how she'd like to move to a place that's barely a dot on the map, a town with a couple of stores and a lot of fresh air. A place to retire, or write. There's one catch, though. If you're black, and the town you happen to fall in love with is white, you never know what kind of experience you might be getting yourself into.

That's why, on the other hand, I have a knee-jerk fear of being in all-white towns. I suspect most black people do. I don't care how irrational it seems: visions of being attacked, or harassed, or simply bombarded by naked looks of hate fill my mind. I can't help from feeling this fear, but I can help how to I react to it. I don't let it stop me from traveling the country, and I keep close tabs on my own personal prejudices so that I don't inflict them on anyone I meet. As I drive toward B. J.'s house, there's another reason I feel fairly comfortable as well. Having gone to Thomasville, Georgia—as deep into the heart of racial darkness as I ever care to be—this has to be a piece of cake by comparison.

B. J.'s house is immaculate and built of gray stone, with the grass neatly trimmed and tidy shrubs lining the front door. I pull up in the driveway behind a Chevy Monte Carlo flanked by two teen boys. The one on the left is taller and muscled, his blond hair pulled under a baseball cap; the one on the right is wiry, his dark hair buzzed and shaved on the sides. He's even got a diagonal shaved-in part, a haircut worn by thousands of black men across America. But the guy who sports this hairdo isn't black. It's my guide to the heartland, B. J.

With a practiced indifference, B. J. ushers me into his living room and stretches out on one of two immense, plushly upholstered recliners. He's wiry and not very tall. The chair swallows him. Their home is an almost self-conscious rendering of a middle-class haven, replete with a big-screen TV, a magazine rack filled with titles like *Country Living* and *Golf Digest,* and dozens of family photographs. It's awfully neat for a full house. B. J. lives here with his sixteen-year-old brother Dustin; his maternal grandmother; his mom Sherri; her second husband, Michael, a medical specialist; and their two young sons. Right now, the news that bomber Timothy McVeigh has been sentenced to death has just hit the airwaves. As the neighborhood kids outside are running around screaming in play, pictures of sobbing, relieved relatives fill the screen.

B. J.'s friend Mark, the owner of the Monte Carlo outside, sits next to me on the couch. He's got the retro charm of a seventies teen idol. Mark's working this summer doing roofing, and Band-Aids and blisters cover his hands. Like B. J., he's one of the sixty-seven teens who graduated from Delphi High a couple of weeks ago. Like B. J., he doesn't say much at first.

Finally Alicia, who's just finished her sophomore year, settles down on the other side of the couch. B. J.'s girlfriend looks even younger than her sixteen years, with braces and a mass of dirty-blond hair. She's as loquacious as the boys are laconic—quizzing me on why I came, telling me about herself, their town, her school.

I sit there fielding questions, trying as hard as I can just to make them comfortable. In my experience, the more you seem like someone—in terms of race, gender, background, income—the more immediately open they are with you. Part of learning how to be a reporter is learning how to make people who are different from you comfortable; and another, more difficult part is learning to accept the fact that most people you interview won't be completely open and honest with you. Even at the ages of sixteen or eighteen, most high school kids are smart enough to know there are certain things they should and shouldn't say to a black person. So as I try to get a sense of these teens' racial attitudes, I have to take with a grain of salt everything they tell me.

I think about one of my best friends, Danzy Senna. She's a racially mixed black novelist who looks white. As a consequence, she hears all sorts of uncensored remarks about blacks that whites would never say to someone of my skin color. She's heard whites talk about the way "they" smell and the fact that "they" (blacks, mind you) are moving into the neighborhood. Eventually, after giving people time to damn themselves with their own words, she reveals that she's black. I don't have to hear the kind of uncensored nonsense that she does. But on the other hand, I never hear the same honest appraisals of race from many whites.

So before I start talking to Mark, Alicia, and B. J. about race, I warm them up by asking about everyday life: things like parents (both B. J. and Alicia live with one parent and one stepparent) and sex (B. J. and Alicia have chosen not to have sex with each other, though he's previously had sex with other girls). These issues rank far higher in their consciousness than any discussion of black and white, as does their constant analysis of how hard it sucks to live in a small town. They tell me with a studied weariness that everyone in Delphi knows everyone, everyone in Delphi is into everyone else's business, and everyone in

Delphi used to date everyone. Before Alicia dated B. J., she dated his younger brother Dustin for a month. Dustin is taller and more muscular, with surfer-blond hair.

Mark also hints at the class differences in Delphi. On paper, Delphi seems pretty comfortable. The average family income is thirty-two thousand, and both the poverty level and unemployment rates are below the national averages.[5] But Mark tells me that there are two groups of kids that just graduated from his high school: the ones who are going on to college, usually at nearby Purdue (just half an hour away in Lafayette), and the ones who are psyching themselves up to risk their lives as miners in Colorado for twenty-five bucks an hour. Mark hopes to end up in the former category, but that's no sure thing.

Mark excuses himself to go to his girlfriend's house, and I go downstairs with Alicia and B. J. to the basement bedroom he shares with Dustin.

A Transplant to All-White America

Sitting in the sprawling basement bachelor pad of these two teen boys, I begin to get a sense of B. J. as a person. "I'm not a wigger," says the now-eighteen-year-old. He doesn't buy into the media's images of white teens out of control. He's not interested in beating up "freaks" (or rednecks, for that matter), nor is he out to save the world. He just likes hip-hop music and the styles that go with it. "It's the shit," he says simply.

When I coax more out of him, B. J. explains that he got into hip-hop for the same reason most black kids do: it's cool. Until B. J. was in eighth grade, he lived in Southern California. He shows me his yearbook from Culver City Middle School. Black, Asian, and Latino faces peer out from the pictures as often as white ones. B. J.'s best friend in junior high was Asian, and some of his other buddies were black. "It was all everything, just like everything [in L.A.] is," he says. "Indian people with those turban things; we had Chinese kids, we had white kids, we had Russian people, we had different kinds of black people from Nigeria, and this one kid from Morocco." He even went to a Spanish bilingual elementary school.

When he was in sixth grade, the new sounds of hip-hop started to hit the charts. "Rock 'n' roll in the eighties was getting a dinosaur feel to it," he says. "Groups like Poison were all doing high hair, makeup. Rap music was something new, something different. It was something fresh." His mom wasn't down with rap, though. When she discovered a tape he bought on the sly during a school field trip, she immediately unspooled it and tore it up.

And then—to hear B. J. tell it—teenage tragedy struck. After his parents' divorce, his mother remarried. His stepfather, Michael, who had roots in Indiana, moved the family to Delphi in October of B. J.'s eighth grade year.

B. J. wasn't just the only kid in Delphi who liked hip-hop and R & B. He was one of the few kids who had ever *listened* to it. He walked through the door of his new school wearing baggy jeans and T-shirt, a baseball cap pushed so low on his forehead you could barely see his eyes. Everyone else was wearing hard-rock T-shirts and tight, cuffed jeans. To them, he was a refugee from planet MTV.

"They never heard of rap music," says B. J. "They were all Metallica freaks. People said, 'Are you a skater? We've seen you in movies.' I was like," he shakes his head remembering, " 'This sucks.' "

The guys in B. J.'s school took an immediate dislike to him for two reasons: one, he was different, and two, the girls really liked him because he was different. But he made the transition into Delphi society with the aid of a couple of things: his athletic ability and drug use. He played basketball until his senior year (he was a point guard) and baseball straight through. "All the boys liked him," says Alicia, "because they were like, oh, he's good, I want him to be on my team."

In a more questionable move, he found acceptance by smoking dope with his classmates. "When I first came out here, people would use that term wigger. But then"—his voice drops almost to a whisper—"when you get high with somebody, everyone sees past it. So, it's messed up that they had to see it that way, but that's when everybody changed their opinions."

"I didn't do too good that first semester," he says. "I'd get high before school, sleep in all my classes, and go get high after school." I ask if his mother tried to stop him. He says she tried almost everything, especially grounding him. "There wasn't nothing she could do," he says, adding, "She used to make us study for two hours a night," as if his mom were administering torture by cattle prod.

It would be tempting—but very wrong—to assume that hip-hop culture corrupted B. J. and led him toward drugs. "You figured that coming from a big city I would know about drugs and about sex," he says. "But I had so much D.A.R.E. [anti-drug-abuse] education up the ass in school, I mean, they did a hell of a job in California teaching us to be aware. I can't believe that when I came out here I was like, 'No, man, you don't want to do drugs, that's bad. You don't want to have sex before you're married.' But that all changed when I moved out here. This is where I lost my virginity. This is where I lost my virginity with drugs, got caught up with all sorts of messed up things. I've learned much more about things out here than back there."

B. J. was even arrested, though not charged, when police raided a house where he and his friends were smoking pot. "I was shitting bricks," he admits. "When I was in that cop station, sitting there, [the officer] was being all relaxed talking to me because he knows I'm scared shitless. 'Who did you get it from?' [I said] 'I don't know' because I would never snitch out anyone. I had the bowl on me, but they didn't find the dope. They searched the whole house." As it turns out, their pot was hidden in a CD case, but not the one the police confiscated. "They took Dr. Dre, because it had the cannabis [a picture of a marijuana leaf] on it, and they took it as paraphernalia."

I'm not one of these people that buys into the false idea that most rap listeners get high, or that rap music is causing teen drug use. But I do see in B. J. and the thousands of teens of all races like him a trend away from the intelligence of hip-hop toward mindless pleasure. When

I was B. J.'s age, the rap music I listened to had a message. In 1988, Public Enemy released one of the all-time great rap albums, *It Takes a Nation of Millions to Hold Us Back.* As strong lyrically as it was musically, the album dealt with prisons, police brutality, crack abuse, and the painful fact that many African Americans weren't focused on dealing with these pressing issues. Years later, I took the title of one of their hits—"Don't Believe the Hype"—as the title of my first book. Some rap music still tries to educate, uplift, chastise, or inspire. But too much of it is booty bump 'n' grind or stream-of-consciousness accounts of violence. In my speeches to teens and students around the country, I take kids to task for listening to music without a message, even though it makes me seem like a crotchety old timer. Like most of the early fans of rap, I wonder how we got where we are today.

Today, white teens like B. J. make up the majority of the rap-buying audience. Some African Americans feel that white listeners are ruining rap. They worry that rappers and music executives are spending more time trying to please white listeners than black ones. They worry, too, that white listeners only want to hear ghetto horror stories, not the more complex music of urban liberation.

B. J. feels hurt by the idea that he's somehow hurting the music he loves. "I don't like that some people think rap is only for blacks and Latinos," he says. "The beats have no color lines." In an effort to learn more about the music biz, B. J.'s even interned at a local radio station, which of course doesn't play hip-hop. He'd love to start his own station, to bring some rhythm to the heartland.

Virtually every house I go to in Delphi has MTV scrolling its image of multicultural pop life across the screen. You've never been to the modern-day heartland until you've seen a kid in a pickup truck blasting R & B star Keith Sweat. (Or weirder yet, a kid walking down a deserted Delphi street pumping country music from a boom box.) I want to know what kind of relationship these kids have to this music. No doubt it's very different from mine. During elementary school, I started hearing these new beats called rap. I remember standing on a hot sidewalk in inner-city Baltimore with some distant cousin whom I probably haven't seen since and discussing how the song "Planet Rock" was the jam. This techno-influenced mix of rhymes and beats, released in 1982, wasn't about money. It wasn't even about fame. It was about the beats—pure party music. The more political rhymes from groups like Public Enemy came later. And after that, rap turned into sex and money music, with rhymes about bitches and hos, Moët and Louis Vuitton and Benzes. As rap's lyrics focused more on sex and money, urban dysfunction and crime, the music became ever more profitable. By the time I graduated from college, rap albums were hitting the Top 40 charts. Today, they routinely enter at the number one position.

While I'm in Delphi, I regale B. J. and Alicia with tales of the time I spent working at MTV. I started there just after I turned twenty-five years old, figuring it was my last chance to have a little fun. Yes, I tell them, I've met Snoop, and Tupac (back when I worked at *Newsweek*, at a party for the hip-hop movie *Juice* that he costarred in), and Biggie, who I even asked a few questions for MTV backstage at the Source Awards. To think that two of these three men are now dead, their killers still unknown, leaves me cold. What a waste of talent, I think. What a blow to the hopes of the young black community. To the parents of kids who like hip-hop, these deaths imply something else: that the music their kids listen to is morally bankrupt.

Multiculturalism via MTV

Teens like B. J. don't have to buy rap to listen to it; it's pumped into their houses every day via MTV. The channel was founded nearly two decades ago, in the days when cable television was a risky, outsider proposition. Today, they are one of the most successful corporations in America—and hands down the most powerful outlet for the transmission of music and pop culture. They are also deeply cognizant of their role in cross-pollinating America's various ethnic and lifestyle subcultures, for example, casting blacks, Asians, Latinos, and gays and lesbians on their popular reality-based show *The Real World.* Todd Cunningham, MTV's vice president of research and planning, keeps close track of his audience. Blacks make up only 13 percent of MTV viewers (perhaps because they're less likely to have cable or more likely to watch other all-rap programming on channels like B.E.T.). Yet black artists blanket MTV 's music video programming. Cunningham chalks up the discrepancy to a simple cultural reality—white kids like B. J. and his friends think black kids are cool.

"What is cool anymore?" Cunningham asks. "Alternative [rock] went mainstream. Today, the whitest of whitest kids in Madison, Wisconsin, is listening to rap and loving it—more for the attitude. It's their own little mini rebellion. It's not about it being black music or it being gangsta-like. But currently, there's nothing these kids have to rebel against." White kids listening to hip-hop are looking for an "escape," he adds, a chance to "be a little different, be in the know." And though he finds that kids in small white towns like Delphi sometimes wish MTV played more rock and less rap, teens across the country are surprisingly similar in their tastes. "With television and the internet, "someone in Des Moines, Iowa, can easily be as plugged in as someone who lives in midtown Manhattan," he says. "They can wear their Tommy Hilfiger shirt in Dubuque and feel as 'in it' as someone in downtown L.A."

A Short History of Rap

The rise of rap music is a perfect way to examine how an ethnic subculture becomes a part of American culture—and the problems that kind of cultural shift entails. The Record Industry Association of America estimates that whites account for 60 percent of rap music sales, which now total over $1 billion per year.[6] Rap is also reshaping the way young America looks, dresses, and acts. The hottest clothing lines among young Americans, like Polo and Nike and Tommy Hilfiger, have used black models and played off the hip-hop mystique. (B. J. has many of these labels in his closet, and a collection of outrageously high-priced Michael Jordan/Nike athletic shoes.) An entire genre of black films, like *Boyz N the Hood* and *Menace II Society*, rose hand-in-hand with the rap industry. And that's just the hip stuff. The biggest testament to rap's popularity may be that it's now used in utterly corny ways as well. (Disney even put out an album called *Rappin' Mickey*.)[7]

Looking back at rap music's beginnings, no one could have predicted it would have become the huge industry—or the racial crossover—that it is today. Rap began in the 1970s, spurred by the influence of West Indian MCs and neighborhood turntable wizards. The first rap hit was 1979's "Rapper's Delight"—a catchy, almost unbelieveably innocent party rhyme. But rap was still largely a subculture. In 1983 only sixteen of the eight hundred bands on MTV's video playlist were black.[8] But the channel hired rapper Fab Five Freddy to host a show called *Yo! MTV Raps* in 1992, around the time B. J. started listening to rap music. The show came on the air right after most high school kids arrived home, and it became a massive hit. By 1993, rap broke another barrier: albums by Ice Cube and Cypress Hill not only hit the pop charts, but debuted in the number one position.[9]

To keep itself fresh enough to attract new audiences, rap music has constantly reinvented itself: party music for blacks; rhythmic black nationalism; pure pop (like M.C. Hammer and Vanilla Ice); and the gangsta rap popularized by the group N.W.A. (Niggers with Attitude) in the early nineties. Perhaps it zigged and zagged to keep the formula fresh for blacks. Perhaps, as a 1991 article in the *New Republic* theorized, the rationale was different. "Although rap is still proportionally more popular among blacks, its primary audience is white and lives in the suburbs," the article reads. "And the history of rap's degeneration from insurgent black street music to mainstream pop points to another dispiriting conclusion: the more rappers were packaged as violent black criminals, the bigger their white audiences became. . . . Rap's appeal to whites rested in its evocation of an age-old image of blackness: a foreign, sexually charged, and criminal underworld against which the norms of white society are defined, and, by extension, through which they may be defied."[10]

In the mid-nineties, rap violence moved from song lyrics to the real world. Rapper Snoop Doggy Dogg was indicted for—and acquitted of—murder charges. (Snoop was the passenger in his own vehicle when his bodyguard shot a man who Snoop claims was stalking him.) Tupac Shakur, who not only sold millions of rap albums, but who starred in several films, was killed in 1996. The year before, he was shot five times in New York, and previous to that he was the target of public outrage when a young man who shot a Texas trooper claimed Tupac's lyrics made him do it.[11] Rapper Biggie Smalls, or the Notorious B.I.G., was no less controversial. The crack-dealer-turned-rapper was shot to death in 1997, just before the release of his album *Life After Death*. That album went on to break Michael Jackson's record for the highest-ever one-day album sales, giving credence to the idea that the "badder" rap gets, the more popular it becomes.[12] B. J. is just one of many young Americans who count albums by Snoop, Tupac, and Biggie among his favorites. And the violence in rap music is one reason why many white parents, and many black ones, wish their kids would listen to something else.

Another reason that baby boomers dislike rap is that many albums emphasize "getting paid" above almost all else. In August 1998, I moderated the keynote panel for *Vibe* magazine's annual music conference. The topic of conversation was nothing less than the economic and racial ramifications of hip-hop, including the question of why materialism dominates so many rap lyrics. The roster of speakers at the panel was high-powered and heterogeneous. There was comedian Chris Rock, recently flushed with the success of his role in the film *Lethal Weapon 4*; *Vibe* owner and veteran music producer Quincy Jones; *Jane* magazine editor Jane Pratt; and Harvard professor Cornel West. During the panel, most of the questions were actually directed at West, whose combination of down-home warmth and razor-sharp intellect charmed the audience out of their seats. But someone else on the panel drew the most stares of awe, envy, and admiration: the twenty-eight-year-old rapper and music producer Sean "Puffy" Combs.

In the past decade, Puffy has gone from chrysalis to butterfly over and over again. He's gone from a business major at Howard University to an intern at the urban music label Uptown Entertainment. He's produced tracks for R & B artists like Mary J. Blige and Jodeci. He became the head of his own record label, Bad Boy, and produced albums for rappers like the Notorious B.I.G., who dominated the number one spot on the charts. Finally, in 1998, Puffy released his own multi-platinum-selling album. It was fitting, perhaps, that Puffy's first hit was "I'll Be Missing You," a tribute to the gunned-down B.I.G. After all, Puffy's hit sampled a song by the Police that had been, itself, a crossover hit from New Wave to pop.

Puffy's story isn't just a tale of an artist, it's the rise of an entrepreneur: a black kid done good in one of the most unexpected of ways. The Cinderella story of the rap industry isn't street kid to artist—we've become used to that—but black youth as C.E.O. The industry couldn't have possibly become as popular as it is without the business savvy of black men and women who began building empires in their twenties: Ice Cube, Queen Latifah, Will Smith. All of them have transitioned from hip-hop into acting and producing as well. All of this background is running through my mind when I first meet Puffy, just minutes before the panel. He rolls with a huge entourage and he's wearing a diamond-encrusted bracelet and watch that probably cost more than four years' worth of tuition at Harvard.

We start out discussing the fact that songs that he produced held the number one spot on the pop charts for more than half of 1997. That means that rap music—the voice of youth, the underdog—has become very much a part of mainstream American life. But Combs says, "I would hope that hip-hop, at the end of the day, has a positive impact on race relations. I think that we can sell millions of records all over the world, and people can buy into our lifestyle . . . [But] because they love Puff, or they love Ice Cube, or they love Tupac, that ain't gonna make them love black people."

A few days later, I read that the albums Puffy has produced for his Bad Boy label have made over $200 million in revenue in just two years. So BMG, the corporation that owns Bad Boy, has decided to give Combs a small token of their appreciation: 40 million dollars.[13] Like Latifah and Cube and Will Smith before him, he's branching out into acting and producing. He owns a $2.5 million vacation home in the Hamptons, and a car worth almost four hundred thousand dollars. On one level, I'm proud of his achievements. On another, I worry that kids hoping for his level of success will think that anything that doesn't pay the big bucks isn't worth doing. Who can blame white kids, and black ones, for idolizing him? According to our cultural mind-set, where wealth not only confers power but implies intelligence and self-worth as well, Puffy is the pinnacle of American achievement.

Most of Puffy's fans listen to his songs for their beats—and to vicariously bask in his hipness. But some rap artists still focus heavily on the messages within their music. In fact, the best-selling rap album of all time is the 1997 album *The Score* by the Fugees, a trio of two male Haitian-American cousins, Wyclef Jean and Pras Michel, and singer-actress-rapper Lauryn Hill. Their raps blend reggae and rock influences, and have helped draw a huge crossover audience. Yet the Fugees have been very vocal about questioning whether their white audience truly understands their music. "White people when they translate black expression, they turn it into something nasty," said Lauryn Hill when I interviewed her after a 1996 show in Harlem. "I saw this girl at a show last night. I guess she was acting black. She was like, 'Shut the fuck up! I'm going to punch you in the face!' . . . She was grabbing her titties . . . Oh! I wanted to punch her in the face so bad." Her bandmate Wyclef Jean hopes that their group gives their white listeners a more nuanced picture of black life than some hip-hop acts. "With us, [white listeners] get reality," Jean says. " 'Cause you know one time the 'burbs thought black kids were just gangsters, 'cause that's what they see."

B. J. considers himself a true fan, not a wigger or a Johnny-come-lately. "The beats have no color lines," he says, repeating a phrase some hip-hop stations use as a slogan. B. J. bristles when he hears criticism like Hill's. "I remember hearing Lauryn Hill saying her music wasn't for white people. Well," he says, as succinctly as ever, "fuck her."

Life Without Diversity

But like Puffy, B. J. acknowledges that being a hip-hop fan is definitely not the same as being familiar with black culture. Just because Delphi's teens now listen to R & B and rap doesn't mean they're any less shocked when a new black face crosses their path. "It bothers me—it's hilarious—that some people report at school that they saw a black person over the weekend," B. J. tells me. "They'll say, 'They dress just like they do on TV.' They watch him or her, everything they did. They just find it very weird. Sometimes it's scary, and sometimes the women are more attracted to them."

Because there are so few blacks in Delphi, the stereotypes have more to do with media image than personal experience. "There is some racism, but it's just against"—and here B. J. goes sotto voce—"see, people say, 'I hate niggers, but I like black people.' " Just like I had to when I was in high school, I point out that there's no white identifier equivalent to the word "nigger." "White trash," as despicable as it is, doesn't even come close. B. J. nods his head as if it's the first time he's thought about it that way. "That's right," he says, warming to the subject. "That is so true. There is no word—that is such a powerful word to call black people. . . . And 'boy,' too. It's like that guy's holding a whip, too, when he's saying it." He continues, 'When people say, 'I like black people and I hate niggers,' what they mean is what they see on TV in the media. The [black] people who are all cocky and things, carrying guns in their belts, that's what [whites] don't like."

The media images are what they base their opinions on "because they don't really know any black people. They don't have any black friends." But it's a two-way street. Some black people "don't give a white person a chance," B. J. says. "They're exactly the same as some rednecks are." B. J. says that his own life, the changes he's had to make going from L.A. to Delphi, have steered him away from making prejudgments. No matter the race or the style of clothing, he says, "You got to give somebody a chance. Got to talk to them first." Most teens in Delphi haven't had a chance to live in a racially mixed city, the way that B. J. has. Alicia, for one, was raised entirely in the Delphi area, in even smaller surrounding towns.

While I'm in town, Alicia takes me to visit her mom, dad (stepdad), sisters, and brother. Their house is large and welcoming—with just a little bit of charming disorganization where B. J.'s parents' house is im- maculate. When Alicia was just two, her mom and her biological dad separated, so Jerry, her stepfather, has really been her dad for most of her life. She has an older sister and brother, and two younger sisters from her mom's second marriage. Alicia's two younger sisters are an elementary-aged tangle of long legs and arms, tearing around the house. They're sweet, friendly, and curious about my being there—not unlike everyone else in her family. After I sit out in the backyard with Alicia and her family for a while, she walks me over to her grandparents' house nearby. They're just as accommodating, and her grandfather shows off some beautiful carpentry work as well. On one level, I'm something of a living, breathing show-and-tell object—the black girl come from the big city. But I appreciate the warmth Alicia and her family show me—and the trust. On the following night, B. J. will want to go into Lafayette and spend the night with his college friends there. Alicia says she wants to go, but only if she has someplace to stay. I suggest she ask her parents if she can stay in my hotel room in Lafayette. They agree—somewhat to my surprise—and we end up hanging out and having girl talk together while B. J. concentrates on bonding with his guy friends.

My race genuinely doesn't seem to make a difference to Alicia, but she's not naïve about how much it matters to some people. That includes her own uncle, who lives on a nearby farm. I end up dropping by his house, where Alicia's mom and younger sisters are visiting. His wife and their children can't wait to say hi. His kids even rush to show me their barn, pigs, and horses. But Alicia's uncle quickly excuses himself.

"He's racist against everything—Mexicans, blacks," Alicia tells me privately. "We used to go on family vacations to King's Island, Ohio, and he used to make fun of the people—I don't know what they are—with the red dot [i.e., South Asians]. He even makes fun of the German Baptists," who, like Mennonites, live for the most part without modern technology, often riding in a horse and buggy. "He doesn't like them because their horses crap on the road and stuff," she says, unconscious of how oddly hilarious her earnest descriptions are.

Yet Alicia adds that her uncle, for all of his racist tendencies, has at least a smidgen of sympathy for the biggest nonwhite group in Delphi: Mexican immigrants who have come to the town in increasing numbers to work long hours for little pay at the new hog plant. It's hard, dirty work, and it doesn't pay very much: a typical point-of-entry job for new immigrants. Alicia says her uncle claims that Mexicans "bring diseases and everything," but he's had one family over to dinner who—desperate for a place to stay—rented a storage cubicle from him and lived there.

Many of the Mexican residents of the town have been migrant workers and speak little or no English. And almost all have been there too short a time to register on Census Bureau surveys and other measures of Delphi's changing demographics. (There are twenty-five Latino residents listed on the most recent survey of Delphi.) But it's almost inevitable that some of these Mexican and Mexican-American newcomers will settle down and begin to change Delphi's culture and self-image. For now, however, Delphi's Latinos seem poor and isolated. One day, as I'm driving around town with Alicia, she directs me to drive until I get to a place where a lot of Mexican families live. Not too far from the country club, there are cobbled-together cabins that look like nothing more than modern-day slave shacks. So on one level, Alicia feels deeply sorry for the families who've come to her town to work. But that doesn't mean she feels comfortable around them, or is free from holding stereotypes. "A lot of them are, like, real perverts," she says. "They're always like, 'Hey, baby, what's your name?' "

Alicia tells me some other Latinos live in run-down apartments above the stores on Main Street. In my entire time in Delphi, I see only one Latino man talking at a pay phone on a street corner. For better or worse, I've made a decision to follow B. J. and Alicia through their town, visiting with the families and friends. No Latino teens are in their inner circle. With school out for the summer, everyone hangs with their own clique.

Alicia, B. J., and his parents tell me Delphi's Latinos keep mostly to themselves because of the hostility directed against them. "Everyone's all like, 'Go back to Mexico,' really rude to them," says Alicia. Adds B. J., "I don't think that a lot of people understand that Mexico, well, it's not as bad as Cuba is. But it's washed up!" One day, while we're standing in the kitchen, I ask B. J.'s mother, Sherri, about the rising Latino population. She's been incredibly warm and open with me on a personal level, letting me spend endless hours at her house, even letting me watch the cartoon *Rugrats* with her adorable young sons. My first night in town, I took a pleasant walk around the neighborhood with her, her husband, the little boys, and their new dog. But when I start quizzing her on race, she becomes very nervous. Yes, she admits, a lot of people are resistant to the Mexicans moving in. No, she doesn't feel the same way, she adds—but from the way she says it, she doesn't quite seem sure.

I'm sure that Sherri felt she couldn't open up to me because I'd judge whatever she had to say. The reaction doesn't surprise me. One day I'm talking things over with Mark and his girlfriend. The girlfriend explains that since she doesn't have a washer and dryer in her apartment, she has to go to the Laundromat, which a lot of Latinos use. "And a lot of them make me uncomfortable," she says. Mark immediately jumps in to say, "She's not a racist! Some people are, but she's not a racist." I haven't said, nor do I necessarily think, that she is. But Mark's media-savvy enough to know that when it comes to race, there's a "right" thing to say.

That sharp plea not to be judged is evidence of how much Delphi is changing, how much all of America has changed. Even in areas where there's little diversity to speak of, people know that they're supposed to embrace other races. Lip service? Sure. But many of the teens I met in Delphi honestly seemed to be trying to go beyond that. It's hard to generalize about an entire generation, but the beginnings of a racial consciousness in small white towns like Delphi is probably a sign of how different this generation is from the last. If this generation is more aware than their parents', it is probably because pop culture helped pave the way, giving people a safe way to experience new cultures. Listening to rap and imitating its styles are a kind of role-playing for white teens. And maybe—just maybe—that role-playing will make the transition from all-white communities to mixed ones a little less jarring.

The Black Girls

What would it be like to be black in a virtually all white town? I never really get a sense of it, since I've so clearly been accorded "cool visitor" status. But one hot Saturday afternoon, I get to ask a couple of people in the know. A group of teens gathers to drink and goof off at their friend Seth's graduation party, conveniently located at a fire station down the street from Alicia's house. One of them is Alicia's classmate Angela, who lives in Camden, one of the many tiny towns that sends its teens to Delphi High. Alicia was in the second grade when Angie moved to Camden. They met at the old-fashioned town store. A couple of days later, Alicia asked her mom if Angie could come spend the night. Her mom gave

Angela's a call, and when she got off the phone, Alicia recalls, her mom turned to her with a question: "Is your new friend Colored?" Alicia, bemused, said no. (Her mom apparently thought she'd detected a "black" accent, though, ironically, Angela's mom is white.) It was only when Angela showed up at her house that Alicia noticed what her mom was talking about—Angela's skin wasn't the same tone as hers.

Sitting on Alicia's stoop, Angela listens to her recount the story. When Alicia asks her if she remembers, Angela shrugs no. She's sitting with her hand on the shoulder of her older sister, Natalie, who just graduated from Delphi High. Together, Angela and Natalie are two-thirds of the entire black population of the school. Both sisters have café au lait skin, shoulder-length braids (done at a black salon in Kokomo where Alicia wants to get her hair braided), flat tummies (Angela's navel is pierced), and thin, athletic bodies covered by sleeveless crop tops and denim short shorts.

A couple of other Delphi High grads sit down as well: Gina, a talkative, tan-skinned brunette, and Laura, a thoughtful girl with blond Breck Girl hair cut into a bob. All three of the graduated seniors—Natalie, Gina, and Laura—are headed to Purdue in the fall.

I ask the group to tell me about Delphi's diversity or lack of thereof, and we launch into a long, free-flowing discussion about race in small-town America. For example, I say, there don't seem to be any Asians around. "There's a Chinese restaurant," says Natalie. "There's some Chinese people." And she has one cousin in nearby Logansport who's half Korean, as well as another in another town who's also black biracial.

I begin to wonder if Angela and Natalie's family has a lock on the whole nonwhite population of the region, but Natalie assures me that's not so. "It's just Delphi, basically [that has no blacks]. Logansport, there's a lot of different races—well, not a lot. It's still predominately white." Their mother is white, and their black father is himself biracial. The sisters identify as mixed more than black. "When it says black, white, or other, I check black and white," says Natalie. "I check black, white, and other," Angela chimes in. "I'm just everything." Then Natalie adds, "Most people probably consider us black because we're the only different ones. But to me it doesn't really matter either way."

But when the two moved to town, the grown-ups took notice. Their friend Laura says, "I remember when she came in fourth grade and Mrs. Drucker was like, 'I just need to tell you she's a little bit different. She's not the same color.' I was like, 'OK.'" "Adults want to make a bigger deal about it than kids," says Angie.

But teens don't exactly ignore the sisters' skin color; sometimes they stare. "Angie gets crappy about it. She's like, 'What are you LOOKIN at?'" Natalie says.

"If they're being rude about it, that's when I'll say something," Angie shrugs. But she admits that even she finds seeing other black people around weird. "In Delphi when you see someone different you stare hard. I know I do. I'll see a black person driving through and I'll be like, 'who's that?'" Adds Natalie, "There was a chick that came in the [grocery] store today. She was black, she was probably, like, sixteen. I just stared. You know everybody [but] you don't know them . . ." she trails off. " She must be just passing through."

They acknowledge they've experienced minor incidents and slights, like when Natalie got a sunburn and the manager of the store she was working at said " 'I didn't know Colored people could burn.'" But when I ask Natalie and Angela if they feel isolated in Delphi, they emphatically reply no. I can't help but wonder if they're fibbing—trying not to say what their friends don't want to hear (or what they can't admit to themselves). But as far as I can tell their race hasn't excluded them from the local social life. Natalie's on-again, off-again boyfriend J. D. is white, as are the several guys that Angie has dated. There aren't any black guys in the town, though all of the girls on the stoop—black and white—admit to having a crush on the Purdue basketball players who they occasionally see while shopping in the Lafayette mall. Natalie and Angela have probably benefited from one of the strongest forces pushing this generation to embrace diversity—the ubiquitous teen quest for coolness. Natalie remembers that when she moved to town, Alicia's sister "Amy said she wanted to be friends with me because I was different." And Angela probably sums up the feelings of a lot of her classmates—ones without a mass of braids or brown skin or biracial families—when she says, "I think it's really cool to be different."

Of course there are some parents and kids who reject them out of hand because they're black, says Angela nonchalantly. "But I probably wouldn't want to associate with them anyway. So it doesn't make that big a difference."

On one level that's certainly true: what black person would willingly hang out with racists? But sometimes, even when you're with friends, you don't know how others around you feel. Alicia tells me privately about the way her uncle reacted to Natalie and Angela. "After church on Sunday we would have family dinners at my grandma's house, and we'd invite friends. Like we'd have Natalie and Angela over one day, and my uncle would be like, 'Are your little nigger friends coming over?' " she says. "My mom would get so upset! He'd say, 'I don't care who you bring over as long as you don't bring them over.' " Alicia makes it clear that her mom and grandparents love Natalie and Angela. Her uncle, for all his protestations, never said anything to Natalie or Angela's face. So they continued to come over for dinner, with many things left unsaid.

Color or Culture?

Alicia adds that her uncle doesn't like B. J. " 'Nigger wannabe'—those were his exact words," she says. "I could see that if B. J. was like, 'All white people are hick people.' But B. J.'s not like that. He's open-minded." (B. J. tells me that even though he's hung out with Alicia's family countless times, the first time her uncle spoke to him was to congratulate him on his graduation.)

In the current battles over issues like affirmative action, many white Americans claim that being white confers no special privileges. Yet in a telling study that author and Queens College professor Andrew Hacker conducted with his students, they had no problem putting a price on "whiteness." He told his students to consider a hypothetical situation. They would wake up tomorrow morning and be black, not white. They would remain black for the rest of their lives. Nothing else would change—their intelligence and life knowledge, for example. But Hacker asked them how much money they would have to be paid to accept this "assignment." "When this parable has been put to white students, most seemed to feel that it would not be out of place to ask for $50 million, or $1 million for each coming black year," writes Hacker.[14] It appears that "whiteness" has a clear value to white Americans.

Being white in America does offer privileges—privileges conferred not only by ability or merit but the accident of birth. This reality is one reason why rap is so transgressive. On some level, when white kids adopt rap styles, they are seeming to reject the privilege of their whiteness. Even if they risk nothing, even if they lose nothing (unlike the wiggers in Morocco, Indiana), they are symbolically thumbing their noses at white culture. To some parents, this minor rebellion is interpreted as wasteful or even shameful.

The Road Back to Home

B. J. misses the ethnic melange of Los Angeles. He tells me he's going to move back there to stay with his dad, and to clean up his own life. "I wanna stop getting high, stop smoking [cigarettes]. I know if I stay around my friends, it'll just be the same thing. We can't have good clean fun." But his plans to leave in a couple months include regrets. "Now I'm comfortable" in Delphi, he says. "I have a strong relationship with my beautiful girlfriend. I don't wanna leave." Besides, he's not an outsider anymore. His friends are here. And his music—the thing that branded him as an outsider—is the most popular thing on the charts. "Everyone in my school has crossed over to listening to hip-hop," he says partly with pride, partly with exasperation. After all, being a rebel was at least half the fun.

I end up speaking to B. J. a few months later. He's made good on his promise to move back to L.A., going to live with his dad a couple of months after graduation and taking a job as a delivery guy for a mattress company. Not only was it hot, heavy work ("We had to stand on the top of the truck and toss one onto a balcony," he says), but B. J. also found he'd fallen out of love with L.A. "All my friends out here have to act hard. They're like, 'Why you sayin' that shit, dog?' . . . What's up with that 'dog' shit?" he asks, questioning the gang-style lingo.

B. J.'s still dating Alicia, long distance. She's part of the reason he decided to move back to Delphi and try to find a job in Lafayette. "I'm not going to fuck around with the factories. I don't want to deal with the pigs and blood and stuff. I want to be in a tie and a dress shirt," he says. "A music store would be good"—no doubt, one with a good hip-hop selection.

Maybe Delphi got to B. J. Maybe the kid who arrived as a bored, pissed-off urban eighth-grader is a country boy now. But he's part of a new breed—kids who lead the rural life with a hip-hop soundtrack.

FIVE

A Nation Within a Nation: Native Americans

Crow Agency, Montana

Sean Morning fits the profile of "minority kid done good." He's obsessed with basketball—but he spends his days taking classes at a community college. His favorite music is anything from the No Limit Records label headed by rap star Master P. He's just twenty years old with an infant son—but he's married. He lives in a community with a 70 percent unemployment rate—but he has a good part-time job.

Based on this brief description, you might assume that Sean is black. But he's not. The tall, heavyset young man has lightly tanned skin and spiky black hair. He's one of seven thousand Crow Indians living on the tribe's reservation in Montana and Wyoming. The 2.2 million acres of Crow land encompass the stunning peaks of the Prior mountains and the prime recreational fishing areas of the Little Bighorn River. "Before the government started reducing our land, we had over 20 million acres," Sean says. Still, his tribe is luckier than many: the reservation that they live on today is part of their original territory.

"The Res," as Sean calls it, is also filled with beaten-down houses, old trailers on bleak patches of land, and a poverty so pervasive that it touches the lives of all around. Sometimes relentless poverty can lead to despair, even cruelty. One day I see a scruffy girl about four years old playing on her battered front porch. She walks over to a puppy lying nearby and kicks it repeatedly until I ask her to stop. The dog flinches but lies there and takes it. I wonder if the girl has had to endure the same thing at someone else's hands.

That small girl lives in Crow Agency, a small, unremarkable town that is the reservation's center. It holds the local Bureau of Indian Affairs office, the tribal council, and the health service. Perhaps most important, it's home to an institution that is helping to transform the bleak socioeconomic terrain of this reservation: Little Big Horn College. The school—Sean Morning's school—may not look like much from the outside: a former gymnasium and a few trailers transformed into a set of classrooms and offices. But this college run by and for Crow Indians is one of the best chances around to break poverty's stranglehold. In fact, I come to Little Big Horn to do a story for ABC. While I'm there with my producer Lenny and the crew, Sean becomes our unofficial guide. He's quiet much of the time—the college president tells me that holding your tongue unless you have something important to say is a prized value in Crow culture—but I find he has good insights on his people and community.

Sean's community is facing huge socioeconomic challenges. With 70 percent unemployment and welfare reform about to push many women and children off the rolls, many on the Crow reservation have nowhere to turn to feed their families. Little Big Horn College, which offers two-year associate degrees, has to reach these impoverished students, many of whom have only a GED or a substandard high school education. In addition to basic liberal arts classes, the school offers specialized majors like computing and forestry management, with a focus on getting its graduates good local jobs. But promoting economic independence is just one part of Little Big Horn's mission. Another is strengthening Crow culture. Even the handful of white students at Little Big Horn, whose families have long owned ranches within the reservation's boundaries, are required to take Crow language classes. Little Big Horn is part of a movement: a collective of thirty "tribal colleges" that are trying to educate Native Americans in or near their communities, giving them both opportunity and self-knowledge. Overall, Native Americans have the lowest rate of college attendance of any racial group in the country. And given the crises facing many Native American communities—unemployment, low life expectancy, the loss of language and culture—these colleges are critical.

In one sense, Native Americans—who make up less than one percent of the U.S. population—are this country's smallest and most forgotten minority. (Many community leaders were incensed that not one Native American was a member of the prestigious Presidential initiative on race.) Just under half of Native Americans live on reservations, and many others live in the cities near them.[1] Nationwide, about half of all Indians on the reservation are on welfare—no surprise, given how isolated they are, and how barren and lacking in jobs much of their land is. Though the perception is that Native communities have gotten rich off of casinos, that's only true for a few tribes, like Connecticut's Pequots. In 1998, they opened a massive Indian cultural center that cost more than $100 million. But most tribes make a modest sum at best—like the Lake Superior Chippewa in Wisconsin, who made a grand total of six thousand dollars from gaming in 1996.[2]

Most Americans know little about Native life or culture except a few positive or negative stereotypes. There are the romanticized images from film and television: the famous seventies commercial showing an Indian crying at litter covering the ground, and the noble Natives of *Dances with Wolves*. But Native Americans are more often demonized than romanticized. On the plane ride I took to Billings, I told a friendly white couple from Wyoming sitting next to me that I was on my way to the Crow reservation. "They take the government's money and what do they do? They drink and they set fires in the middle of their living rooms," the husband said. "I guess it's like your [i.e., blacks'] housing projects." (What a nice welcome to the state, I thought, to hear blacks and Indians insulted simultaneously.)

Like most other nonwhite groups, Native Americans face both racism and a lack of economic opportunity. But they are not simply another "minority." Each tribe is a sovereign entity with the power to create its own laws on the reservation; run its own government and police force; and, hopefully, help chart a path from poverty to prosperity. My friend Bird Runningwater, a twenty-seven-year-old Apache-Cheyenne who's worked on Native issues for the Ford Foundation in New York, paraphrases a bit of wisdom from college classes on Indian law: "Other ethnic minority groups have laws designed to integrate them. Native American laws are designed to protect cultural separateness and political autonomy." To Bird, who grew up on the Mescalero Apache reservation in New Mexico, the differences between Native Americans and other nonwhite groups are myriad. "Whenever people try to lump Native Americans in with other minorities, I try to remind them it transcends the race thing," says Bird. "The term Native American isn't a racial categorization, it's a political recognition. As long as you have your citizenship," meaning that a person is an enrolled member of a federally recognized tribe, "you're regarded as Native American. The race of a Native American could be African American, white, brown. Anything." Today's Native Americans include not only the children of years of mixing with blacks and whites, but individuals who've grown up in any number of circumstances: among other races in big cities; near Indians of many other tribes on family "allotments"; or with members of their own tribes on the reservations that dot the West and Southwest.

The Next Bill Gates

Sean Morning has experienced life both on and off the reservation. Until he was in sixth grade, he lived with the woman he calls "Mom"—his biological aunt—in Billings, Montana, about an hour away from the reservation. Montana's largest city is businesslike and utilitarian, a commercial hub whose downtown architecture is virtually indistinguishable from hundreds of other cities' across America. Sean went to a majority-white elementary school, where he got a good education but sometimes felt out of place because there were only a few Indian kids. "But we had a rule that I had to speak Crow when I got home," he recalls, so today—unlike many other Crow his age—he's fluent in his language.

Sean's life changed dramatically when his mom decided to move back to the reservation. "I was scared, because I had never been around Native Americans," he says. "Moving to the Res, I had culture shock, even though they were my own people." First of all, he moved from an apartment with heat and running water to a bare-bones ranch in the tiny town of Lodge Grass. Second, he says, "Times were harsh for me because I learned so much more in the white school that [Native] kids were dogging me." Just like black kids who are teased for being "white" when they do well in school, Sean was deemed an outsider because he was ahead of the other kids in class. "I had to mess around just to get along," he says.

Sean finished junior high school on the reservation, then chose to attend a majority-white high school in Tongue River, Wyoming. It wasn't easy. The school was ranked fifteenth in the state academically, and it took Sean a while to get back up to speed. "A couple times I felt like giving up and going back to the reservation," he says. "Freshman year, the principal was on my back. I felt like giving up, but my Mom told me not to." Sean knew five other Indian students at Tongue River. Like him, they were on the basketball team. But unlike Sean, all five of them were enrolled in special education classes. Sean constantly had to prove his intellectual abilities to his white classmates, enduring round after round of their impromptu quizzes designed to see if he was really smart or not.

In the same way some black inner-city kids are recruited to play ball for white prep schools, Crow kids are prized for their skills on the court. When I arrive at Little Big Horn, I'm shocked to find out how many people are consumed by basketball mania. Men and women alike play in league games in the nearby town of Hardin, and when I walk the halls of Little Big Horn I see kids sporting the latest team jackets for George-town and the Chicago Bulls. But it's easy to imagine how kids who grew up going to reservation schools could founder when sent into the more challenging—and often more hostile—environment off the reservation.

Even Sean, who took advantage of the strong academics at Tongue River, let basketball rule his life. He broke his ankle sophomore year, and the high school gave his spot on the team to someone else. He had a choice: stay at Tongue River, where the education was better but he wouldn't be able to play ball, or go home to the reservation, where they'd find a spot on the team for him once he mended. For Sean, that was no choice. He transferred to the high school in Lodge Grass, where he still lives today. As soon as he got his cast off, he started playing for their team.

How different were the two high schools that Sean went to? "In Tongue River, if I was even late for class I'd be suspended. At Lodge Grass, people could turn in their work a week late and still get full credit." At the time, he was happy to get a chance to slack off. But now, as a college computer major, he regrets not having been able to take advanced high school classes like calculus. Sean has two younger brothers who are being raised by his biological mother. He's trying to get the youngest to transfer to a "tough school, a white school" in the nearby town of Hardin, off the reservation. "The teachers [at the tribal high schools] don't push people," Sean says. If he were a teacher, he muses, he would "create a disciplined atmosphere, encourage everyone to come to class on time. I'd tell them life stories of how I struggled through college, little pep talks. I'd get in the flow with the students, let them see eye to eye."

Sean already offers help to other students as a tutor in Little Big Horn College's computer lab. When I first walk into the computer labs, I'm astounded. Three rooms are filled with desktop computers. They're not a bunch of junk, a pile of outdated boards and circuits, but up-to-date equipment and software, with a school website and an e-mail address available for every student.* One Little Big Horn graduate works as a computer technician, salvaging parts from old computers and upgrading them at a fraction of the cost it would take to buy brand new machines.

"I want to be the next Bill Gates," Sean says with a self-depreciating laugh. What he'd really like to do is bring some kind of computing industry to a reservation with few high-paying jobs. "I want to get them up to date with computers," he says. "Like, at the hospital, some of the people go home without seeing a doctor, because it's too long a wait. So you could get computers to each district. Get everyone e-mail. Get quick-cam [so that you can see video over the computer] and get the doctor to talk to people over the computer." Before he can put these grand plans in place, Sean has to finish his coursework at Little Big Horn. And then he'll have to leave the reservation to get a four-year degree. He's already had to face the fact that, in order to succeed in his field, he'll have to leave the reservation, at least temporarily. Sean's got an adorably chubby nine-month-old son named Quadon, and an eighteen-year-old wife, Tamra, who's just finishing high school. But last summer he left them to take a prestigious government internship near the nation's capital; and he's planning to take another internship out of state before his time at Little Big Horn is done.

"I want to come back to the reservation and help my people," Sean says. But he's also keenly aware of just how hard starting a computer services company could be. First of all, he would have to learn to run a business. He went to a conference of entrepreneurs and heard them tell their tales of how tough they've had it, forgoing their own paychecks to make sure their businesses stay afloat. With the kind of skills he's learning in his internships, he'd find a lot better pay—at least at first—off the reservation. And Sean isn't immune to a certain amount of cynicism about what kind of businesses the reservation could support. I ask him if there's anything he could do on the Res that would be a sure money

*http://www.lbhc.cc.mt.us/

maker. "I could sell drugs," he says sarcastically. But that's not an option Sean takes in any way seriously. His mom, who now works at the college, has constantly pushed him to do well in school. As he gets closer to a life of independence, he looks to education as the one clear path toward success.

Perhaps Sean's dedication to education runs in the family. He's a seventh-generation descendant of Chief Plenty Coups, whose words are printed in the Little Big Horn brochure. "With an education, you're the white man's equal," the powerful nineteenth-century Crow chief said. "Without an education, you're his victim."

Success on a Shoestring Budget

Dr. Janine Pease Pretty On Top supervises everything at Little Big Horn College, from making sure the computer labs are maintained to placing that quote from Chief Plenty Coups in the school brochure. This tall, beautiful woman, with a regal bearing yet an easy warmth, is one of the founders of Little Big Horn, and its president. "We are a nation of people, with our own government and our own language," Pease Pretty On Top emphasizes. By tailoring Little Big Horn to Native needs, "We're building our own communities, not someone else's." She is talking about the fact that her college provides its 300 students with a strong education in their own culture, which in turn forms a strong foundation for acquiring other knowledge.

Nearly two decades ago, Pease Pretty On Top taught at Navajo Community College. When that school was founded in 1968, it was the only tribal college in America. She decided her people needed their own college, too. Sixteen years ago, Pease Pretty On Top arranged college classes in a couple of used trailers. (She was happy to have them.) Today, Little Big Horn fills a converted gymnasium. Students built most of the internal walls and partitions—even adding a second level within the structure for administrative offices. Pease Pretty On Top has accomplished so much with so little. She makes sure that she gets every penny of funding she can from federal education, welfare-to-work, and jobs programs, and several of her students have won impressive national internships. For her efforts, Pease Pretty On Top won a McArthur Genius Award, among many others. (Not that she'd tell you herself; that would be bragging. But I spotted a framed copy of the letter they sent her tucked away on a shelf in her office.)

Pease Pretty On Top believes deeply in the potential of tribal colleges to help transform the communities around them. In Crow lands, not only is there a dearth of good jobs, there's a lack of Indians trained to do the few high-skill positions on the reservation. The tribe has had to hire white professionals for many of the high-level jobs at the Bureau of Indian Affairs and the local tribal hospital. "Crow Indians should be trained so when a job comes open, they can qualify for that job," Pease Pretty On Top says. But even if Crow Indians filled all the available positions on the reservation, it wouldn't make much of a dent in the massive 70 percent unemployment rate. So Little Big Horn is set on training people to be entrepreneurial and create jobs for themselves and other tribe members. The school won a concession to give tours at the nearby Little Big Horn Battlefield, where General George Custer was killed by Sioux and Cheyenne warriors. (The Crow actually fought on the side of Custer, something which a college employee tells me produces lingering tensions with some other tribes to this day.) "It's a good seasonal income," Pease Pretty On Top says. But the school's main focus is training people in education (to be teachers and aides), technology, and environmental sciences. If they choose biology and natural resource studies, they might find jobs as experts with the Fish and Wildlife Service, or with the businesses that serve the anglers who come to fish the river. Perhaps they will find new ways of utilizing tribal land. The reservation is home to elk and buffalo, animals that need to be tracked and monitored. Or, if students choose computing, there are jobs in nearby cities like Billings and Hardin that pay a lot better than minimum wage.

Most of the people I meet at Little Big Horn, even ones as young as Sean, are married or divorced with kids. What they earn is not just a matter of personal survival, but their family's, and their tribe's.

Little Big Horn and the twenty-nine other tribal colleges like it have a clear record of success. Nearly 70 percent of Indians who attend colleges off the reservation end up dropping out. But those who attend tribal colleges have a higher graduation rate than other community college students. And 85 percent of those who graduate find jobs. Today, over twenty-five thousand Native students attend tribal colleges, most of them located on reservations. Virtually all offer specially tailored courses and majors, from tribal management to Pacific Northwest Native art. A 1995 report by the Carnegie Foundation for the Advancement of Teaching highlights these institutions' importance. "Without question, the most significant development in American Indian communities since World War II, was the creation of tribally controlled colleges," says the report. "More than any other single institution, they are changing lives and offering real hope for the future."[3]

The Carnegie report also calls tribal colleges "underfunded miracles." Tribal colleges get no state or local money, since they're considered to be on federal lands. Given the fact that virtually none of the students can afford the already low tuition, that leaves the colleges in dire financial straits. Some have no heat, or operate in unsafe buildings. Virtually all can't enroll as many students as they'd like. And things may get worse. Because of the impending welfare cutoffs, many more unemployed tribe members will have to seek jobs and job training immediately. Congress initially authorized nearly $6,000 per student for tribal colleges. But each year, when the legislature votes on federal appropriations, the schools get only half that money. That wouldn't happen if Native Americans were a bigger and more powerful group. Senator John McCain (R-AZ), who's tried hard to raise support for tribal colleges, bluntly assesses the political calculus: "Native Americans aren't much of a constituency in Washington." Pease Pretty On Top testified before

Congress in 1996, to little avail. The Kellogg Foundation has tried to step into the funding breach, offering a $22.2 million grant to help out tribal colleges.[4] And, in a parallel to the United Negro College Fund, the Native American College Fund has started running television advertisements to gain donations.*

Pease Pretty On Top empathizes deeply with the hardships facing her students. She describes the typical Little Big Horn College student as "a woman with children, on welfare." Pease Pretty On Top seems like the kind of person who has never seen hard times, never struggled the way so many of her students do. But she goes out of her way to make it clear to me that that's not true. When her first husband, a "not-quite-recovered alcoholic," lost his job, she and her two children briefly went on welfare. "I canned. I dried meat. I dried berries and I did everything to make ends meet. I was making handcrafts just to buy sugar," she says.

Pease Pretty On Top introduces me to a student named Loraine Hogan. Like many other students, Hogan has a GED rather than a high school diploma, and her self-confidence has been worn down by years of receiving welfare. I go out to Hogan's trailer one freezing, foggy morning. Though run-down on the outside, it's cozy on the inside. But the night before, Hogan and her four children slept together in the living room. She'd bought fuel, but couldn't find anyone to light her heater. Hogan and her children had to rely on one electric space heater in the living room to keep them safe from the penetrating cold of the mountain air.

Lorraine Hogan's children are all in preschool or elementary school. She's divorced, and she's raising them alone. She wants to get an education, but it's hard. A few years ago, Hogan dropped out of a college farther away. "I don't like being off the reservation. I miss home," she says. "I miss the mountains" whose beauty greets her every time she

---

*http://www.collegefund.org/toc.htm

walks out the door. The reason she's enrolled at Little Big Horn is simple. "I want a better life for my kids," she says. "I'm tired of being on welfare. I want to get a job, and we'll be happy."

Pease Pretty On Top knows the education that women like Loraine Hogan get at Little Big Horn has a ripple effect. "Someone came into my office from Head Start and said that they'd seen an educational improvement in the students," the college president says. "And the only thing that was happening differently was that many of their parents went to this college. It made me feel really good."

Preserving a Culture

Tribal leaders and educators like Pease Pretty On Top hope tribal colleges will also help preserve Native languages and culture. Even though 85 percent of adults speak Crow—one of the highest native-language rates of all tribes—the numbers are far lower among children. "You might find only 10 percent of children speaking Crow with their playmates," she says. Like other governments including Australia's, the U.S. government once fought an undisguised battle to erase Native culture. During the eighteenth and nineteenth centuries, tribes were pushed from their lands and sometimes massacred, like the slaughter of unarmed women and children at Wounded Knee. At the turn of the last century, the Native American population had shrunk to just a quarter of a million, compared to 2 million today.

But Pease Pretty On Top points out there is a much more recent history of dispersing tribal members. In the fifties, she says, the government ran a relocation program to disperse what officials saw as the surplus Indian population. Then, as is true today, there were few jobs on the reservation. Many young Native Americans leapt at the chance to get a couple of months of rent subsidy and food assistance and a job placement in a big city. But the job placements were often at minimum wage, and the housing was often in the toughest of neighborhoods. Some Crow Indians went to Cleveland, Minneapolis, Los Angeles, and Oakland, says Pease Pretty On Top. Some, no doubt, have lost their ties to the tribe. If you move to a big city, Pease Pretty On Top says, "You lose your language, you lose your culture."

Preserving the Culture . . . in the Big City

Bird Runningwater, twenty-seven, believes that's not always the case. As someone who grew up on the reservation and now lives in New York City, he acknowledges that keeping ties to the home community is hard, but can be done. Tall and handsome, with his once-long hair cut to chin length in keeping with traditional mourning processes following a death in the family, Bird looks like a consummate downtown New Yorker in his dark suits, constantly talking on his tiny StarTAC mobile phone. He's friends with Native Amerian director Chris Eyre, who directed the award-winning film on Native life, *Smoke Signals,* and he's always going to chic Manhattan benefits for Native causes. But despite his fast-paced New York lifestyle, Bird's home is, and always will be, in the mountains of southern New Mexico. That's the land his father's tribe, the Mescalero Apache, calls home.

Bird grew up on the reservation until he was fourteen. "I was in an environment where I was a majority: ethnically, culturally, racially, everything. I knew what it was like to be in that role. When outsiders came in, even Anglos, I had a sense of being in the majority culture." In addition, compared to many other tribes, Bird's was well-to-do. Like the Crow, the Mescalero are living on lands that they traditionally occupied. But the Mescalero were able to build a ski resort and a hotel complex in the mountains, and run a cattle operation. "My tribe was a political and economic power in the region," he says.

Bird went to elementary school on the reservation, and then to a junior high school in a border town called Tularosa. The other students were primarily Latino. Cultural differences were acknowledged, but never in a way that implied one group or the other was better.

And then, when Bird was in ninth grade, his mother was offered a job in western Oklahoma. That's where she, as a Cheyenne, grew up. Unlike the system of reservations in much of the West and Southwest, federal officials placed Indian families on piecemeal "allotments" throughout Oklahoma. Members of a single tribe were often assigned to allotments far from each other, in an effort by officials to erode tribal unity and diminish any threat of group actions. Members of one tribe may live next to whites who then live next to members of an entirely different tribe.

In Oklahoma, says Bird, relations between Indians and whites were strained. "That's when I went into an environment of stereotypes," Bird recalls of his arrival at Clinton High School. "In a way, all of a sudden I realized I was Indian."

By Bird's estimate, only about 10 percent of the students at his high school were Indian. And as in Sean Morning's case, many of them were left behind academically. When Bird went to enroll in classes, his parents provided records from his previous school placing him in honors classes. But high school officials argued against letting him into the classes, until his parents argued back. Bird found he was usually the only Indian in the advanced classes. "The white kids didn't really care for me," he says, echoing what Sean Morning told me about going to a white high school, "And the Indians were like, 'He's trying to be white.' " Today, Bird still analyzes his experiences at the high school. "I was at home in June, talking to one of my cousins," he says. "He was a big football star. They used him to win championships, but he graduated high school basically not knowing how to read. We were both in completely different situations, but we both said, 'Can you believe we survived that place?' "

Today Bird has just finished two years of working on Native American issues at the prestigious philanthropic group the Ford Foundation. He sees a common challenge facing most Native Americans. "Among the Native people in the United States there's a dedication to remembering who they are: an indigenous person in their own land. They're working to maintain that identity while mastering the ways of the white man. Just kidding," he laughs, "—while mastering what's needed to advance in a mainstream context. It's so complicated." The lack of good jobs on the reservations complicates Bird's life as well as those of other young Native Americans who have less education and far fewer opportunities. In the weeks ahead, Bird hopes to find a position or two that will let him lead his ideal life: splitting his time between the reservation in New Mexico and his urban life in New York City. "There's this trend toward leaving home, especially if you're a professional and educated Native person," Bird says. "Most of the reservations don't have strong economies and opportunities, outside of tribal government and the Bureau of Indian Affairs. But I'm convinced there must be some young people at home on the reservation, doing things in their communities. I don't come across them because I've been in the very mainstream nonprofit world. But I know they're out there. Some day I want to travel Indian country, write a book and show people. There are so many stereotypes of Native Americans in the media, and we absorb a lot of those stereotypes."

Bird has a simple, personal antidote to seeing the secondhand images of Native life, and to the grind of living in a demanding city like New York. "Going home to me is like returning to a natural state and function, a way of thinking and being," he says. "The hard part is leaving home and coming back here. It's a shock. I'm usually out of commission for a week. But going home is easy. To them, no matter what my job, I'm Bird. I always will be Bird. I find that affirming." Bird has important reasons to return home so frequently. "I'm ceremonially involved with both my tribes," he says. Every summer, Bird performs a role in tribal coming-of-age services. "That's what differentiates me from the average twenty-something Native American professional. They have a freedom to be who they want to be and not go home. But I have to go home."

A Tie to the Land

Of course, Bird Runningwater wants to go home. And so does Sean Morning. The question for both of them is how to make a way in the world and earn a living while maintaining the ties to their land.

"I love them," Sean says of life with his family on the reservation. "But if we're going to live, I gotta make money." And to continue to make money, he may ultimately have to take a job in a big city. Even though the pay is bound to be better, on his internship he saw evidence of the racial tension that exists in many workplaces. "In one of my big corporate jobs, you worked in teams," he says. "There was one black guy. Everyone would express their idea, but every time the black guy made a good point, no one would say 'Yeah, yeah, yeah.' I was thinking, Damn, it's still like that." He stayed at a dorm for the summer, and ended up hanging out with the black students there, chilling and playing some basketball. "I couldn't really hang with the white people," he says. Needless to say, he met virtually no other Native Americans. If he does go to work outside the reservation, he'll miss it tremendously.

"It is beautiful here," Sean says of Crow country. "It's laid back. As soon as you get off the plane, you feel the tension getting off your back. You feel your blood pressure go down. As soon as you get off the plane in D.C. [where he did his internship], you feel your blood pressure go up." Sean takes me to the site near town where thousands gather for the annual Crow Fair, living in massive teepees over the course of the four-day festival. He describes with obvious pride the arrow-throwing contests and feeling of solidarity he has every time the summer festival rolls around.

When I ask Sean whether it's an advantage or disadvantage to be Indian, given all of the socioeconomic troubles in the community, he answers without hesitation. "It's an advantage. Spiritually and culturally, I have a lot more. Indians are at one with the earth, we have a more mutual feeling with things on earth. White people just want to destroy it and look for resources." Recently, Sean joined thousands of other Indians from seven Montana tribes to protest a plan to compromise Indian sovereignty. Republican state Senator Conrad Burns tried to push through a plan that would force tribes that take federal money to give up their sovereignty. With sovereignty, tribes can set their own laws (for example, permitting gambling in states that don't otherwise allow it) and remain free from some forms of taxes. The antisovereignty plans, which some Capitol Hill lawmakers also tried to advance, have been squashed—for now.[5] "They want to go back and change the treaties so we have to pay taxes on our land," Sean says. "What they promised us a long time ago, they're trying to take away. It makes me angry."

For now, Sean plans to leave the reservation in order to return to it a stronger and more educated person. He plans to apply to four-year schools next winter, probably the University of Montana at Missoula, eight hours away. If so, he'll probably live in married student housing with his wife and son. Sean's infant son Quadon said one of his first words recently. He said it in Crow: "Igah," or "Look at that." Sean hopes that by the time Quadon's a little older, what he sees when looks around the reservation will be less poverty and despair, more jobs and more hope.

SIX

"Perfect" Diversity in an Imperfect World

Aurora and Colorado Springs, Colorado

High school's pretty rough on the ego no matter who you are. It's even tougher if you don't have a group of friends to provide emotional shelter—in other words, a clique, a crew, a posse, a group, a scene.

Gina Perez is a crew of one, someone who feels little kinship to most of the kids at her school. Plump, with permed dirty-blond hair, she rarely smiles. Always observing, examining, watching, her pretty eyes don't register anything that makes them light up with pleasure. Gina wants to be able to have friends of all races, but her school is divided: whites with whites, blacks with blacks, Asians with Asians. "Whites rule the school," Gina says of Smoky Hill High, an exceptional public school in an affluent district of Aurora, Colorado. Most whites, she claims, are too stuck up to deign to talk to anyone else. She transferred to Smoky Hill from Gateway, a school with lots of blacks and Latinos where the academics weren't very good, but where she had lots of friends. "Everybody called me Rainbow Girl," because she had both friends of every race and a penchant for dying her hair different colors. But when she got to her new high school, Gina was surprised to get attitude from the black students as well as the whites. "At Smoky Hill, it was like I tried to make friends with different races. I look white even though I'm Spanish, and when I would try to make friends with [black] people, it's like they just, you know, turned their head. It was so hard."

Students like Gina all around the country are trying their best to live the promise of an integrated America. Sometimes the areas where they live, like parts of the Deep South, have deep-seated racial tensions. Other times, as in parts of the all-white heartland, there aren't enough members of different races to provide much diversity. The irony here is that Gina is trying to mix in an area that should already be mixed. Aurora, Colorado, is about as close to matching America's racial demographics as you can get.

A City with Near-"Perfect" Diversity

I got to know Gina—whose mother works with a friend of mine—only after I decided to check out her city. I was looking specifically for a place with "perfect diversity"—a community which exactly matched America's racial mix. Right now, America is 73 percent non-Hispanic white, 12 percent black, 3 percent Asian, 11 percent Latino, and 1 percent Native American. At my request, the U.S. Census Bureau's special tabulations office generated a list of places that closely matched those numbers.* Of the top fifty places the Census computers turned up—cities ranging from Denton, Texas, to Sierra Vista, Arizona, to Lorain, Ohio—none was a perfect match. Few were on the East or West coasts—cities there tend to have more nonwhites than the country overall. That fact didn't surprise me. This one did: the majority of the cities that came close to matching America's mix either contained or adjoined military installations. America hasn't yet managed to integrate on its own, but the U.S. military is exceptionally integrated. The army is 27 percent black (including 9 percent of the generals), and Asian Americans are particularly well-represented in the Navy.[1] Of course, the military is

*U.S. Bureau of the Census, Population Division, special tabulations (Rose Cowan, 12 June 1996).

more than just a job. Entire families move where they're told, creating new housing patterns and mandating integration the way almost nothing else does. Aurora's largest employer is Buckley Air National Guard Base. Now Colorado's third largest city, Aurora is a pretty good match for the United States as a whole. It's 78 percent non-Hispanic white, 11 percent black, 7 percent Hispanic, 4 percent Asian, and 1 percent Native American.[2]

Not only is Aurora an example of "perfect diversity," at least on paper, it also illustrates the regional differences in America's racial mix. Unlike water on a perfectly flat surface, diversity doesn't spread evenly across the nation. It's regional. The states at the top of the U.S. map are among the whitest. Ninety-one percent of Idaho residents and 94 percent of North Dakotans are non-Hispanic white. By contrast, blacks, Latinos, Asians, and immigrants tend to be more heavily concentrated in urban areas and on the coasts. Three-quarters of America's Latinos live in just five states: California, Texas, New York, Florida, and Illinois. And 54 percent of blacks live in the South, compared to 32 percent of whites. But the most obvious example of ethnic concentration may be Asian Americans, a third of whom live in California.[3] We live in a stratified nation. According to one Loyola University study, only 5 percent of America's neighborhoods are racially diverse and stable (rather than in transition from, say, mostly white to mostly black).[4]

Segregation has been and still is the key issue in where different races live. Many Americans would like to think that nonwhites live together only by choice, but white flight plays a major role. If a neighborhood becomes 8 percent black, whites start to move out. The more black residents the neighborhood has, the more whites move. To this day, one-third of all African Americans across the nation live in conditions of intense segregation, with smaller numbers of Latinos and Asians bumping up against the same barriers.[5]

The images of a segregated America are familiar ones, from the Civil Rights movement to the inner cities of today. But we're less familiar with the images of an integrated America. Some of us don't even know if such a thing exists. Does it? And how do young Americans who live there feel about it? To try to find out, I decided to visit Aurora, where Gina lives, and Colorado Springs, a city surrounded by natural beauty two hours to the south. Both ranked high on the list of places that matched America's racial mix. Both have the military influence that seems to help produce a "perfect" demographic picture. And both, unfortunately, show how "perfect diversity" is an awfully hard thing to find, or define.

An Overgrown Suburb

It's the last day of the third quarter of Gina's junior year of high school. Later in the day she'll make up some quizzes and get the skinny on a couple of her grades, but right now—despite the anti-tobacco admonishments of President Clinton—the sixteen-year-old is taking a break in what's arguably the most integrated part of Smoky Hill High School: the concrete courtyard out back where students sneak a smoke. It's chilly outside but Gina and her classmates, some of them wearing shorts, would rather shiver than miss their chance to get a couple of puffs in between classes. "Skaters, freaks, Asians hang outside," Gina says, lighting up on my left. ("Skaters rule!" yells a blond buzz-cut guy on my right.) "Blacks hang inside," she informs me—at least the ones who don't smoke.

Like many high schools, Smoky Hill has a mix of students—but the students just don't mix. The massive school enrolls nearly three thousand students, over 80 percent of them white. That's significantly whiter than Aurora, and than America as a whole. Virtually every city school system is internally segregated, and Aurora is no exception. Some of its schools are mostly black; others are 90 percent white. Smoky Hill is in one of the wealthier (and whiter) neighborhoods in Aurora. In 1996, Smoky Hill's Mary Jarvis was named national principal of the year.[6] The school has top-notch facilities and a full compliment of high-level academic classes. But the number of Latinos and Asians is growing rapidly, and that's making some parents panicky. One math teacher tells me she worries that, despite its present demographics, Smoky Hill could become a victim of white flight. The district is building a new high school even farther south, in the whitest area of town. Aurora started as a suburban refuge. Now it has "inner-city issues," she says. "We never wanted to deal with Denver's urban problems. Now we have problems, and we don't know how to deal with it."

It's a common story. The growth of new cities like Aurora was once viewed as the nation's best hope for integration, a place where arriving blacks, Asians and Latinos would be accepted by whites who already lived there. The former Denver bedroom community has the confused, decentralized layout of a suburb that's outgrown its own expectations. Enclaves of townhouses lead to highways lead to strip malls lead to soccer fields lead to business districts. In 1970, Aurora's population was seventy-five thousand; by 1990, it had tripled. But local residents say the bigger Aurora gets, the more segregated it gets. What happens if you're someone like Gina Perez, someone who really wants to be friends with all races? What happens to the young Americans like her who've decided they want integration to work?

Master and Slave

According to Gina (and newspaper clips on a handful of incidents) Smoky Hill is a place where students are playing out long-standing racial anxieties. Gina's first week at school, she saw some kids in her French class playing "master and slave" with a black puppet. The teacher didn't do anything about it, Gina says, so she went to her dean and complained. "The kid got suspended. But I was like, 'That's unbelievable!' " she says. "That was my first impression of Smoky Hill." To this day, she says, "I've heard some people saying 'chink' or 'nigger' in the halls. It kind of forces people away."

A couple of years before Gina arrived, students reported that Ku Klux Klan members had distributed literature at the school. After she got there, the Smoky Hill newspaper lampooned blacks, including a proposed story on "Minority scholarships—white man's burden," and tales of a black Smoky Hill student "cutting off his Afro curls and selling them to the Colorado Paintbrush Co." It could be, and has been, worse: a student at nearby (and even wealthier) Cherry Creek High performed at a school show in blackface.[7] Stereotypes aren't the only hot issue. The civil rights division of the Department of Education is investigating apparent inequalities in Aurora's disciplinary standards. Black middle and high school students in the district are suspended three times as often as the statewide rate, and much more than whites in their own districts.[8]

Gina loves her school's academics, but she hates the tension she sees between students. And perhaps because she sees white students as privileged and smug, Gina has chosen to identify herself as nonwhite. Given Gina's looks and her background, choosing her race is a complicated issue. But then again, so are most things with her family. Her mom, Kathy, who's an executive secretary at a technology firm, is Italian American. She's divorced from Gina's dad, who's Mexican American. Gina has a full sister, Angie, who's two years older; younger twin brothers from her mom's second marriage (which also ended); and a brother and sister from her dad's second marriage, which ended as well. The twin boys live with Gina's stepdad; the other siblings live with Gina's stepmom. "I've been through three divorces and I'm only sixteen," says Gina with a mix of amazement and exasperation. "At one point, my sister was living with my dad, and then my brother and sister were living with my stepmom, and then my twin brothers were living with my stepdad, and I was living with my mom, so we were split up in four different households." Gina and her sister Angie are living together again with their mother. They both have pale skin with tawny undertones and hair they dye dirty blond. "I put down 'Hispanic' " on forms that ask for race "because I am Hispanic and Italian. I am not white at all," Gina says adamantly. She sees white kids as racially prejudiced and snooty, and she sees herself as a working-class girl in a school full of upper-class kids. They don't have to work as hard as she does (or at all) to make their car payments. Their parents don't have to sweat money issues. "Almost every single kid at this school has a computer at home," says Gina, who doesn't. "If not one, then like three, you know, one for each family member." Gina's profoundly grateful that her mom has spent so much time making sure the family was secure. Kathy moved them into a two-bedroom townhouse near Smoky Hill so they'd be in the right district to go to the school. Now she's moving them again, to a bigger three-bedroom in the same complex. "My mom works so hard," says Gina.

But the irony is that Kathy's hard work to make sure her daughters had the best educational opportunities has also made them socially vulnerable. The high school Gina and Angie used to go to, Gateway, is largely black and Latino. It's not affluent like Smoky Hill, and it doesn't match the wealthier school's academic reputation. Angie was a scene queen at Gateway, a social hub of the school. Gina, who only went there freshman year, was able to coast in on her sister's popularity. She was happy there—"I was friends with the whole school"—but she had a dismal 1.8 GPA. That was enough for Kathy. She moved the family so Gina and Angie could go to a better school. But Angie hated Smoky Hill immediately. "She's really good at art and stuff, and they have thirty different art classes she could take," says Gina. "But she thought it was too hard, and she saw people being rude about black people and stuff, and she just dropped out. . . . So I honestly think that if she had stayed at Gateway, even if she was cutting class, she would have still stayed in school, because she had so many friends there." Angie, who's as thin as her sister is curvy, is as outgoing as her sister is reserved. The three of us hang out together—going to a Mexican restaurant they used to love when they were younger, hanging out at their favorite coffee shop in Denver. Angie's all wisecracks and attitudes on the surface . . . but she's worried about the future. She signed up for an alternative school—and then dropped out of that as well. Now she's looking for a job and thinking about getting a GED.

The move to Smoky Hill worked much better for Gina academically— she got a 3.1 GPA sophomore year—but she sees firsthand the racial tensions that helped drive her sister away. "I have like four friends, four friends that I made the whole year," says Gina. " 'Cause even the people that talk to me a little bit, I got to know them a little bit better, and I was like, 'No way, you're not my friend. You make fun of everybody around you. You bring twenty bucks every day for lunch,' " she says. Speaking of lunch, she breaks down the income and class differences between her old school and her current one by looking at what's on the menu. "They had a Subway in Gateway—and then at Smoky Hill they have Taco Bell, McDonald's, Chick-Fil-A, Arby's, Subway, Pizza Hut, Dominoes, Chinese food," she says. And like many schools, the cafeteria is a place where racial segregation becomes clear. "There's like one section where all the black people sit and then one section where all the Asian people sit, and there's like a few Spanish people up here and the rest is all white."

Many of Gina's friends are black, but she introduces me to Katy, a curvy white girl in hippie clothing whose birthday falls just a day after Gina's. Katy doesn't make racial judgments about who she hangs out with, but she doesn't exactly fit in with the preppy cheerleader types either. The metalhead kids who share the smoking area with Gina don't fit in either. "They don't like me because I wear leather, I smoke, I drive a fast car," says a guy in a chain draped leather jacket. The ultimate dividing line in high school is insider-outsider. Being nonwhite is one easy way of being branded an outsider.

Lasana and Dana, two black friends of Gina's, tell me the place to go to see how segregated the school is, is "Activities," an open area with thirty-foot-high ceilings, brick and white cinderblock walls, and black columns. The black students hang toward one end of Activities; cheerleader-blond white girls and white guys in backward baseball caps take over the rest of the room. One white girl sucks on a lollipop; a guy surreptitiously adjusts his jock. Some look as if they should be playing with Barbies and Tonka trucks; other look like extras on *Melrose Place*. Even though some teachers are giving out grades today, sex is the topic of choice. Four boys, all white, discuss partying and girls; "fucking" and "bitch" seem to be the two most crucial words in their vocabulary. "She said, 'The only reason I won't have sex with you is that it'll fuck up our friendship,' " one says. A kid walks by in a HOOTERS KITCHEN STAFF T-shirt and baseball cap. A girl wears lavender pants, a teeny T-shirt, and Farrah Fawcett hair. Race isn't the only issue of diversity in high school, just one of the most obvious.

Everyone's got an angle on what's going on at the school. The black students roll their eyes when I ask them if the school is truly integrated. The white kids sheepishly shrug their shoulders. And several of the students refer to a group called "Asian Pride" as a gang, even though, as far as I can see, the Asian kids are just hanging out like all of the other students do. It's an odd double standard, especially given who applies it. Ashley is a white, seventeen-year-old senior with a calm, mature demeanor. She says she has friends of all races, and went to a middle school, Harrington, where whites were a minority. She wants the classes to include more topics on nonwhites—"In U.S. history, we only did a little bit on the slave trade," she says—and she's upset by the divisions between the students. "There's a white clique and a black. The message is, I will tolerate you, but I will not accept you," she says. But she still calls Asian Pride a gang, though she can't really explain why.

It might help things a bit if the school provided some structured way of dealing with racial issues. But Gina says that the school doesn't foster any meaningful discussions of the issues dividing the school; it just has a sort of feel-good world cultures week. That means that people like Gina have no outlet for their feelings of frustration and isolation. She doesn't identify with the white students. She hasn't really grown up around a lot of Mexican-American culture. And the fact that she's light-skinned means that she sometimes faces the prejudices of blacks. "Blacks talk shit about whites," Gina complains. "I've walked into parties with like all black people and they're like, 'Oh, my God, you're glowing.' They'll talk behind your back to their homies and they'll be like, 'Why is she here?' " So now when she goes to parties, she asks her friends beforehand, " 'Are there going to be other white people there, you know, people with white skins?' because I hate getting that crap from people," she says.

Gina has casual friends of almost every race, but she seems to feel close to few of them. The ones she feels closest to are black, perhaps because they were the majority of her old school, or perhaps because she sees them as an antidote to the elitist white culture of her new school. Gina wishes she had a more racially mixed group of friends, and that they could all party together instead of separately. She loves taking friends who've never stepped outside of their white or black or Mexican cliques to a whole new scene. "If I can take someone to a mixed party, I mean, that's something that they've probably never been to. You know, it's a major experience," she says. Most of the guys she dates are black. "I don't get along with white guys that much, you know. I mean, every once in a while, I'll go out with one, but most of them are assholes, you know. . . . They just don't know how to have fun. Like black guys will take me to parties, drive around in their nice car," she says. The black parties are mostly about dancing. And the white parties are mostly about drinking, something Gina's not down with.

Junior year's been harder for Gina than sophomore year was. The strain of working a forty-hour week as well as taking a challenging course load is taking its toll. She goes to school from 7:30 A.M. to 1:30 P.M. (under pressure from Aurora's growth, the school staggers its schedules so more kids can attend). Then she does an hour of homework; then she drives to the local mall and works at the fast-food restaurant Chick-Fil-A from the afternoon until she closes the place at 9:30. She drives back home in a car that much of her salary goes to pay for, then does some more homework before she goes to bed. "Sometimes I get totally tired. Another day, another dollar, another grade," she says. After a disastrous first semester of junior year, she's started lifting her grades this term. The easy solution would be to work fewer hours, but it's easy to understand the lure of making money if you're not rich and most of the kids at school get a king-sized allowance from Mom and Dad. Despite the difficult juggling act, Gina feels committed to learning, an attitude she credits her mom with having instilled in her. "Even though I get stressed out, it's like I always have to be learning," she says. "I love the world and I love learning about stuff in the world. You know, it's like I'm just totally like, 'Wow!' "

Gina's love for learning helps mitigate a little of the pain she feels because her fellow students are so divided. Even in cities like Aurora that represent the nation's racial mix, there is no "perfect diversity." There are only people—in this case, teenagers—trying to figure out how to get along. Gina has one suggestion: start judging others by the way you're treated, not by the way you *think* you'll be treated. "There's some white people and all their friends are white people [who say], 'Well, black people hate us.' Or [black students who say], 'White people hate us.' " Gina tells them, " 'You guys don't give each other a chance. You guys assume everything about each other.' " And because she's borne the brunt of some of these judgments, she tells her black classmates, " 'You guys don't even give me a chance. I'm a really good friend and everything and I'm not racist at all. But you guys, you know, you look at me and all you see is light skin. That's what you assume. You automatically hate me.' " All one of her classmates could say was, " 'Oh, well, that's just the way it is.' "

Even in "integrated" America, is that the way it always will be?

"An Insulated White Town"

There's a flip side to Gina's story of being rejected by blacks, what makes black students in cities like Aurora fed up with mixing with whites. It's been called "black self-segregation" and decried by conservative critics across America. But many black Americans say they have no choice: in ways ranging from blatant racism to honest gaffes, whites don't understand or respect black culture.

The feelings of isolation that lead to black self-segregation are exactly what I found in another city that roughly matches America's racial mix—

Colorado Springs. Just two hours to the south of Aurora, Colorado Springs is a world away in geography, attitude, and culture. Aurora is a city built on urban sprawl. Colorado Springs, by contrast, grew from a small Old West town into a thriving city ringed by the beauty of the mountains— and by a series of military installations. The Springs region has an army base, two air force bases, the Air Force Academy, and heavily guarded missile warning facilities. The military isn't just an employer; it helps set the tone for the city's straight-laced civic culture. Another major influence on the city's character (and economy) is an astounding array of Christian Right organizations. The Promise Keepers, who brought hundreds of thousands of men to the nation's capital in 1997, are headquartered in the area, as is Focus on the Family, a broadcast and publishing empire whose radio show reaches over 2 million listeners across the United States each day. Both are multi-million-dollar businesses as well as religious organizations. (Focus on the Family, which has an official sign marking its exit on the highway, gets a quarter of a million visitors and generates over $100 million each year.)[9] The city's conservative character has brought it its share of controversy, leading to what many call a city divided. In 1992, the Colorado Springs religious community helped pass Amendment 2, a statewide ordinance banning any antidiscrimination laws protecting gays and lesbians. Rather than joining with the gay community to fight discrimination, which might have forged a greater coalition on diversity, some blacks and Latinos berated gays and lesbians for comparing gay rights to civil rights. After the vote, attacks on gays tripled, and the local community became divided even further.[10]

So what are the locals like? The bunch I meet at a bar called the Clubhouse paint a vivid picture of a place where small town meets big city, and majority-white Western America meets an influx of outsiders from different backgrounds. It's not just race that makes someone an outsider in the Springs; it can be ethnicity as well. I meet Ray DeGeorge, a solidly built Italian American who served in the air force and the marines, at a local bar. He still exudes New Yawkness from every pore even though he's lived in Colorado for eleven years. "Back home, I'm an Italian with Italians. Here . . ." He simply shrugs to indicate how out of place he feels. "It's a city without a soul," he says.

Twenty-six-year-old Seth Crane cuts a unique figure among the crowd at the Clubhouse. When I first see him, he's on stage playing bass in nothing but a T-shirt and jockstrap. Seth calls Colorado Springs "an insulated white town." Seth looks Latino, but he's half Seneca Indian and half self-described "poor white trash from Northern California." Both sides of his family are staunchly Mormon, and he went to Brigham Young University and did his Mormon mission on Indian reservations before pursuing a decidedly less orthodox lifestyle. He's bandmates with the husband of Amanda Stettler, a pregnant twenty-two-year-old who sees the culture clash in Colorado Springs as generational. "Focus on the Family brings upper-middle-class, conservative people. Our half is the younger generation; we're different. So it's divided." Colorado Springs, she says, is "kinda split 50/50 between right wing religious groups" and people who either lead or respect alternative lifestyles. "There are KKK rallies, gay marches, religious marches all within a week in the summer," she says.

And then there are people for whom Colorado Springs is an oasis of diversity. Shannon Mangum, an athletically built twenty-one-year-old former rodeo rider and beer promotin' "Bud Girl" with pale skin, dark brown hair, and a nose ring who's studying to be a beautician. Now she's engaged to a man she met in the Springs who grew up in Buenos Aires. She grew up in a town called Eaton in the rural north of Colorado near the Wyoming border—pure ranch land. "I got up at four in the morning to feed the cows," she says. "I was in the NHSRA—National High School Roping Association; the CHSRA, Colorado High School Roping Association; the Colorado Girls Barrel Racing Association. . . . I'm only friends with a few people from home. There were a lot of people who put people down, racist people," she says of her high school days. "I like knowing people who are different. You learn something."

"A Disaster for Diversity"

Colorado Springs was summed up by young residents as everything from "an insulated white town" to an oasis of diversity in a mostly white state. Obviously, diversity is in the eye of the beholder.

I head to Colorado Springs to gauge its diversity myself just weeks after the *Wall Street Journal* published an article that sparked racial debate. The front-page story detailed how black employees of MCI Telecommunications' software development division absolutely hated the white-bread culture of Colorado Springs, charm or no charm. When the company moved the division from majority-black Washington, D.C., some black employees refused to move in the first place, and others quit after coming to Colorado. The article quoted MCI's chief information officer, who called the move "a disaster for diversity."[11]

Judging by the strength of the reaction to the article, the issue of race doesn't bubble to the surface in Colorado Springs very often—but when it does, it's a doozy. John Fowler, the head of the local chamber of commerce, went into damage-control mode, eager to refute the article's charges. "We were shocked and surprised by the tone of the MCI article. . . . There are not extremes in race relations," he says. Fowler, who appears to be in his forties, has sandy hair and wears a gray suit; he seems almost overwhelmed by the scale of his large, traditionally furnished office. The entire space seems a fitting cocoon for Colorado Springs' business class. "Neighborhoods are integrated," Fowler continues. The racial atmosphere is "positive, but there are always incidents where people believe discrimination exists." He paints a picture of a rapidly growing and changing city—one that a few decades ago hardly qualified as a city at all—where 20 percent of the population exits, to be replaced by newcomers, each year. The revolving-door effect is due in large part to the military, which deploys its members throughout the world.

Rather than characterize the city as conservative, Fowler calls it "populist," and the religious influence "overstated" by the media. "Colorado Springs is a Western town. It's fiercely independent. There's an ethic that says everybody has equal opportunity but no special favors," he says, consciously or not using phrases often used by affirmative-action opponents. Diversity is "exciting," though competition between groups occasionally drives up tensions. "We're economically strong, we're on the cutting edge. . . . That rising tide's the best thing that can happen for all of us [and] ethnic minorities benefit from it."

Jerome Page, president of the local chapter of the Urban League, sees the city far differently. The Denver native is tall and trim, with the thoughtful demeanor of a college professor. "The trust and communication level is at zero in a community like this," Page says. "White people like to think there's . . . only two percent minority population here." In fact, while the number of Latinos in the city is close to the 11 percent nationwide figure, the proportion of blacks in Colorado Springs— 7 percent—is lower than average. The upside is that blacks are not segregated in Colorado Springs, something that happens to blacks in virtually every other part of the nation. Perhaps that's because the 7 percent figure is just below what's called the tipping point—the threshold at which white flight begins. Demographic studies show that when neighborhoods become 8 percent black, some white residents begin to move out. Considering that America is 13 percent black, the tipping point is a real barrier to integration. In one study, if a neighborhood became 21 percent black, half of whites would refuse to move in—and a quarter would move out.[12] Today, even well-off black families are usually segregated. African Americans earning over fifty thousand dollars per year are more likely to be segregated than Latino families earning just twenty-five hundred dollars per year.[13]

Whether it's due to the deplorable existence of the tipping point or because of true enlightenment, Colorado Springs has no "black neighborhood," something that could be seen as a positive leap forward. Yet according to Page, black families are integrated into white neighborhoods, but they're not faring as well in the schools or job market as whites. "Private business is a problem here—they're not hiring blacks," he says, and while those seeking careers in the military fare better, not everyone should or will follow that path. "Minorities are invisible in this community," he says. "We don't have a ghetto here, but we are ghetto-izing people in our minds."

Page went to Venezuela with the Peace Corps, and has served the Urban League in cities from Washington, D.C., to Chattanooga, Tennessee for over thirty years. Though becoming the head of the traditionally black group in Colorado Springs was a homecoming for the Colorado native, it was also a wake-up call. Page thinks that the Springs' small, scattered black community contributes to a sense of frustration among young African Americans. Because there are so few blacks, they are constantly asked to explain or defend their race. After a while, they simply stop trying. "My youngest son is twenty-two," says Page. "He's moved to an angrier posture to the point where he went wild [with his hair] and my wife pulled out a picture from the sixties and we looked like twins." Page wishes his son, who attends the University of Colorado in Boulder, had more white friends. "It's painful to me because I've always felt that to get there [i.e., to racial equality] we need a partnership." Instead, he pictures the crop of black kids on today's campuses in "an angry stance, with earphones on to block out the white kids."

The views of a group of black teenagers who meet me at the Urban League's offices seem to bear out Page's fears. The five range from Arema, a petite, high-voiced, fifteen-year-old sophomore, to Reginald (the only guy among them), an athletic college freshman. Most come from military families. Unlike their parents' generation, they're the beneficiaries of being able to live in racially integrated neighborhoods, something they acknowledge. Says Arema, "Our generation is different because we've been around white people and stuff and different cultures more. My dad, when he was in high school in Arkansas, his senior year, got bused to high school. There were little riots every time they played 'Dixie' at the school." But these teens feel as if something's missing—a connection to black culture on one side, and a true bond with white students on the other. Says Monica, a fourteen-year-old sophomore with dimples who sports a Mickey Mouse watch, "All blacks are spread out. That's both good and bad." "The good is, being isolated from the black community makes me independent," Reginald picks up seamlessly. "It makes me strive. The bad is that you're robbed of your culture." When festivals like Juneteenth (which originated with the liberation of slaves in Texas) come around, kids in Colorado Springs choose to go someplace with a larger black community, like Denver's Montbello neighborhood.

These kids are fluent in the ways of white culture and the nuances of living in a mostly white town. But they feel as if many people would like them to give up their sense of black culture—something that only makes them stick more closely with other blacks and with Mexicans. They cite incidents ranging from blatant prejudice to more farcical misunderstandings as evidence of what they have to put up with. When fifteen-year-old Dara was in seventh grade, she punched a white boy out for repeatedly calling her a nigger at school. (She says the teacher did nothing.) Today, most of her close friends are black and one is Mexican. She also recounts a more benign (though annoying) incident. "My sister had pineapple waves [a fragile, heavily gelled hairstyle] and she went to a job interview and all the white people were squishing them," she says. "If you put grease in your hair, [whites are] like, what kind of grease, cooking grease? They don't understand." Natoshia, a seventeen-year-old who was actually born in Colorado Springs, says "I don't have to explain things about my hair, whatever, because I don't interact with [whites] as much as I—I don't want to say should—but as much as I do with my other black friends. I don't think I'm missing anything. And I don't think they're missing anything either." Just as Jerome Page worries, these students are tired of being cultural ambassadors to white America.

This is the classic dilemma of what many (from a cover story in *U.S. News and World Report* to conservative Robert Bork) call black self-segregation, the idea that blacks are clumping together, rebuffing the best efforts of whites to get to know them. A report by a black think tank makes it clear the issue is far more complex. The Joint Center on Political and Economic Studies warned black college students against creating "self-segregating cocoons . . . [which enforce] feelings of paranoia." But it also added: "It is disquieting to be taken into a college dining room and be shown row upon row of tables occupied solely by white students and one or two tables of black students, and then ask why blacks insist on segregating themselves. . . . The assumption [is] that black students should make concessions to the predominance of whites, and also represent their race."[14] In a majority-white environment, many black students feel like they have to stick together, either for camaraderie or to avoid harassment.

These students suspect that blacks are singled out for disciplinary action at local high schools, something borne out by statistics. Arema attends Air Academy High School. "The teachers are OK [but] the hall monitors follow you if you're in too big of a group." And recently, a black student was expelled for fixing his eyeglasses with a pen knife—something forbidden by the school's zero-tolerance law on weapons. "White people couldn't really understand why we were getting offended [by the laws]. It doesn't really affect them because they're not being watched as closely as we are. . . . And we were talking about how if he was white, he would probably not be kicked out."

All of these students are eager to talk about issues like zero tolerance and self-segregation. But they say they've only got each other to turn to: their teachers and principals aren't helping them deal with these tough, controversial issues. In a vacuum of school leadership, these teens are left to make their own decisions about how to treat whites who don't know much about black culture. I tell them that the idea that blacks bear all the responsibility for segregating, and whites are simply befuddled bystanders, is naïve. But I also push the black students to tell me one thing: if they don't teach white America about black life, who will? Arema replies that she does spend some time with white students. "At lunch, there's a black lunch group and a white lunch group," and she switches between the two. But if they want to know about black history, Arema says they better go look in a book. "We learn about their history all the time," she says, musing that there ought to be more taught about nonwhites in class. Once white students get the basics from a book, they can come to her, she says, adding, "You don't have to be friends to ask a little question." "I'm not gonna be explaining to nobody, unless they ask and they truly want to know," chimes in Monica, who has a close white friend she met in junior high school. "When I had my braids, a boy said, 'Do you wash them?' He didn't want to know—he was just trying to be funny. I was kind of upset about that."

But the oldest and most mature of the students realizes that he's probably going to have to make some time to talk about black culture. Reginald goes to Drake University, which he calls similar to Colorado Springs in its racial mix and its attitudes. This year, he chaired the speaker's and issues committee at his school and organized roundtables on race. During Black History Month, "a lot of white students, because we're the minority and stuff, are making such an uproar about our culture. They come in and they say they want to learn a lot more about it. And if they were willing to come in and not be sarcastic about it, or even if they were sarcastic but willing to sit down and listen . . . we would have little conversations," he says. "And the more we would do it, the more we would see people open up and talk, and kind of erase a lot of the racial tension we had."

But Reginald doesn't have much faith that Colorado Springs offers blacks equal opportunity. "I kind of see things through my brother's eyes right now," he says. "He just got a degree in mechanical engineering, and he's still looking for a job. I guess it's kind of tough because a lot of businesses don't want to give him the first step. Every job, he's either over- or underqualified. But on the other hand, he could go to a town like Atlanta and put in his first application and get a job. I couldn't really say what the difference is with these companies out here, why aren't they hiring black people the same way they hire white people?"

Is there anyone in this group who really likes living in Colorado Springs? I learn that Natoshia alone finds the racial mix of Colorado Springs familiar and comforting. "I mostly spent my summers in Alabama, where my parents are from. It's a culture shock, because you've never seen so many black people. When you see 'em, you don't see just one, you see all of them," she says. "I do like it for visiting and for the summers. But I don't think I'd be able to stay down there. It's not something I'm used to—being around black people all the time. My dad asked me if I wanted to go to school down there, and I said, "No: it's too many of them!" she says to the laughter of her friends. It's clear that having grown up in a majority-white environment, she's as uncomfortable in an all-black area as most whites would be. She adds, "I didn't even think white people lived in Alabama, because I never see them." But most of the other teens have had enough of being a small, scattered minority. They want to move away, preferably to somewhere with a larger black population. They're among the first generation of blacks living in integrated America—and most of them are dying to get out.

Older African Americans in Colorado Springs grew up with mandatory legal segregation, and they're worried about the next generation's attitude. James Smith, Sr., is a loquacious eighty-three-year-old retired civil servant known throughout Colorado Springs society. He absolutely rejects the idea that blacks are unwelcome in the Springs, and says they're treated with a neighborliness not found in most urban areas. "In Detroit [where he grew up] they looked down their nose at you. Here they say, 'Have a nice day!' " But when I ask him about the black community, he admits, "There ain't no black community." Even though he has an appreciation for the Springs that the next generation doesn't, he admits that most black neighborhoods seem to have something that Colorado Springs doesn't—a sense of history and solidarity.

What will happen to our ideas of integration and segregation as the number of cities like Aurora and Colorado Springs grow? Even though their demographics match America's as a whole, it's hard to see these cities as paragons of racial enlightenment. On the one hand, in the case of Gina, it seems that the few kids who really do want a multiracial group of friends are rebuffed. On the other hand, conservative Colorado Springs may have literally integrated blacks in terms of housing and schools— an admirable accomplishment in and of itself. But these kids, who should be the most privileged of the post–Civil Rights generation, feel as if they're being asked to set aside their own culture in order to fit in with white society. They show that literal integration isn't enough to create real understanding and harmony. That takes more work: talking, perhaps even arguing, then coming to a true common ground. Public school systems already have enough on their plate that they may feel dealing with racial issues is extraneous. But until someone helps the next generation deal with modern-day racial issues, "perfect diversity" seems destined to exist only as a demographic concept, or a doomed dream.

III

The **Political** as **Personal**

Some racial issues take on so much significance that they are constantly in the news. But the news coverage doesn't always do the subjects justice. The 1990s have seen strident battles over affirmative action, over failing urban schools (and whether the only way to save them is to dismantle them in favor of a voucher system), and, of course, over immigration. Young Americans rarely have a voice in these debates, but they are often buffeted by the decisions the officials and politicians make. The following chapters give some of the young Americans in the crosshairs of American public policy a chance to speak their mind and explain their own lives.

SEVEN

Good Kids and Bad Schools: The Black and Brown Future of America's Urban Schools

Oakland, California

Fremont High School lies on Foothill Boulevard just off of Oakland's East Fourteenth Street corridor. The wide, charmless main streets are lined by mom-and-pop shops and low-rent chain stores like Payless Shoes. The blocks surrounding Fremont hold modest wood-frame houses and a few scruffy apartment buildings. Most of the entrances to the school—a solid, aesthetically challenged structure—are padlocked. You can go in and out only through one gate, where two monitors stand to keep an eye on the flow. Just beyond the gate is a central courtyard, a place where kids goof off, mack the cute boys and girls, and eat plates of goopy chili cheese fries for lunch. The skin colors of the students chillin' in the California sunshine run from paler golds to warm tans to mahogany. Nearly every single one of the kids is Asian or Latino or black.

Oakland is no example of "perfect" demographic diversity, like the cities of Aurora and Colorado Springs. Where those cities closely matched America's racial mix, Oakland is overwhelmingly black and brown. The city's history encompasses black power, white flight, and multiethnic immigration. Oakland is the birthplace of the Black Panther Party, where founding members had their first meeting in 1966. A decade later, their political clout helped elect Lionel Wilson the city's first black mayor.[1] Since then, Oakland has become less black and more Asian and Hispanic. (The 1990 census put the figures at 43 percent black, 12 percent Asian, 14 percent Hispanic, and 19 percent non-Hispanic white.)[2] As has happened in other parts of the country, many Asians and Latinos have moved into what used to be all-black neighborhoods. While many of the whites live together in the affluent Oakland hills, most of the blacks and Hispanics are what locals call "flatlanders," living in the less expensive areas downhill.

You can take East Fourteenth Street straight out to Fremont High. The road runs from the tame waterfront shopping complex at Jack London Square to the barrio, the 'hood. Traveling out from the waterfront you pass Vietnamese storefronts, Mexican *taquerias,* black beauty shops. More and more of America's neighborhoods will come to look like Oakland's East Fourteenth Street corridor, places where you can hear dozens of languages including Vietnamese, Spanish, Tongan, and Tagalog—even what some people in the Oakland school system called Ebonics. But they're places where you rarely find the group that remains, for the moment at least, America's racial majority: whites.

Only 6 percent of the kids in Oakland's school system are white. With those kinds of numbers, it's virtually impossible to talk about integration—at least in the traditional sense.[3] We think about integration as black and white. But how do you classify neighborhoods that lack whites but are mixed black/Latino/Asian? Immigrants from around the world have brought their cultures—and over eighty languages—to this city. Virtually all of the schools in Oakland have to provide some bilingual or English as a second language (ESL) services, especially for members of the large Vietnamese and Mexican immigrant communities. Because race is almost always framed in terms of black and white, "majority" and "minority," it might be tempting to think that all these different "minority" kids would automatically get along. The reality is far different. There have been black/Mexican riots at some of the junior and senior high schools. The racial groups in Oakland's schools, including Fremont, tend to clump together as much as the blacks and whites do in places like Colorado.

A Place for Learning, and Understanding

I visited Fremont High School over the course of a month, attending classes, hanging out with students, even (against my best judgment) eating the lunchroom food. I chose Fremont in large part because it exemplified the issues and problems facing black and brown neighbor-hoods—places that are racially diverse, but devoid of whites. In one way, all the students from the East Fourteenth Street corridor are in the same boat: poor or working class and minority. But how do the differences in language and culture, and the inevitable stereotypes and prejudices, affect their ability to get along? And how do the incredible challenges that face all of them affect their ability to get a good education?

I also choose Fremont because it illustrates the issues of race and opportunity that have come to dominate the affirmative action debates. Oakland is right next door to Berkeley, home to the university of the same name. (I explore the issue of affirmative action at Berkeley in the next chapter.) But most students in the Oakland system can't qualify to attend the highly ranked public university just a few miles away. Their grades and test scores are too low. Some critics, like the authors of *The Bell Curve*, argue that the black and brown students of the inner city don't measure up because of genetics.[4] I decided to take a look at Fremont to gauge whether they were ever given a chance—if the education these students receive places them in a position to compete.

I was prepared to be thoroughly depressed by what I found in Oak-land, both in terms of black-brown racial tensions and what we've come to accept as the typical problems of urban schools. What I found was an extraordinary program within Fremont High that made me alternately hopeful and angry: hopeful because it offers a clear road map for success, and angry because this kind of success is so seldom replicated.

It's called the Fremont Media Academy, and it's tucked away—sheltered, perhaps—at the back of the overcrowded school. You walk through the courtyard and past the main classroom buildings to what used to be open space. But after parts of the school were demolished by the 1989 San Francisco earthquake, portable classroom units, large trailers, were plunked down in rows. At one time they were probably utilitarian and new. Now they're utilitarian and crumbling, a temporary solution turned permanent eyesore.

But what's inside is more of a sight for sore eyes: teenagers working in groups and clusters, planning newspaper stories and magazine articles and television spots. That's because these portables contain the Media Academy, a journalism program that is partially funded by the state. I was introduced to a handful of Media Academy students at the Freedom Forum Pacific Coast Center, a well-funded nonprofit organization that had reached out to the Oakland school. After I met them, I decided I had to learn more about their program. Students are grouped together for journalism and English classes, but take their electives, math, and science with a mix of Media Academy and other teens. Even then, however, they hang out mostly with their Media Academy friends. With a loyalty to their fellow students and the intense attention of their teachers, Media Academy students go on to schools as competitive as Berkeley, some even becoming journalists themselves.

Steve O'Donoghue, a wiry Irish American with graying hair and an easy laugh, has been teaching at the Media Academy for thirteen years. His portable classroom has desks in one section and a computer lab and darkroom in back. As the kids file in, O'Donoghue warns them that if they use foul language they'll have to "drop a quarter in the curse box," a bank he uses as a gentle way of enforcing genteel behavior in the classroom. The fact that it actually works probably has less to do with the quarter fine than the fact that the students respect O'Donoghue, who they usually call by the shortened term of endearment "Mr. O'D." Much of the time, he treats them as if they're valued employees and he's the supervisor. Instead of babying or bossing them, he gives them enough autonomy to make some decisions (and mistakes) on their own. The students write, edit, and shoot their own photographs in O'Donoghue's newspaper class. They even learn to lay out the paper themselves on the Media Academy's computers. O'Donoghue and (a white, nonsinging) Michael Jackson, the Academy's other journalism teacher, teach and supervise the production not only of the newspaper, but the magazine, and the student-shot and -edited television show that airs on the local public-access cable channel. If they can find the funds, they plan to purchase equipment to air a radio show from a booth above the school auditorium as well.

Students have to apply to the Media Academy in ninth grade for admission sophomore year, but there's no firm benchmark of grades or test scores they have to meet. The students are a mixed bag in terms of academic preparation, English speaking and writing ability, race, and family background.

The students in O'Donoghue's classes are mostly Mexican American, with a healthy helping of black students and a few Asian Americans as well. There's Jackie, who is dark-skinned and curly-haired, half black and half Filipina. Her constant companion is a student I'll call Jorge,* a heavyset, baby-faced Mexican American with a troubled home life and gang affiliations in his past. Jorge, who exhibits a keen intelligence in our conversations, constantly cuts class and is failing. Ricarlo is tall and skinny, an ambitious African American who lives to put out the Academy's television show. There's even one white kid, Justin, who probably could be spotted by aerial radar because of his blond hair.

This is the first time I've been back to high school for more than a quick speech or reporting trip since I graduated a decade ago. I'm sur-

*Name changed.

prised by how quickly I fit into the rhythms of the school, and how quickly I blend in. (Sometimes too well—some of the guys in the other divisions of the school end up checking me out because they think I'm enrolled there.) I spend almost all of my time with the students of the Media Academy, and they're amazingly open given my constant questions. One of the first people I meet is Sandra, who was born a year after her parents moved here from Mexico. At sixteen, she's one of the youngest seniors; quiet and pretty with brown eyes, long brown hair, and braces, and an extremely observant gaze. She takes me on a drive around the neighborhood, pointing out areas that are more heavily black or Asian or Mexican; the ones that are OK and the ones that are dangerous. "Some of the drug dealers aren't that bad," she says. "But I don't know, are they just lazy that they don't want to go out and look for a job? If they can stand on a street corner, you know, nine in the morning 'til nine at night," she muses, "why can't they take a job?"

And then there's Mimi, who immigrated from Vietnam a decade ago. She and I first become friends when I accidentally squirt ketchup on her bright, white CK T-shirt during lunch. Mimi's well under five feet tall. The huge T-shirt reaches down to her knees. "Don't worry," she says as I daub gingerly at the red stain. I continue to murmur apologies while she gets down to what's really on her mind: "So you work at MTV, huh?" she says of the job I held at the time. "I *love* [female R & B trio] TLC. Have you ever met them? Have you met [host] Bill Bellamy? I love Bill." As we walk back to the Media Academy's classrooms, she walks trapeze-style on a concrete curb and stops to play-box with a football player literally twice her size. Irrepressibly full of energy, she and I remain friends to this day.

Over the time I'm at Fremont, I learn that not only do students like Sandra and Mimi produce good work together; they also know how to get along. All of the Media Academy students I speak to say that the racial atmosphere is calm and friendly. I see the occasional minor spat—one time Ricarlo tells a group working on the television show that they *know* they're not supposed to be speaking Spanish in class. But that's about it. There are no big racial dramas, no major rifts. The way their classes are structured helps. Journalism "is a class, but it's almost like a sport in the sense that you have practice," says O'Donoghue. "They put in a tremendous amount of time working together." Just as sports teams foster cross-racial friendships in many of America's high schools, the devotion to putting out the newspaper, magazine, and television show helps the students bond. Drawn together by their work, the students in the Media Academy have created an oasis of racial unity within a divided school, city, and community.

The Media Academy also uses programs and excursions to draw the students closer. The Academy begins in sophomore year. One of the first things they do is a two-day program at the Center for Living Skills, where they do trust-building exercises to make sure the students learn to work as a team. But the big event comes near the end of that year—the group trip to Yosemite. Most of the kids are ecstatic (and sometimes a little scared) because they've never been out in the open. In the outdoors, they bond even more. "We say, 'We're all going to go to the top of the mountain. We're a team, and we have a goal,'" says O'Donoghue.

Mimi, who's one of the few Vietnamese Americans in the program, says that "the sophomore trip really helps. We get to know each other. We know that we all have the same problems and we're all dealing with the same thing." And they put that into practice with the groups of friends they choose. One of Mimi's closest friends is April, a quiet, studious African American. And Sandra's boyfriend is Filipino, and one of her closest friends is Jackie, the half-African American, half-Filipina teen. Race is a complicated issue for Jackie. She chooses "other" when she has to put her race on a form, but she was named the Black Student Association's homecoming queen. In addition to an all-around homecoming king and queen, each of the school's ethnic clubs—like the Cambodian student association—chooses a pair as well.

"The Only White Kid"

One of the biggest testimonials to the Media Academy's harmony comes from someone whose racial group makes up less than one percent of the school. He's Justin Killian, and he isn't afraid to describe himself as "the only white kid." The handsome, athletic blond credits the Yosemite class trip with helping him get to know the classmates he now counts as friends. "People really opened up," he says. "We ended up having forty kids in the same two-bedroom tent talking. We didn't care who we were sitting on and who was sitting on us. It's the glue that kept us together."

And even though Justin is racially isolated from other whites—there aren't even two dozen of them at the school—this hasn't stopped him from fitting in at Fremont. He plays several sports, including being a member (yes, the only white one) of the school's four-man golf team. He loves his classes at the Media Academy, and he wants to go on to be a teacher. One reason Justin has no trepidation about being immersed in black, Latino, and Asian cultures is because his parents have taught him by example. Both his mom and dad, whom he goes so far as to call "perfect," grew up in Oakland and went to Fremont. They're one of the few white families that didn't move away, and even today, they live a mere two blocks from the school. Justin credits his dad, who works in a clock shop, with teaching him patience, and his mom with urging him always to do the right thing. For this family, that includes being open to people of all races.

That hasn't always been easy. Justin's junior high school, Calvin Simmons, had roughly the same demographics as Fremont but was very racially divided. "There would be fights every other week—just enough to keep the kids coming back to school," he jokes. During the L.A. riots, a white teacher drove him home in case anything bad was going to go down. But neither he nor his parents ever had any doubts about going to Fremont. "I would be the person most likely to get beat up in high school if they held a vote, based on ethnicity," he says. "But I know how to carry myself. I know how to get along with people," he says.

Justin's romantic life shows just how much he fits in. At one time, he dated a Latina named Rosa, but his longtime girlfriend is Phoutsavanh, who fled Laos with her family. "She has eight brothers and two sisters; I'm the only child," he says, beginning to list their differences. "She's Mormon [her parents converted] and I'm no religion. She's Asian and I'm white. Her parents don't really speak English and they weren't for the relationship at first. My parents love her to death," he says. To get on her parents' good side, Justin learned a few words of Laotian. It worked: now the family accepts him, and he even talks cars and sports with Phoutsavanh's dad.

"I've always felt more privileged than others to be in a school that has so many different cultures and traditions," Justin says. But many white kids he meets ask him if he feels out of place, even seeming to pity him. "When I tell people I'm from Oakland, they give me a funny look," Justin says. "When I tell them what school I go to, if they know where it is, I get an even funnier look." Many of the white kids in Oakland who go to a public school at all go to Skyline, "in the hills." In fact, the existence of Skyline High, which was built during the era of legal desegregation and de facto white flight, is a surprisingly blatant example of modern-day resistance to integration. As O'Donoghue puts it, "When Skyline was built in the early sixties, all of the high schools in Oakland [except one, which was the segregated all-black school] had attendance areas that ran from the Bay to the hill line. This meant they had kids from blue-collar (flatland), middle-income (semi-hilly), and upper-income (very hilly) neighborhoods in every school. But Skyline's attendance area was drawn all along the ridge line, which immediately skimmed the high income kids out of the other schools and insured it would be a white bastion." Over time, many nonwhite parents made sure their kids got into Skyline as well. In fact, because of the numbers of white students who attend private schools and the fact that the Oakland School District is so heavily black, even Skyline is majority black. But that hasn't exactly eliminated the zoning problem. First, the school has more whites than any other in the district. And, second, it also contributes to what O'Donoghue calls a "brain drain" of talented nonwhite students from other attendance areas, who sometimes lie about what neighborhood they live in to get districted to the better school. As for Fremont High, it's somewhere in the middle of the overall rankings for Oakland high schools, but the Media Academy's grades and test scores are significantly higher.

"I love my school," Justin says. "I feel proud because my school is so interracial. America is the melting pot. If [other white students] spent a week down here, they wouldn't feel the same." Once he becomes a teacher, "I'm going to do my part," he says enthusiastically. "Most teachers don't talk to students. You have to talk to students like you're their friends. Then you won't have a noisy class, students will learn, test scores will go up." If everyone was like that—like many of the teachers he's had—then "you would have students wanting to go to school, not clinging to the gates waiting for the bell to ring. 'Let me out!!!' "

As he prepares to enter the wider world, Justin has only one trepidation, a fear that seems particularly ironic. "I really don't know how to hang around white people," he confesses. "If I go to businesses and where I work is mostly white, I'll probably feel uncomfortable. It's weird. I've never been exposed."

Up in the Hills

Justin's final words are particularly noteworthy not just because he himself is white, but because learning how to interact with white society is still an important life and job skill. Most Americans are white, as are most employers and supervisors. Even though Fremont is racially mixed on one level, it's clear that the students are still segregated on another.

No Media Academy student expresses as much frustration at their segregation as Nicole, a black sixteen-year-old whose body is sculpted by the modern dance she loves. I meet her while she's crying during TV production class; a boy has done her wrong. After I cheer her up, we spend a lot of time talking about love and life—and race, of course. I ask her if it bothers her that there are virtually no white kids at the school. "Yeah, it bothers me because that shows that there is still separation." She says the Hill schools like Skyline have much better facilities. "You can tell which school has more white people because of what the school looks like," she says. "They get more privileges and all their extracurricular activities are different."

Like Justin, Nicole lives just blocks from the school. Her family, Jehovah's Witnesses, have a neat, well-appointed home full of pictures of Nicole's grandparents and siblings. Her father's a supervisor at Gatorade; her mother, who used to run a small computer-accessories business, is an at-home mom. They're precisely the kind of lower-middle-income family that manages to persevere even in neighborhoods like this, neighborhoods where the problems of poverty lie not far outside the door.

Nicole wishes there were more white kids at the flatland schools so they could see that blacks, Asians, and Latinos "are just like them. We have our educated, just like they have their educated; we have our dummies, just like they have their dummies, and I think it would be better if it was just a mixture of kids at every school." The white kids, she says, aren't so much afraid of blacks as "sheltered. Some don't care [about whether they interact with nonwhites or not] because they are in their own world."

She thinks her peers' prejudices are passed down from their parents. "Older people tend to poison minds," she says. Nicole, whose maternal grandfather was Jewish, sees people as "cultures, not races. . . . Someone could have dark skin and maybe have a European cultural background, that's the way they were raised, someone could have fair skin and have maybe an Indian background. People put so much importance on visual things, it's funny. You don't look at a book and say, 'Oh that's an English book.' You have to open it up and dissect it."

Segregated, and Stymied

Unfortunately, the open attitude of Media Academy kids like Justin and Nicole isn't uniformly replicated throughout the school. There's some tension between black and Mexican students, a small portion of it inspired by gang affiliations. But the main reason most kids hang in race-based groups is lack of exposure and fear of being rejected. Blacks have always hung out with blacks; Mexicans with Mexicans; Asians with Asians. Unless someone teaches them differently, each new class of students simply walks down well-worn roads of social conduct. Unintentionally adding to the segregation, Fremont's sixteen hundred students are divided into a series of specialty "houses," including the Media Academy. By Fremont students' own descriptions, the architecture house is mostly Asian and studious; despite the passage of laws to crack down on students without papers, the ESL house has lots of undocumented immigrants; and the business house is "ghetto"—loud, boisterous, and black. With the exception of the ESL house, where administrators try to place students with limited English abilities, students have a chance to try to choose which house they go into. But many of them go where their brothers or sister or friends have already gone, continuing the existing patterns of segregation.

One day on my way to the Media Academy's portables I run into a group of black teens sitting in the courtyard near the principal's office during the middle of the class period. I ask them if they're cutting. "No," says sixteen-year-old Zalika firmly. "I got sent to the office because a couple of friends, we all walked out of the class because my teacher wasn't teaching nothing," she says. The office told her they're supposed to get a new teacher on Monday, but they've already wasted two months of the school year. "I walked out because I am not really concerned about my grade, I am just concerned about what I learn," she continues. "And if I go to college I am not going to know nothing, because my teacher didn't teach me anything, and some of these teachers, they are so scared they will pass you without you even knowing anything." I ask her what house she's in and what the students are like. "Business. It's mostly black. But we ain't did nothing in business [skills]," she says with disgust. It's clear that Zalika wants to learn. If she and the other students in the business house aren't getting much out of school, it doesn't appear to be their fault alone.

The Ebonic Plague

The plight of students like Zalika inspired one of the fiercest educational debates of this decade. In December 1996, the Oakland school board voted unanimously to declare that "black English" was a whole new language. They called it "Ebonics," a "genetically based language structure" originating in Africa, adding that blacks are its "native speakers."[5] To say that the story was huge is an understatement. If filled more national headlines than if a tsunami had swept away Los Angeles. Op-ed pages were clotted with essays proclaiming outrage (and making use of handy puns like "The Ebonic Plague"). Prominent African Americans ranging from the NAACP's Kweisi Mfume to Maya Angelou decried the decision. Claiming blacks "genetically" spoke a separate language simply played right into the hands of whites who saw blacks as inferior, they said. Polls showed most Americans didn't believe Ebonics was a separate language, but the measure had strong support among many black Oakland parents.

Why was their support so strong? Black parents in Oakland have every reason to search for anything that will help their children, students like Zalika, get a decent education. The average GPA for black students is only 1.8, or academic failure. Blacks make up 52 percent of Oakland students—and 80 percent of students suspended, 64 percent of students held back a grade each year, and 71 percent of those in special education classes. How exactly would Ebonics help improve this dismal situation? The resolution contained language that said blacks "are not native speakers of a black dialect or any other dialect of English"—that in other words, they spoke a foreign language, just as Vietnamese and Mexican natives do.[6] And since those immigrants receive extra federal funds to take bilingual or English as a second language classes, why shouldn't blacks?

The fight over Ebonics was not a fight over language per se but a fight over money, the scarce pool of resources available to black and brown children in America's urban neighborhoods. The Council of Great City Schools, which encompasses the fifty largest urban districts, says that urban schools receive four to five hundred dollars less per student than those in nearby suburbs, or nearly $3 billion less in funding for inner-city schools each year.[7] The parents and officials in Oakland seemed to think they could get extra money for much-needed improvements by declaring Ebonics a language. (The federal government disagreed.) But as they were looking for a way out of the system's dismal record of failure, the Oakland school board could have looked to a better model than inventing a new language. They could have looked to programs like the Media Academy.

A Program for at-Risk Teens

In formal terms, the Media Academy is just one of several dozen state-funded programs around called California State Partnership Academies. Located in schools around the state, these academies provide a curriculum centered around one subject area—whether that's aerospace or computers or, like Fremont, media—in order to decrease the dropout rate at schools where kids are at risk. The state funds can be used however they're needed, but they usually help provide new computers and extra supplies and help fund summer job and industry mentor programs. One of the current political debates is over whether to start school voucher programs. Proponents argue that vouchers are cheaper and more effective than funding some public schools. Opponents say it's premature to give up on public schools, especially since these schools will continue to serve a disproportionately poor and nonwhite population. The Partnership Academies show that with a lot of effort and a relatively modest investment—about eighty thousand dollars per year by the state—schools can show major educational gains. At Fremont, where the overall dropout rate is over 20 percent, the Media Academy dropout rate is under 10 percent. More kids graduate; more kids take AP exams; more kids go to colleges, and good ones at that.

While Media Academy students are from the same neighborhoods and homes as the rest of the kids at Fremont—some stable, some violent, some troubled—they've got dedicated teachers leading them in hands-on learning. First, they offer concrete goals, like putting out the newspaper. Second, the teachers pay close attention to the students and track both their personalities and their performances over time. And third—the ultimate intangible—they seem to believe in the students, in their inherent ability to succeed.

O'Donoghue explains what he and the other journalism teacher, Michael Jackson, have to do in order to transform a bunch of kids "running on hormones" into scholar-journalists. "We really work a lot on kind of like home training in terms of behavior," O'Donoghue says. "If there's an assignment on the board, you bring it in the next day. You walk in late—you have to call home. You have to be responsible. The dog doesn't eat your homework; you just didn't do it." Some students come into the Media Academy thinking they know everything—"they just automatically got A's if they were good kids in class"—and other kids are beaten down because they've never succeeded before. They're placed in an environment where they get a newspaper every day and newsmagazines every week. By the time they're introduced to the computers and the cameras and the videocams, they have a sense of "ownership, so it doesn't make any sense for them to trash the place because it's theirs."

Real Jobs, Real Experience

One of O'Donoghue's students is Deborah Montalvo, a seventeen-year-old senior whose older brother also went through the Media Academy. She feels she's benefited a lot from another core aspect of the program—

internships. Last summer she worked at a summer program for high schoolers at the *San Francisco Chronicle,* updating archival reference materials. "We did a lot of research—a *lot* of research!" she says proudly. She and the others also learned how to do computer graphics and lay out their stories using the Pagemaker program. "I never worked in that kind of place before," Debra says. "The only place I really worked is like where I have my job right now, at Burger King." Debra's mother was ill, and she wanted to make extra money to help her family. So she worked at Burger King after her job at the newspaper; in all, a twelve-hour workday.

The summer internship program illustrates another powerful reason why students in the Media Academy succeed: they get a guided tour of the American mainstream. Students have worked at television station KTVU, as well as reporting for *YO!* (Youth Outlook) magazine, a scrappy, uncompromising San Francisco-based publication written by and for teens, and for the *Oakland Tribune.* Nineteen percent of Oakland residents live below the poverty level; numbers are far higher for blacks and Latinos. The East Fourteenth strip is not exactly rife with white-collar businesses; what little industry there is tends to be service-oriented (*taquerias,* beauty parlors, drugstores). If they fail to find one of these service jobs, their choices are too often working poverty or unemployment. The Media Academy's internships provide them with the guidance they need to begin to make informed choices about the possibilities open to their lives.

Teaching the Wounded

Even given all of the advantages of this program—the strong teachers, the sense of community, the hands-on job experience—the Media Academy can't help or save every student. All high school students major in angst. But many of the kids in America's urban schools deal not just in the typical coming-of-age emotional growing pains, but in more profound, destructive pain inflicted by poverty, family dysfunction, or abuse. Too often we mistake the color of teens' skin or their accents for the underlying cause of their problems. The reality is more complex. Skin color can be an indicator of risk (for poverty or dropout rate), but the problems that affect each student's life are individual and complex.

One girl in the program is a rape victim who was hospitalized after drinking drain cleaner in an effort to die. But she has not only moved past her suicide attempt; she's among the most hardworking and perceptive students in the school. "I know so much about how pain feels that I can describe it," she tells me. "I can just write a whole book on what pain is and how it feels and what it does to you." She understands the mentality of black and Latino students who feel there's nothing left. "When you don't have anything to look forward to, you feel hopeless. So [urban teens] can rule the streets, they can gamble, they can win the crap games, and they can sell the dope, and buy the fancy cars that they can't get if they went to work in McDonald's. We try to get it the easy way, and it is not going to work like that, so we need programs for us. We need internships, we need job programs, we need people to sponsor African-American kids to go see the world. So many kids in Oakland, this is so sad, don't even go around their city," she continues. "They are scared to leave their block, [but] they need to go see pretty things, they need open surroundings. Our surroundings are depressing, if you are living around garbage and trash and it's just ugly, you're going to feel ugly. Now when you get out of bed and the sun is in your face," she says, "and the trees, and you go out to the green grass, and the fresh air, of course you got beautiful surroundings, so you feel good about yourself." Where in particular, I ask, might kids from Oakland benefit from going? "Kansas," she says. It strikes me as almost unbelievable, and sad, that a teen who's been through as much as she has would choose Dorothy and Toto's home state as her fantasy refuge.

A melancholy senior named Diana, who first immigrated from Mexico when she was only two, is grappling with another problem entirely. Diana is withdrawn not because of limited English proficiency, as some of her teachers originally thought, but because of dejection. Despite having lived in the United States most of her life, she doesn't have a green card, spoiling most chances that she'll be able to go to college or get a decent job. Her father has a green card; two of her four siblings were born here and are U.S. citizens. But since she doesn't have the money to hire an immigration lawyer—and as the public sentiment against illegal immigrants grows harsher—her options have narrowed. "I try to hope for the best," she says. But her struggle to live in the United States without a green card "makes me feel inferior," she says.

Two Lives, Two Outcomes

As the challenges facing the rape victim and the undocumented immigrant illustrate, these kids have a lot more to deal with than your typical high school students. Sometimes the Media Academy is powerless to overcome the profound problems in a student's life, and the school provides little formal counseling. Many school employees do what they can. One aide who's seen me interviewing kids volunteers that he lets a couple of kids sleep on his floor when their parents kick them out. Sometimes, even these small actions make all the difference to a struggling student. Other times, no amount of attention seems to help. Nothing illustrates that better than the lives of "Jorge" and Mimi.

Jorge has just wisps of a mustache and beard on his baby face and acts as if he doesn't have a care in the world. He and his classmates Sandra and Jackie are inseparable—a dynamic trio whose fun Jackie describes as "wild, but safe." But Jorge's life isn't limited to his escapades with Sandra and Jackie, and it isn't all safe. "I cut school more often than they do. I get high more often than they do. I get drunk more often than they do," he says. "If it's illegal, it's me."

Several people I meet think Jorge is tortured by his knowledge— though not acceptance—that he is gay. All he will tell me when I ask is, "I've wondered." He admits that the carefree demeanor he effects is "a facade I let everybody believe," a clear effort to hide the hurt he harbors. He's got a smart-aleck attitude about his classes to match, though it can't quite hide his impressive intelligence. When I tell Jorge that I think he's purposely trying to fail, trying so hard to disguise how smart he is because he wouldn't know what to do if he succeeded, he admits that might be true.

What Jorge knows best is fear and failure. He used to sell drugs, and he used to be in a gang. You wouldn't expect that by looking at his home, a neat, well-furnished one-family house near school. When I stop by, his mother is sitting on the couch cradling her new baby. Her other daughters, young and adorable, run happily in and out of the room. The walls are hung with picture-studio portraits of the girls and their young brother. Jorge is from his mother's first, unhappy marriage. The rest of the children are the products of Jorge's mother and stepfather's union.

The placid picture painted by Jorge's home doesn't reveal the truth of the family's history, he claims. "My family is the biggest gang family you ever did want to meet," he says. "My great-grandmother was a *pachuca* [Mexican gangster moll] back in the thirties," he says, adding that his grandparents, mother, aunts, and uncles all ran with Chicano gangs in Texas and California. "I guess I ended the cycle, because I don't . . . well, for a while, I ran with it, too, but I didn't let it take over my life," he says.

Jorge joined a local gang called the Border Brothers in order to gain protection from what he describes as his stepfather's abuse. The way that he got his stepfather to stop beating him was to walk into his room one day and say, coldly: " 'If you ever hit me again, my friends are going to kill you, so you better not. It wouldn't be advisable.' " At the time Jorge was just thirteen. Even though he did actually belong to the gang, he didn't have enough clout to carry out his hastily articulated threat. "I was scared," he says, recalling that day. "They wouldn't have beat his ass; they wouldn't have killed him. It was an empty threat. So I risked a lot." But his stepfather didn't know that. "He didn't say anything," Jorge recounts. "He was very quiet."

The Border Brothers used to be small-time hoodlums, but since Jorge's gotten out, the game has gotten tougher. "Back then, it was more of a turf thing and of respect. Nowadays, it's gone to the shits. It's all drug-based." When he was in junior high school, they dealt a bit of weed. "Now," he says, "it's heroin; it's crack." Jorge dealt marijuana for a while, and got his first gun, a .38, when he was in seventh grade. Someone gave it to him to hold (so they wouldn't be caught with it on them) but never requested it back. "The biggest gun I ever had was a nine millimeter," which he got in trade for drugs, "but I got rid of it. . . . I was really comfortable around guns. I was really comfortable with the lifestyle because that's all I had known when I was young, you know." Guns "have no class," he says now. "They really don't. I would much rather just sit there and fight somebody than just pull out a gun and shoot them."

Jorge didn't just sell drugs; he used them as well. He started smoking weed in the seventh grade. By eighth grade, he'd moved on to other and heavier drugs: 'shrooms, acid, coke. But his drug of choice was crystal methamphetamine, or crank—a much higher-powered version of speed. "It was making me lose weight. I felt good. I had a lot of energy. It was just so uplifting. It was just so uplifting," he repeats as if once again entranced by the high. He didn't stop using crank of his own volition. He stopped because he was busted by one of his own gang brothers. After he grudgingly made himself go to school, he decided he needed a reward. "I was waiting for the bus to come and so I pulled out the sack [of crank] and I dumped it out on this little compact thing that girls use for makeup. And I separated it into two lines and hit it. I hit both lines. And my cousin comes driving by in a car." His cousin, who was also in the gang, made an immediate U-turn "and beat the holy shit out of me. He took off his belt and whupped me. I didn't feel it [because of the drugs], but I did get the point."

Jorge doesn't deal anymore, and he uses much less frequently. To get him out of the gang life, his mother decided to send him to Fremont, a school ruled by a gang that hates the Border Brothers. Because he's on enemy turf, Jorge let his gang affiliation slide. She didn't want "to see me get my ass whupped, but she knows that if I came here, that I would not be causing all kind of mess," he says of his mom. "Honestly, I'm glad I'm here. It keeps me more or less on the straight and narrow." Had he gone to Castlemont, a school he claims is "ruled" by the Border Brothers, "I would have been getting high on school grounds."

While Jorge isn't spending most days getting high, he's falling ever farther behind in school. He's behind on the number of credits he should have as a first-semester senior, and shows little enthusiasm for doing the hard work most of the Media Academy students embrace. The only thing motivating him to try to straighten up and fly right is that he'd set a good example for his twelve-year-old brother. "The image I try to set for him is, Jorge is my older brother and he goes to school and maybe cuts school once in a while and gets high occasionally, but my older brother has class," he says, almost slipping into a reverie. "My older brother goes to plays in Berkeley at the Berkeley Repertory Theater—I do do these things. My brother goes out on weekends with his friends, and they go drink cappuccino in Berkeley and sit and talk and have intelligent conversations. My brother's in the Media Academy at Fremont High School. My brother does good things; my brother gets to be on TV once in a while and makes radio shows and goes on nice field trips with his school to Disneyland and to Yosemite and to Lake Tahoe. And my brother is a really good person, but at the same time is still having fun no matter what."

Things don't turn out the way Jorge dreams. Despite his friends' and teachers efforts to get him to focus, Jorge continues to cut school and fails his senior year. He doesn't return the next fall; he simply drops out. The last I hear, his friends say they've seen him hanging, maybe small-time dealing, on the streets, "looking really rugged," or worn down.

Asian Hip-hop Queen

Mimi, the Vietnamese immigrant who's *ALL* about the R & B group TLC, doesn't have the burden of coming from a gang family to deal with. But she's got plenty of issues to face. Mimi came to the States with her mother and three siblings when she was seven, a Vietnamese refugee. Many days after classes end, Mimi's older sister picks her up and they drive to the nearby junior high school they both attended. Mimi and her sister set up shop in the gym tutoring young Vietnamese immigrants. After telling the kids in Vietnamese and English to sit down and *be quiet*, they begin tutoring. In between lessons, Mimi trades playful karate kicks with the adoring young boys, most of whom have already reached her height. Her sister, a buttoned-down student at Laney Community College, simply rolls her eyes at the antics.

The fact that Mimi is offering tutoring help rather than receiving it is a testament to her hard work and determination. Not only has she learned English and adjusted to life in the United States, she fought to avoid getting stuck in the ESL ghetto. When Mimi came to Fremont, advisors wanted to put her in the ESL house because they felt her written English wasn't up to speed. She fought to get into the Media Academy, a program that's become almost a second home.

How to teach newcomers to speak English has become one of the hottest educational debates in America. In California and several other states including New York, at least 20 percent of students are nonnative English speakers. About 4 percent of students in California are "linguistically isolated," or living in homes where no one speaks English proficiently.[8] Students from limited-English households have little chance of continuing their education or getting a toehold in the workplace if they don't master English at school. But how should they be taught English, and for how long? In June 1998, California voters passed a referendum ending bilingual education in the state. Most Latinos voted to keep bilingual education, despite deep reservations about how well the programs were being run. In the fall, many parents signed waivers allowing their children to be taught in Spanish once again, rather than kept in "English immersion" classes.[9] Bilingual education programs have often become the target of critics who say they don't push students into English proficiency quickly enough. On the flipside, parents and watchdog groups see ESL programs like the one at Fremont as de facto segregation, since depending on the makeup of the community, the entire

ESL population may be composed of minority groups. Steve O'Donoghue says this is a "big political issue" at Fremont. "The Feds are on our case." The Department of Education threatened to cut off funds to the entire Oakland School District because it said the district denied non–English speaking students an equal education.[10] So the school is looking into ways to incorporate English language training into a different program.

O'Donoghue favors letting students like Mimi into the Media Academy. If their English isn't strong enough—as ocassionally happens—he urges them to take ESL classes for the time being and re-enter the media program the next year. Some choose to return; some don't. But Mimi doesn't seem as if she'd belong anywhere else. She's in complete command of spoken English and does a good job of writing for the Media Academy's newspaper. (She also enjoys shooting photos.) She not only acclimatized in school, she's also chosen to strongly identity with American pop culture. Her older sister is all business, wearing skirts and sheer hose to college. Mimi is rarely caught in anything other than jeans and sneaks. Her mother and oldest brother are devout in their adherence to Buddhism, including remaining vegetarians. Mimi's cool with grabbing a burger from Mickey D's, but (to be respectful) she wouldn't bring it into the house.

Mimi's home, just off of East Fourteenth Street, lies in an undistinguished boxy structure that contains two small apartments on each of its two floors. A tall black sliding fence in front adds a modicum of protection. The apartment's front door opens directly into the small living room, with a cramped kitchen off to the side. The living room contains two worn leather couches and brown carpeting. It also holds two massive and competing emblems of immigrant life and urban status. The first is a battered gray metal school desk with a three-tiered altar. One is dedicated to Mimi's grandmother (who died when Mimi was in utero), one to a goddess, and one to Buddha himself. The other emblem, which rivals the altar for size, is a big-screen TV, the ultimate symbol of Americanization. Mimi herself is a mix of American pop identity and immigrant culture. In addition to being devoted to hip-hop, TLC, and MTV, Mimi participates in local Vietnamese cultural events. They are large lavish affairs where she gets to hang out with Vietnamese pop stars and Vietnamese-American beauty queens.

One day Mimi and I are sitting in her living room watching rap videos when her brother comes in. He is a pale-skinned, brown-haired, bearded man who from a distance looks more white than Amerasian. I'm not shocked. I know that many Vietnamese families gained entrance to the United States because some or all of their children were fathered by American servicemen. But Mimi's brother feels obligated to explain why he's biracial and she's not. He pulls Mimi close to him and says, "It's weird, huh? We don't look alike, but we're brother and sister." Then he goes back to talking to his mom, a small woman in house slippers, in Vietnamese.

There are over six hundred thousand Vietnamese Americans living in the United States, nearly half of them in California. Many are refugees who came to the United States scarred by atrocities in Vietnam and bereft of any material possessions. Vietnamese Americans are one of the poorest Asian ethnic groups. Their lives are far more complex than the stereotype of the Asian "model minority." A small but significant group of these kids, first- and second-generation Vietnamese Americans, fall through the cracks and end up in gangs. Many more, like their black and Latino peers, end up in second- or third-rate jobs with no security and little prospect for advancement.

Mimi already had some good role models: one brother who finished college and lives on the East Coast; her sister, who's going to college now. But the Media Academy helped Mimi avoid the pitfalls of staying only in English as a second language classes and opened whole new worlds to her. Several months after she's graduated, I meet her in a glitzy high-rise office tower where she holds a part-time job. She's in an associates program that Steve O'Donoghue and the Center for Living Skills hooked her up with. In addition to making much-needed money, she's also meeting other young business associates from all over the country.

Mimi is going to community college, and thinking about applying to four-year schools including Berkeley, where her old classmates Sandra and Jackie ended up. Her friend April, who's black, goes to a four-year college out of state, as do several other Media Academy grads from her year. The Media Academy kids have faced down this society's presumption that they wouldn't, or couldn't succeed. Though they've suffered losses along the way, like Jorge, most of them are still following their dreams.

The Future of Urban America

Students like the ones at Fremont represent the future of urban America. The quality of that future depends fundamentally on the quality of the education they receive. Despite the forty years between now and the *Brown v. Board of Education* decision, many of America's schools remain segregated. According to Deval Patrick, former head of the Civil Rights division of the Justice Department, two-thirds of black kids still attend segregated schools. In many places, Latinos and Asians experience segregation as well. But instead of searching for solutions, the government—particularly the courts—have dismantled them. Busing was dismantled; the Supreme Court overturned the use of magnet schools as a way of attracting white students to city schools; and for the most part, the courts have avoided equalizing funding to urban and suburban districts. What's left? Maybe targeted, hands-on learning like the Media Academy is part of the answer. It mixes typical classroom teaching; production experience on the newspaper, TV show, and magazine; and the bonding experiences that help the students work together well. The one thing it does not do is take anything for granted: not the English proficiency of its students, not their study habits, not their ability to get along with classmates of other races. The Media Academy is so successful precisely because it assumes nothing—except the inherent worth of its students. Says Steve O'Donoghue, with a mix of frustration and determination, "Except for the normal percentage of hoodlums you get anywhere, it is not the kids that have screwed things up. It is the adults. These kids are victims."

EIGHT

The End of
Affirmative Action

I feel sorry for the white students, because they don't have
anyplace that's their own, except maybe the frats.
—TON DANG, VIETNAMESE AMERICAN JUNIOR,
UNIVERSITY OF CALIFORNIA AT BERKELEY

October 12, 1995: The bodies are packed in tighter than at a rock concert; the mood is edgy and expectant. The location is Sproul Plaza, the
University of California at Berkeley's main courtyard and thoroughfare.
It's bustling even on normal days, as students rush between classes, stop
to buy lunch from a cart, or sit, sun, and gossip on Sproul Hall's marble
steps. But today the bustle has become a jostle. Today, thousands of
students, faculty, administrators, and onlookers have gathered to protest
the end of affirmative action at a school once known as one of the most
liberal in the nation—and one of the most diverse. The heads of all nine
campuses of the University of California—including UCLA and Berkeley—supported affirmative action. But the Board of Regents set a meeting during the middle of the summer and ended the program with one
vote.

I've come to Berkeley to witness the end of an era. Only a few decades
after the Civil Rights movement forced us to try to find solutions for
discrimination, the nation's focus has turned to dismantling the few lim-

ited programs we bothered to set up. On one level, Berkeley's liberal reputation makes it an unlikely site for the demise of affirmative action. But on another, it's just the kind of volatile environment where major social changes occur. While most colleges are still wrestling with black-white racial tensions, the University of California at Berkeley is over 40 percent Asian and only 30 percent white.[1] Berkeley is one of the most selective universities in the country; it's also state run. And California is not just any state. With over 30 million residents, it's the most populous in the nation. And over 40 percent of its residents are nonwhite, a number that is steadily increasing.[2]

Soon California will have no racial majority. The battle over affirmative action, over what helps and hurts racial "equality," is no dry academic matter here. It is a matter of intense personal self-interest, and often one of clashing individual and group demands. Asian Americans, one of the fastest-growing groups in California and America as a whole, have been torn by the question of affirmative action. The community is heterogenous—rich, poor, U.S.-born, refugee, immigrant. But overall, Asian Americans have the highest education rate in the country, regardless of income, and they tend to lose out rather than benefit from affirmative action policies. Black and Latino Californians, the latter of which will one day become the dominant ethnic group within the state, still often attend subpar public schools and are the most likely to be hurt by affirmative action's end. It's easy to guess the problems which lie ahead if a rapidly growing number of California's children are not receiving an education that prepares them for the upper echelons of the state's schools and workforce. The result will be—and many argue, already is—a bifurcated society, stratified by both race and class, with a white minority holding the power and a brown majority filling the low-wage, low-skill job pool. But the most powerful group in the state, and for now the majority, is white Americans. California lost 1.5 million jobs between 1990 and 1992, most of them in the wholesale and retail industries.[3] In a time of economic crisis, white Californians began to fear for their children's futures. Individuals who'd once supported affirmative action began to worry that it would undermine their own offspring's chances for success.

In 1995, a three-pronged attack toppled affirmative action within the state. The Regents' vote killed the program at the state's top public colleges; two academics began promoting an anti-affirmative-action referendum, Proposition 209 or the California Civil Rights Initiative, which passed in 1996; and Governor Pete Wilson decided that hammering away at affirmative action was just the tonic his flagging Presidential candidacy needed. (His presidential aspirations proved abortive, but his attacks on affirmative action landed a crushing blow.) Berkeley's reputation as the last bastion of liberalism—as a political biosphere enclosing tree-hugging environmentalists, feminists, and multiculturalists—is yielding to one as affirmative action's Waterloo.

Protesting a Done Deal

By the time Berkeley students returned to campus in the fall, the Regents' vote was a done deal—a deft political move made without student input or administration consent. A small group of student activists immediately began planning a massive rally: leader Rona Fernandez, a tough, introspective Filipina writer and union organizer who'd graduated from Cal the year before; Josh Franco, a well-heeled white eighteen-year-old freshman from L.A.; and José Palafox, a junior who transferred from a community college. Short and wiry, with buzz-cut black hair and worn Converse tennis shoes, José is a Mexican immigrant who's been told to his face by classmates that "you probably got in here because of affirmative action or something. . . . It's really sad because we as Chicanos, or other oppressed people in this country, have to be on the defensive." The young Chicano-studies major and punk-rock musician worries about divisions in the activists' ranks. He hears disgruntled anti-white murmurings among some of the black and Latino students. "I plead for more unity," says José, "and that has brought problems with some of the activists. It's like, 'No, we don't want to deal with them. Fuck them.' And I know where that [sentiment] is coming from, but it's a dead-end road."

José is caught in the California equivalent of double jeopardy, squeezed by anti-affirmative-action referendums on one side and anti-immigrant legislation on the other. A couple of weeks ago he picked up the school newspaper and read about the proposals to strip legal immigrants of financial aid benefits. He's a legal resident whose mother and father earn poverty-level wages. The fact that the bill will probably not succeed (I later learn it fails) doesn't ease the hurt that people are debating the measure. "It's like debating whether slavery is good or not," José sighs. Many of the students he lives with in Casa Joaquim Murrieta would be affected by any curbs on funding for immigrants. The Chicano dorm is a large, plain house nestled among the spit-shined mansions of Berkeley's fraternity row. It's named for a Mexican martyr—a Robin Hood-like bandit who fought against and stole from the whites who'd taken Mexican land until he was executed. Today, forty-five Mexican-American and Latino students sleep, share cooking and cleaning duties, offer support to each other, and fight fiery intellectual battles with each other in the co-op. José knows that Mexican Americans are already the dominant ethnicity in Los Angeles; one day, they will be the largest in the entire state of California as well. But without access to adequate schooling, he worries they'll become a permanent underclass in the state they demographically dominate.

Josh Franco agrees. He's one of the handful of whites deeply involved with the protest. The night before, the freshman sits in a dimly lit graduate student office the organizers have commandeered as a place to paint signs for the following day. "I love it here," says Josh of the school he's attended for a mere matter of weeks. Handsome, curly-haired, and introspective, he's trying to find his place within a campus divided. Josh describes his best friend as a "Republican frat boy. He's convinced Berkeley is just separatist cliques of every type. . . . But the only way this problem is going to be solved is if we can all make sacrifices and pull together. I grew up very wealthy. My dad is a doctor; I went to prep school. But I don't like being handed everything in life. It doesn't seem right to revel in advantages if everyone doesn't have it."

Josh sits next to another volunteer, Sascha Bittner. Sascha can't make signs. Her delicate face, surrounded by a halo of blond curls, tends to loll unpredictably to the side. She's been disabled since birth, so she uses a motorized wheelchair (equipped with cell phone) to get around. Because her speech is difficult to understand, she writes on my notepad in painstaking print: "After the egregious decision by the Regents, I decided I had to get involved somehow." I tell her to go ahead and talk; I'll listen. So the twenty-two-year-old junior (who participates in a program Berkeley runs to insure access to students with disabilities) tells me why she felt she had to support the affirmative action march. "For me, because I have a disability, I think I have empathy with other minorities." I ask her if the solidarity is reciprocal. "I think I support them more than they support me. But look at Christopher Reeve. Anyone can become disabled. There's certainly some difference between all minorities, but there's a commonality as well: discrimination."

"Focus Not on the Top, But on the Bottom"

The day of the protest, I wander through Sproul Plaza talking to students instead of listening to the speeches. Predictably, most of those who've shown up support affirmative action; a handful have come to support the Regents; and many have shown up just to see what the fuss is all about. One of the last is a stunning twenty-three-year old junior with brown skin, almond eyes, and cheekbones sharp enough to cut steel. Ché— half Swedish, half black American—was born and raised in Sweden and came to the United States in 1983. While many of the black kids at Berkeley were making their way through urban schools, Ché says he was receiving lessons from a private tutor on African-American culture, paid for by the Swedish government. He thinks affirmative action is a great idea in concept, but "when you look at the effects, I'm against it. It lets people in, but the dropout rate is really high. It doesn't mean they [affirmative action admits] are underqualified in terms of intellect, but in terms of knowledge." The solution, Ché says "is not to focus on the top but on the bottom"—on ensuring that students in preschool and elementary schools get a decent education. "But," he shrugs his shoulders, "that's too much of a long-term solution for American politics."

The Reverend Jesse Jackson takes the stage to a chorus of cheers and one lone heckler. "You who did not vote . . . elected Pete Wilson and Newt Gingrich," he says, urging the crowd to "vote our hopes and not our fears. . . . This is your moment to choose multiculturalism and diversity over racial isolation and polarization. . . . We must choose schools over jails. We must choose affirmative action and inclusion over negative action and exclusion. We must make some choices."

The crowd has swollen to over three thousand students, staff, and faculty members. Though she's worked her ass off to make this protest a success, activist Rona Fernandez is far from convinced that the numbers on Sproul Plaza represent any real long-term commitment to fighting the Regents' decision. The entire day's events have been planned by only a tiny handful of the campus community, and she suspects that tomorrow the same few will be back to square one. "If you do activism, you see the same one hundred people," she says. "Berkeley students have more racial awareness than in most places, but they're cynical. The black students, Chicanos, Asians, and Latinos, are all separate. I would like to see them be more politicized."

Raichelle Jordan, a black twenty-six-year-old psychology major standing at the base of the steps, agrees with Fernandez. She doesn't see a lot of cohesiveness among the black students who have the most to lose, while she does see a growing cohesion among those who oppose affirmative action. "Berkeley has become a lot more conservative," she says. "People want me to jeopardize my future. If I flunk out, people will say, 'See!' " Her friend Christina Battle, a black twenty-seven-year-old junior who's also majoring in psychology, adds, "My main reason for picking this campus was diversity. Now a lot of people are going to go without a good education." She also questions the way the issue is being played for political gain. "Affirmative action shouldn't be revoked, it should be modified. Pete Wilson hasn't been in a Regents meeting for three years. Now that he's running for President . . ." she trails off, dejected.

Max Lau, a tall twenty-three-year-old senior, came with a large contingent from Cal BiGay, a gay Asian-American group. Chinese by ethnicity, Latino (he was raised in Brazil) by acculturation, Max realizes that Berkeley, for all of its tensions, provides an extraordinarily rare campus environment. At how many schools could he comfortably assert his identity as an Asian-Latino-American gay man? "Living in California, in Berkeley especially, it's like we live in a different country," he admits. But he's troubled by the way the Asian-American community is torn by the issue of affirmative action. "The whole model minority theory pits ethnic groups against each other. A lot of my Asian-American friends are very apolitical, conservative. They try to segregate themselves from blacks, but only by being together will these things end." Asian Americans probably have the most complex vantage point on affirmative action. On the one hand, they tend not to benefit from affirmative action in education. They have the highest college graduation rate of any racial group, including whites. But on the other hand, despite the fact that Asians are more highly educated than whites, they earn less on average; and in recent years, greater numbers of Asian Americans have begun to benefit from affirmative action programs for businesses.[4]

Shu Ming Cheer, the head of the Asian Students Union, is trying to puzzle through these contradictions. Shu Ming supports affirmative action—she's also a member of Asian Pacific Islander Students for Affirmative Action—but many of her friends don't. They're not helped by affirmative action in admissions; they receive no benefit and tend to have the highest high school GPAs and test scores. So how does Shu Ming defend affirmative action to other Asian Americans? "Usually, to me, I think of affirmative action as being long-term. I mean, short-term we are very well represented here at UCs or whatnot. But long-term, when we look at graduate level or tenured professors, we're really underrepresented and, to me, there's definitely a glass ceiling." She also thinks that socioeconomics affect the "meritocracy" more than most people would like to admit. "I mean when I was in high school, I took a prep course and that raised my SAT score by two hundred points and that's not because of my intelligence or anything. It's based on the fact that my parents could afford it. And grades are also based on the fact that you have the privilege of going to a school with AP courses and if you don't have to work, say, twenty hours a week to support your family." But Shu Ming's arguments don't hold much water with Asian Americans who routinely get better grades and test scores than not only blacks and Latinos but whites. Organizing Asian Americans for any cause, let alone affirmative action, is "really hard," she says. What many Americans fail to realize are the deep cultural biases—and histories of animosity— between different Asian nations, including the Chinese and Japanese. Feeling a sense of Asian-American unity requires that students let go of the tensions between their cultures. But at Berkeley, many students belong to ethnic affinity groups like Chinese, Filipino, Vietnamese, and Pacific Islander associations, but they don't join broader-based groups like the Asian Students Union.

The Sun Has Set

As the litany of speeches winds to a close, the energy level in Sproul rises rather than dissipates. The organizers have planned a winding march through Berkeley and a possible blockade of Interstate 80. (At UCLA's sister protest, thousands of students swarm the busy intersection of Westwood and Wilshire boulevards. Thirty-three are arrested.)[5] The phalanx of students takes off down Telegraph Road, a main Berkeley thoroughfare filled with restaurants and shops both trendy and practical. Within ten minutes, we have left the familiar environs of the Berkeley campus and entered a run-down neighborhood few students have probably ever seen. Black families peer from their porches, some dispassionately, others cheering when they learn the reason for the march. One student murmurs, "I didn't know Berkeley had a 'hood." A few stop and lean against the gates bordering the minuscule lawns of the equally minuscule homes, urging the kids and teenagers to apply to Berkeley when they're old enough. Unspoken is the fact that attending Cal is a dream few of these poor black kids will realize.

I walk alongside Sascha Bittner, who manages to navigate the crowded streets and sidewalks in her wheelchair. A few other students in wheelchairs are on the trek as well, most of them black. A ripple of tension runs through the crowd—they've neared a drab industrial area deserted except for a wall of police in riot gear. It's here that students, if they choose, can try to hop a fence and block the interstate. But the riot police, many of them blacks, Latinos, and women, form a near-impassable barrier against the waves of students who, like they, are a mix of genders and hues.

After a few tense minutes of chanting slogans and singing "We Shall Not Be Moved," Berkeley's affirmative action supporters do just that. They turn and march back the way they've come, toward campus, where the sun is now setting over Berkeley. They all know that the sun has already set on affirmative action.

Affirmative Action and Morality

So who wins, now that affirmative action is gone, and who loses? Whites have generally been the biggest opponents of affirmative action, and people tend to assume they'll benefit the most when programs are killed. That's probably true in most of the country, but not at the UC schools. Asian Americans, already the biggest group on campus, will gain the most new admissions slots. But the groups who lose are just what we expect. Two years after the Regents' decision, the numbers start coming in for UC graduate school admissions. (Undergraduate admissions will change the following year.) The numbers are stark. Black admissions at Berkeley's law school dropped by 81 percent. Fourteen African Americans were admitted, and none of them chose to attend.[6] Latino admissions dropped by half. It's not just that admissions went down; applications did as well. Talented black and Latino students apparently decided to go somewhere where their race wasn't such an obvious bone of contention.

I look at the group of people organizing the October 12 protest and see what I expect to: a bunch of nonwhites, mostly black and Latino; women of a variety of races. Then there's Sascha and a tiny cluster of white men. With a few exceptions, like Josh, the group of people gathering here is the group that must: people directly threatened by the end of affirmative action. Discrimination is about demographics, affirmative action is about demographics, and the way these issues are playing out at Berkeley are all about the demographics of power. Even though I support affirmative action, I can easily understand the abstract moral arguments against it. But what I find disturbing—what's always been the crux of racial (and gender) struggles—is the way in which we deny that self-interest creates morality. Most people who argue for abolishing affirmative action say that theirs is a pure moral position, that they simply endorse each American being judged as an individual, not a race. They argue affirmative action punishes them for discrimination committed in the past, but they won't admit that they're still benefiting from educational and employment advantages accorded whites. By the same token, nonwhites and women who believe in affirmative action claim they've got a pure moral position as well: that no just society would allow itself to continually favor whites and men over all others. The sad truth about affirmative action is that, on the simplest level, both of these pure moral positions are right. Endorsing individual achievement is crucial; so is endorsing a society that allows and encourages achievement from all members. But can we really make moral decisions about concepts like "equality" and "opportunity" in a vacuum, where we forget not only America's history but the discrimination that continues to this day? Even the staunchest anti-affirmative-action crusaders can't do it.

As a contributing editor of *Vibe* magazine, I commissioned an interview with the hottest figure in the affirmative action debate, California businessman Ward Connerly. As a member of the Board of Regents, he helped dismantle affirmative action at Berkeley. He went on to push through Proposition 209, a ballot dismantling affirmative action across the state.[7] And even though he has decried the idea of "preferences" and "special consideration" for nonwhite students, he didn't hesitate to put in a letter requesting special consideration of an application to UC Davis law school. He told a moving story about the woman he championed, someone who fought her way through the educational system after an accident left her disabled. "And so I felt like, hey, this is a person who needs some special consideration," Connerly told the reporter for *Vibe*. But when asked how he could reconcile his belief that a disabled student deserved special consideration, but that students facing hardship because of race did not, Connerly dodged the question—and made a blanket statement reaffirming his moral absolutism. Discrimination "is wrong all of the time," he said. "Moral judgments are not relative."

Connerly's actions—many would say, his hypocrisy—illustrate that we can't argue these issues as abstractions. The most common criticism of affirmative action is that it tries to make up for "past discrimination." First of all, that's a misreading of the definition of affirmative action. The federal government defines the program as "action taken first to remedy patterns which show flagrant underutilization of minorities or women as a consequence of past discrimination perpetuated in *present . . . systems*, and secondly, to prevent future . . . discrimination which would prolong these patterns. [emphasis mine]"[8] The focus is not on the past but on the present and future—on people (blacks, women, Latinos) who've historically experienced job discrimination and *still* are to this day. If the discrimination weren't ongoing, affirmative action wouldn't be needed. But just look at the numbers. Black family income, on average, rarely tops 60 percent of white income.[9] And *The Bell Curve*, which advocated against affirmative action, compared blacks and whites of what they termed "equal IQ." They found the blacks were more highly educated than the whites, yet they still earned hundreds of dollars less.[10]

And what about the perception that reverse discrimination has reached epidemic proportions? Of the more than three thousand discrimination cases decided by federal courts between 1990 and 1994, only one hundred claimed reverse discrimination. Of those one hundred, only six were actually proven.[11] Or what about the argument that affirmative action is bad because it embraces what critics call "group rights"? Well, our government has no problem making distinctions between groups of adult citizens for any number of reasons. The U.S. military tells a large proportion of its armed forces—women—that members of their gender cannot go into combat, despite the fact that the opportunity to engage in combat is a crucial part of attaining higher rank. The federal government tells adult U.S. citizens between the ages of eighteen and twenty that they are not allowed to consume alcohol. Everything from homeowner tax credits to Social Security benefits is based upon the concept of aiding groups when there is a compelling state interest to do so. Some opponents of affirmative action think race is the only category *not* worthy of being considered under that same standard.

Do we even know what affirmative action is? According to a 1995 study, up to half of all Americans don't have the foggiest idea.[12] The first programs were initiated by President John F. Kennedy and institutionalized by Richard Nixon. Today, it's almost impossible to define. There are state, local, federal, and private programs that encompass everything from minority internships to funds for female business owners. Says Troy Duster, a Berkeley sociology professor who is himself considered an expert on the issues, "There are no experts on affirmative action, only pretenders. There's nobody in this country who understands the gender and racial issues, the public and the private. The people who know about fire and police departments don't know what's going on at Texaco [which paid $187 million to settle a massive discrimination suit filed by black employees]."

In 1998, some persuasive evidence emerged that affirmative action both serves higher education well and often helps whites as well as "minorities." *The Shape of the River*, a book by the former presidents of Princeton and Harvard, documents these benefits. Authors William G.

Bowen and Derek Bok analyzed a database tracking forty-five thousand students who attended twenty-eight of the nation's top colleges. They found that black students who attended the most selective schools were more likely to graduate and to get high-paying jobs than black students with similar test scores who attended less competitive schools. And the black college graduates at these top schools were more likely than their white counterparts to take leadership positions in their local communities. Bowen and Bok say that affirmative action benefits whites by giving them a hands-on experience of integration, knowledge that most professionals today can't do business without.[13] Ironically, another study supporting affirmative action comes from the state where programs were abolished by popular vote in 1998. A study of admissions at the public universities in Washington found that white students made up three-quarters of "special admissions," which take into account race, income, and socioeconomic factors.[14] Nonetheless, the majority-white voter pool dismantled affirmative action at state colleges.

All of this illustrates that when it comes to affirmative action, we can't argue abstractions. We *must* argue realities. The only way to understand affirmative action is to understand our history, our current socioeconomics—and the reasons why Americans of different backgrounds feel so strongly about their positions. If I weren't a black person raised to empathize with the struggles of other African Americans, I'd probably feel a lot less passionate about the battles over affirmative action. And for those who don't have strong opinions either way, the fairness of the media's coverage is critically important. We don't have a balanced debate. We've ceded the moral high ground to those who argue that programs like affirmative action, designed to foster equality, are actually thwarting it. Lost somewhere in the rhetoric and abstractions are the stories of the people with the most to lose, people like LaShunda Prescott.

Seven Years of Hard Time

LaShunda entered UC Berkeley in the fall of 1988. What happened over the course of the next seven years is an incredible tale of hardship and determination—and an illustration of how hollow the hypothetical debates over "qualifications" ring when measured against the reality of race and income.

Who knows if LaShunda would have qualified to enter UC Berkeley had affirmative action not existed? She was the valedictorian at Castlemont, her high school in inner-city Oakland, but even the best education her school had to offer didn't prepare her for the academic rigors of Berkeley. While she was struggling to learn new concepts in her first semester math and science classes, she says, the other kids from private and public prep schools were coasting, reviewing old material.

Oakland's East Fourteenth Street corridor, the violence-plagued neighborhood where LaShunda grew up, is just miles away but worlds apart from the manicured lawns of Berkeley. A brown-skinned woman with close-cropped natural hair and mischief in her eyes, LaShunda lost the first boy she ever had a crush on to gunfire. Her two brothers, one older than she, one younger, still carry inside their bodies the bullets that she thanks God did not kill them. Her father, a traumatized Vietnam vet, drank and smoked crack to block out the graphic flashbacks. Her sister is a recovering crack addict with two young daughters. The day her sister went to jail, LaShunda found one of her nieces abandoned and sobbing. It also happened to be the day of one of her engineering midterms. She flunked.

LaShunda never complains about the hard hand life's dealt her, nor have her trials eroded what can only be called her joie de vivre. Her speech, peppered with colloquialisms, her walk, even the ease with which she allows emotion to register on her face, all illustrate that she has not let life shut her off or shut her down. Despite her packed academic schedule, she's taking an elective class on black women's history. It inspired a desire to pull together an anthology of young black women's writing. "Do you remember [Toni Morrison's] *The Bluest Eye*?" she says, recalling the book where a black girl named Pecola goes insane because she wants so desperately to be white. "I never wanted the blue eyes, but I wanted the long hair. Pecola is the victim in the book. When I write, I want to make Pecola not a victim. I want to give her back her beauty."

LaShunda's seven years at Berkeley include time away from school after she was expelled for failing her classes, and the extra time it's taken to make the work up. Though she's had to step into the role of mommy, had to take exams just after her brother was shot and her grandmother died, and had to study in an apartment without hot water or heat, she never wraps herself in the mantle of victimization. She also wants to make one thing clear: though she may have moved heaven and earth to get to where she is, she considers herself no better than other African Americans who haven't made it out of the 'hood. "Sometimes I don't like telling my story because I'm not"—she affects a TV newscaster's voice— " 'that black girl from the ghetto that made it.' I'm not the exception."

She rightly fears being cast into the role of "the exception that proves the rule"—the hardworking black youth who proves that if she can triumph over adversity, we don't need to change the playing field to get rid of the adversity in the first place. While everybody else is talking about how to save the tiniest vestige of affirmative action, LaShunda feels the problem of inequality is far larger and more profound. A new student at Berkeley came from her old high school and reported the changes: some of the good teachers are burning out, some of the new teachers are terrible, and there aren't even enough books to go around. "You know, people act like we're complaining. And I'm like, that shit is so . . . !" She trails off. "That's why I get mad with this affirmative action thing, 'cause I'm like we are sitting here begging for crumbs. How few of us do you see up here [at Berkeley]? We are protesting and begging them to be able to go to this school, and instead of protesting, what we need to do is go to Castlemont, make sure the kids are proficient, help them learn how to start up businesses."

The Future of America's Most Populous State

LaShunda sees something that a lot of people don't—at least not yet. California is becoming increasingly black and brown. And if something isn't done to make sure that black and Latino students have a shot at getting a good education, it's going to tear the state apart. Schools like Castlemont (and Fremont High) aren't giving smart kids the education they deserve, making it hard for them to compete at schools like Berkeley. Many urban blacks and Latinos attend segregated schools; in fact, according to the Justice Department, two-thirds of black students still do. And the Supreme Court hasn't helped matters either, ruling that remedies for segregation (like magnet schools) and school funding discrepancies between urban and suburban schools shouldn't be widely implemented. We seem to have given up on providing equal opportunity at the primary and secondary levels; now the end of affirmative action is cutting students off at the college level as well.

In a nutshell, affirmative action hinges on two issues: the inherent quality of the student (or worker) and the readiness to get the education (or job). Students like LaShunda tend to get lower test scores than whites and Asians. The first fork in the road is why they score lower: nature or nurture. Some, like Charles Murray, argue that blacks and Latinos are inherently less intelligent. If you don't believe books like *The Bell Curve* (which came under attack three years after it was published for errors and failing to have its findings reviewed by other social scientists), then you probably believe that blacks and Latinos have the potential to learn just as much as anyone else does, but they haven't reached their full potential because of poor schooling. Again we reach a fork in the road: what to do with these undereducated students. If we go by current qualifications alone, these students are less qualified. There's no point in arguing that they're not. (Take LaShunda's evaluation of how she stacked up versus other first-year engineering students.) But do you take smart kids who are "less qualified" because of a bad education and tell them they shouldn't ever get a better one? At its best, affirmative action provides a means of allowing these students to finally get the chance to compete—and to catch up. If they aren't offered the chance to run the race, they certainly won't be able to finish.

Racial discrepancies in education are going to hit states like California particularly hard. California, already 40 percent nonwhite, will be majority-minority much sooner than most of the nation. To have a majority nonwhite state where the education, and the jobs, and the power remained concentrated among whites would be nothing less than economic apartheid—far from the "equal opportunity" anti-affirmative-action forces claim they seek. Berkeley's chancellor, Chang Lin Tien, argued for the necessity of widespread educational opportunity after the Regents' vote. The campus publication *The Berkeleyan* carried his statement, along with a large photo of him seated stiffly with his hands clasped firmly together. No doubt the pose was designed to look authoritative, but it conveyed a sense of nervousness, even dread. Tien vowed that the Regents' decision would not end his "belief that excellence and diversity go hand in hand. . . . Our workforce and student population must reflect the ethnic, racial and gender composition of the world around us. . . . Today the fate of youngsters in California's elementary schools is in our hands. We must be sure to send a message to the next generation of undergraduates that our doors will be open to them if they are committed to their studies and excel academically."[15]

It's easy to argue that making sure kids of all races have access to the universities is in the state's best interest. But given the rancor of the affirmative action debates, it's an argument we rarely hear. In fact, it seems like race is one of the only things UC admissions officers *can't* consider when they choose who to let in. "SP-1," the technical name for the Regents' vote barring affirmative action, stated that race could no longer be a factor in undergraduate admissions—though whether or not your parents were alumni, whether or not you are an athlete, and whether or not you are disabled, for example, are all categories that can be considered. So can socioeconomics: consideration for students who have "suffered disadvantage economically or in terms of their social environment (such as an abusive or otherwise dysfunctional home or a neighborhood of unwholesome or antisocial influences)."[16] The policy was set to take full effect with the admission of the class of 1997, but fewer blacks and Latinos began applying to Berkeley immediately. In 1996, the year before the affirmative action ban officially took effect, the percentage of black applicants fell by 8 percent; for Hispanics, the figure was 6 percent.[17]

LaShunda is precisely the kind of student Berkely's affirmative action program was set up to help, someone whose race, gender, and socioeconomic background have all made it harder for her to get the education she deserves. But why should a talented young white man give up his space at the school even for someone as deserving as she is? That question is at the heart of the current affirmative action debate, and we can all understand the moral reasoning behind arguing that the white guy shouldn't have to pay. The opponents of affirmative action have wrapped themselves in the mantle of morality, saying they simply want each person judged as an individual. But a closer look reveals they aren't the champions of pure equality they claim to be. They're more than happy to advocate for the special admissions needs of some students—as long as those students are politically well connected.

In 1996, the Los Angeles Times broke what should have come as shocking allegations: top schools like Berkeley and UCLA routinely received requests from politically well-connected Californians, and many of those requests were honored.[18] One regent sent thirty-two admissions requests to UCLA, including one for a friend's son whose grades and SAT scores were below the school's standards. He was admitted. A state assemblywoman lobbied for a school transfer that was approved even though the student had both low test scores and had missed the admissions deadline. Terry Lightfoot, a spokesman for the UC President, admitted: "In some cases . . . you had students who had been denied admittance on one or two occasions, who were then granted admission solely on the basis of who these students were connected with." Connerly, of course, put in a letter. And even Governor Wilson, the self-styled champion of the meritocracy, put in two special requests, though both his candidates were denied.[19] But Connerly's hypocrisy on affirmative action goes deeper. He made the emphatic statement that being seen as an "affirmative action businessman" would be just as degrading as drinking from "colored only" water fountains in the pre–Civil Rights Deep South. Yet he drank from the fountain, and drank deep. During the six years before he voted to overturn affirmative action as a member of the UC Regents, he accepted fully one million dollars in state contracts for minority business owners.[20] LaShunda Prescott wants to be a business owner one day too. She won't have the advantage of the programs Ward Connerly used to make his way.

In addition to taking high-level engineering classes, working, and volunteering, LaShunda helps out at the school's chapter of the black engineering society. She keeps a suit hanging in the association's office so she can change between classes and go on job interviews. Between her student loans and her job, she has enough money to rent a one-bedroom apartment in a working-class area a fair distance from campus. It's filled with used furniture, engineering texts, and photo upon photo of the friends and family she credits with helping her move on through.

LaShunda tells me about her family one afternoon as we sit in Berkeley's People's Park, a place filled with a mix of undergrads, local residents, and homeless people. Her mother and father met in Mississippi when they were twelve and thirteen respectively. Roger, her oldest brother, is thirty, a married man with two kids who works double shifts at an Oakland factory to support them. Derek, her baby brother, is twenty-two, working at UPS and trying to find a way to go to school. Jackie, her twenty-six-year-old sister, is off of crack and trying to get off of welfare. If LaShunda gets a job outside of Oakland, she wants to take her sister and her sister's two daughters along, moving them away from any echoes of the life they'd known.

She shakes her head with a loving but knowing smile as she describes her father. "My daddy is the most brilliant man I have ever met, but he is a drunk. I am happy because he finally got his VA money, so it is like we don't have to worry about him any more. We don't have to worry about him being on the street being hurt." He was a medic in Vietnam, a man whose daily experiences consisted of treating the bleeding, maimed, mutilated, and dying. "He will cry sometimes, sometimes he'll get up and have dreams. We were watching *Platoon* and he started throwing up because the smells came back." Now that she has less reason to worry about him, she's more able to enjoy the parts of his personality that weren't corroded by the war. "It's a trip—I am starting to like my daddy a lot. I know I love him, but I didn't used to like him."

Her mother is "a sweetie. She's real strong. She had four kids by my age." Without any real financial support from LaShunda's father, her mother sewed the children's clothes and rifled through bins at Goodwill to find shoes. "She just thought she was going to go crazy a lot of times," LaShunda says. "But that's the beauty of mothers. Sometimes they are able to have a little bit of happiness because they're there working ten times as hard."

LaShunda worked her butt off in high school because she knew that was the only way she had a prayer of getting enough money to go on to college. She wanted to go a black school, especially Howard, but they didn't offer her any financial aid. So she ended up a stone's throw from home at Cal.

Not only did she face the hurdle of being underprepared for the rigorous math and science courses, as a black woman she got the cold shoulder from a lot of her white peers, who assumed her work wouldn't be up to snuff. She practically had to beg for someone to be her lab partner. "When you start taking the science classes, it is like, you hope there is another black person in the class, or somebody of color, because nobody wants to work with you. 'Will you be my partner? Will you be my partner?' " she recalls. "First I tried with the women because women are more approachable—and they are like, one of the last ones to be picked too. And a lot of times my partners were actually Mexican because we didn't have a lot of blacks. I was the only black woman going into electrical engineering in my year." But even having black students in the class was no guarantee things would work out. "A lot of the black students are afraid to work with another black student, because *we* still think the other black person might not be a good student. A friend of mine from Ethiopia, he has too much pride to beg anybody, so he is doing the labs by himself. But that's not smart." Today things are a bit better. "When you get to the higher classes, the fact that you made it this far, they say, well she's in the class with me, she must not be that dumb," she says.

LaShunda first ran into academic trouble during her sophomore year. Her younger brother, Derrick, got shot during finals week. Her mother told LaShunda's sister Jackie to hold off on the news until finals were over—but Jackie blurted it out anyway. "It was [the class] E-40, my first D+ at Cal, the first class I had to repeat. I think that started shaking my confidence. But my sister and my father was like, don't try to blame what happens outside on your performance in school. I think that's because they had to deal with it at home."

During her junior year, family and money woes combined to erode her performance further. "My first upper-division semester I took E-104, E-105. Because the numbers were low I assumed it was easy, but 104 is a super-theoretical class. And that semester we hosted the National Society of Black Engineers regional job conference. I was on the job fair committee, working, and trying to date, so of course I bombed." During the same semester, an agent at the financial aid office misrouted her check—meaning she was behind on her tuition payments and technically not enrolled in the classes at all until they sorted out the mistake. "Do you know how horrible that is, to take classes and know you can't pay for it? They accused me of taking the money from my financial aid and spending it. When they found out [the payment went astray] they had no apologies. But I'd already stressed myself out so much I was failing."

A series of minor misfortunes and major tragedies combined to make the semester a complete disaster. "The day of my 105 final, my grandmother died. That was just kind of a climax to a semester where me and my roommate, we were both working but we didn't have any financial aid so our PGE [utilities] and our water got cut off. And I had to take my sister's daughter because she had went to jail for stealing." LaShunda found out that her five-year-old niece had effectively been abandoned on the day of her E-104 midterm. She picked the child up and took her to campus in order to try to take her test—only to be told that because of her financial aid woes, she wasn't listed on the class rolls. "I started crying," she says, "and my niece said, 'Auntie, why are you crying?'" LaShunda convinced officials to let her take the test, but she still had her niece to deal with. "So I ended up taking her to the [black engineering students'] office and somebody watched her while I was taking the test. I was crying throughout. I ended up getting a C+ out of the class, but that's all right, because"—she punches the air to underscore a determination born of love—"that is my motherfucking baby too."

If only someone else had stepped into the breach, LaShunda might not have lost so much time from school. But most of her family couldn't, because of poverty or drug use, and those who could have didn't. One of those who didn't was the family of LaShunda's other niece. Her sister's two daughters have different fathers. The family of the older girl came and picked up their granddaughter—but they left her half sister behind in the apartment with relatives who'd been smoking crack. LaShunda will never forget their callousness, though she hopes her niece will some day. "My niece came out crying, 'They left me!'" she remembers. "I was like, how could these other niece's folks leave the baby there just because she is not their belonging?"

Today, LaShunda's sister and nieces live in a different city and are living a life of "stability." "My sister has seen some things I have never seen. It hurt me, my sister was looking like an old lady, her face was so tired." Her nieces have seen too much as well: the older one saw her father shot and paralyzed. "Now she don't want to be around him no more," LaShunda says. But back in the fall of 1993, when LaShunda failed her classes, no one was there to lend her the helping hand she'd lent her family. The school kicked her out. "The spring after I got dismissed," she says. "I thought my life was over."

"This Handout Welfare Thing"

If LaShunda's story ended there, it would provide perfect evidence for the opponents of affirmative action—another black kid out of her educational league. But that feeling isn't isolated to critics outside of Berkeley's halls. Some of LaShunda's fellow students are as vehemently and vocally opposed to affirmative action as any national spokesperson. One of them is Steve Mohebi. A tall, nineteen-year-old Persian American, he has long sweeping eyelashes, olive skin, thick dark hair, and a Semitic nose. Persian- and Arab Americans, and Indians and other South Asians, don't fit into the narrow boundaries of American racial classifications. Mohebi has more freedom than most students to define his place within the racial power struggles, and he's made a clear choice to identify with and advocate for conservative whites.

We meet a few days after the October 12 protest. Black Republican presidential candidate Alan Keyes is coming to speak on campus that afternoon at the behest of the Berkeley College Republicans, a group Steve is the vice president of. Keyes is a political anomaly, an outsider desperately trying to squirm his way into the bosom of the GOP. A favorite of the religious right, Keyes will rarely capture more than 1 or 2 percent of the vote in Republican primaries but spends his media time on favorite issues: decrying abortion and welfare and promoting values and prayer. Regardless of how in sync his message is with the Republican ideal, Steve doesn't think Keyes has a chance. "It's a racist society," he says. Party officials "are going to advance whoever can get the votes. If you're going to advance a minority candidate, the constituency is not there. [Colin] Powell is what they call a whitewashed black guy. He gets criticism from blacks—he seems to distance himself from the black population. He's the only guy who has a glimmer of hope because he's shunned his ethnicity. America is highly racist, mostly against blacks," he admits. "For a black candidate to have any prayer of winning, he's going to have to distance himself from the black community."

Steve's own organization, the Berkeley College Republicans, has by his count three hundred and fifty dues-paying members and a mailing list of seven hundred. The largest racial group on Cal's campus is also the largest within the organization—Asian Americans. But he doesn't think an Asian American has much of a shot at being nominated for president either. That doesn't bother him terribly much, because he feels that the racism that shapes the American socioeconomic and cultural system pales in comparison to the new ill of reverse racism.

"We all know the double standard. A white male club would be firebombed. A black woman's club is OK," he says. The debate over affirmative action is the one arena in which "you can have white males band together and say, 'We're being screwed.' The affirmative action vote is a step in the right direction. My friends and I had chilled champagne bottles waiting for [the announcement of] the Regents' vote."

"You might say," he smiles, "that our position was, 'Ban affirmative action by any means necessary.' "

Steve's well aware of the political maneuvering behind the affirmative action issue. Even the most impartial observers saw Governor Pete Wilson's strident opposition to affirmative action as a ploy to revive his flagging presidential campaign. Wilson once strongly supported the Republican presidential nominee, Bob Dole. As Wilson pushed the issue through California, Senate Majority Leader Dole attempted to do the same thing on a national level. He addressed the Senate floor, telling his colleagues that he would push for a national law banning affirmative action. Political strategists saw affirmative action as a "wedge issue" that could drive more white men from the Democratic party. Dole was backed up by conservative pundits like George Will, who calls affirmative action a "racial spoils system." In a 1996 essay, Will also calls diversity a "cult" in higher education, "an aggressive ideology concerning the meaning of culture, the aims of education and the merits of the United States."[21] But the cult-like behavior was apparent at the Republican National Convention when conservatives booed Colin Powell for even *mentioning* his support of affirmative action.

Steve's ideas lie to the right of some of his idols in the Republican party. He wouldn't go so far as Dinesh D'Souza, who advocates dismantling the existing Civil Rights Act, but neither is he keen on upping the penalties for discrimination in the workplace, something conservatives like Bob Dole tout as a solution to inequality. "I don't know how you could police individual discrimination," he says. "I don't support the criminalization of racism. Certain people are socialized differently." Dole declared on the Senate floor that he would introduce legislation abolishing affirmative action, stating: "After nearly thirty years of Government sanctioned quotas, timetables, set-asides, and other racial preferences, the American people sense all too clearly that the race-counting game has gone too far." But his proposal to increase enforcement of antidiscrimination laws seemed ludicrously limited. The EEOC—the government agency that handles discrimination cases—has a backlog of ninety thousand claims, making any search for individual justice difficult if not impossible.[22]

But the same day that an article outlining Dole's attacks ran on the front page of *The New York Times,* a very different article did as well. A piece on the government's "Glass Ceiling" report revealed that while white men make up 43 percent of U.S. workers, they hold all but 5 percent of top management positions. In other words, despite the supposed ravages of affirmative action wreaked by blacks, Latinos, and women, white men are 95 percent of America's corporate vice presidents, presidents, and CEOs. White women are well represented in middle management, while black and Latino men are scarce there as well. The Commission's report also found that in every category of employment, white men earned more than either black men or white women. In manufacturing, for example, one of the higher-paying fields studied, white men earned approximately $60,000 per year; black men, close to

$50,000; black women, not quite $40,000; and white women, just over $30,000.[23]

What did the report pinpoint as the chief reason why blacks and women failed to move up the corporate ladder? "The perception of many white males that as a group they are losing—losing the corporate game, losing control, and losing opportunity. . . . Many middle- and upper-level white male managers view the inclusion of minorities and women in management as a direct threat to their own chances for advancement." The report concludes: "Corporate leaders are talking the talk of inclusion. Yet minorities and women express dismay and anger when they describe what they perceive to be innumerable obstacles to their corporate advancement. In short, there is a difference between what corporate leadership says it wants to happen and what is actually happening."[24] Yet many Americans, including Steve, see blacks and Latinos as beneficiaries of government largesse rather than people facing discrimination.

Steve had some experience with discrimination. He grew up in Seattle and Silicon Valley, arriving in America as an infant after his family fled the Iranian revolution. His father was an ambassador to Israel under the Shah. "He was aristocracy," Steve says. Immigrating to the United States "was a socioeconomic rude awakening"—no more servants, no more chauffeur, no more royal treatment. But his family did well. His father now does import-export; his mother is a homemaker. One of this two brothers studies artificial intelligence and the other went to college at the ripe age of fourteen. But Steve's family lived through racism as well. During the tense, economically tight days of the U.S. hostage crisis in 1980, white Americans looked at them and saw the face of the Ayatollah—a man the Mohebis hated. But Steve says the in-your-face racism his family experienced didn't foster any solidarity with blacks. "Ninety-nine percent of Persians are conservative. They're racist, mostly against blacks. They don't support welfare. 'To hell with these ethnic groups.' " I point out that the largest group of women on welfare are whites.[25] "Persians don't know that," he says.

It's one of many times that the facts about race in America seem almost immaterial to Steve. He says he's become convinced that "racism will always exist to some extent"—and that it circumscribes everything from the political ambitions to the job prospects of blacks and other groups. But "in some situations it may be OK to let it go," he says. He talks one moment about the racism of the present, then uses the rhetoric of "past discrimination" to describe affirmative action. "It's bad to penalize the white males of today for what happened in the past. What do you tell a guy who didn't get his place in grad school? We need eighteen percent Chicanos? You're qualified but you just can't get in? . . . Read Shelby Steele—why should black people have to accept the stigma" of being labeled affirmative action recipients? He believes the "mental advantage" blacks will receive from giving up affirmative action will far outweigh "this handout welfare thing."

The idea that affirmative action is a "handout welfare thing" is often reinforced by what we read in the papers and see on TV. Instead of staying neutral in this political debate, the news media—often accused of having a liberal bias—chose sides by mimicking the language of its opponents. Headlines in *The New York Times, Washingon Post,* and *Wall Street Journal* screamed "preference" and "bias" when talking about affirmative action. When racial code words masquerade as journalistic objectivity, it has a profound effect on the American public. In 1992, pollster Lou Harris found that Americans supported affirmative action 70 percent to 24 percent, but decried racial "preferences" by a margin of 48 to 46 percent.[26] A *Los Angeles Times* poll found a similar split: people opposed "preferences" for blacks and women by 72 and 70 percent respectively; only 29 percent and 24 percent opposed affirmative action for blacks and women.[27] Or look at a *Washington Post* poll that contained a double dose of bias, asking: Do you "favor preferences for blacks and other minorities to make up for past discrimination?" The words "preference" and "past discrimination" both tilt this question. Yet to this day, national papers like *The New York Times* use the word "preference" in headlines when talking about affirmative action, reinforcing the most negative vision of the program.

Steve says the issue of affirmative action is poisoning Berkeley's atmosphere. "White America is mad at black America for taking handouts," says Steve. "Everybody's racist to a certain extent. [But] however racist you are when you enter Berkeley, you will be ten times more when you graduate. It's appalling to hear people brag about taking handouts." Steve's words echo those of Charles Murray and Richard Herrnstein. They wrote in *The Bell Curve* that white students resent black [and in schools like Cal, Latino] students because they "are in fact getting a large edge in the admissions process and often in scholarship assistance. . . . [They] 'don't belong there' academically."[28]

Steve sees the professors as enemies, too. "They've been here for twenty or thirty years. They're liberal." He's fairly pleased with the student body, which is divided but "more conservative than liberal. But there's so much leftist rhetoric," he claims, "it's hard for them to voice opinions." Far from being a cultural melting pot, Berkeley in Mohebi's eyes is a place where even the dorms are "segregated. Unit 2 is far away. It's cheaper. It's Chicano. Chicanos are financially less sound than other groups. Foothill is expensive. There are a high amount of Asians. They've got their cell phones. A lot of them are from Taiwan."

Right now, the Berkeley College Republicans are "targeting the Greek system for membership. "The frats are white guy clubs," he says. "Minorities are not welcome." I ask if this is a problem. "Not if there are clubs on the other side. The Chinese Students Association has all-Chinese-guy dances and they don't invite other people." While many conservatives decry Balkanization as a byproduct of multiculturalism, Steve seems to find it comforting, if it means no one need interact with people they don't like. "I'm not sure I believe in a cohesive American culture," he says. "American culture is a patchwork quilt—more patches than quilt." He has no desire to recruit more blacks for the Berkeley Republicans, for example. "I'm not convinced that would be a good place to concentrate our efforts. I think we're strong as we are."

Is there any solution to the affirmative action conundrum? Education. "It's cost-inefficient for the government to police discrimination. We should spend more money on education," he says. Of course, providing education to blacks and Latinos was precisely the point of the University of California's affirmative action program. Are Steve's beliefs a paradox? If so, he doesn't have to puzzle it out. He doesn't feel the need to. The inequality isn't his problem.

Ahistorical Equality

Mohebi, like many opponents of affirmative action, justifies his position as a simple quest for individual fairness. But does fairness constitute ignoring decades—even centuries—of both government- and privately sanctioned discrimination? Or does the fairness truly come into play when we chose to do something about it?

Troy Duster, the Berkeley sociology professor who has studied affirmative action, compares our current situation to two real-life case studies: South Africa under apartheid and India under the caste system. Yes, he realizes their situations have many differences from our own. But we share a common, current reality—those societies (and ours) are dealing with how to redress ongoing discrimination on the one hand while dealing with the protests of individuals who've benefited from that discrimination in the past.

Those who claim eliminating affirmative action is simply "fair" are being ahistorical, Duster argues. In South Africa, whites forcibly removed blacks from their farms and ranches, corralled them into impoverished "homelands," and refused to pay for running water or even minimally sufficient schools. By the time forty-five years of apartheid ended, whites (less than 10 percent of the population) had ten times the wealth of blacks (over 80 percent of the population). Duster writes, "In 1992, when the writing was on the wall and apartheid's days were numbered, the corporate managers at Telkom, South Africa's national telephone company, an organization with more than fifty-eight thousand employees, did a quick review of the racial composition of its corporate structure. In late 1993, they found one more black manager than many expected—this is, they found one. By the second half of 1995, Telkom employed eighty-three black managers and has since embarked upon an aggressive affirmative action program to recruit and hire more." What was the reaction to this significant, though still *very* modest, bit of progress? "More than five thousand white workers have threatened to strike to protest the new policy." If affirmative action is about group versus individual, so is the history of race that precedes it. No doubt these workers were not protesting when they were judged as a group before—as a white group accorded tremendous privilege. Now that their seniority is entrenched, they demand to be treated as individuals alone.

At the heart of the debate over affirmative action is our belief in a meritocracy. But one of the conundrums we face in puzzling a way out of racial discrimination is how to judge the *potential* for achievement when individuals have not yet been given the tools to succeed. Many black South Africans who didn't have the same education and training as whites could assume prominent positions should they be given the opportunity to get education and training. Of course, that requires money, time—and the political will to devote both to changing the status quo. It would be foolhardy, in South Africa or Berkeley, California, to place blacks in positions where they didn't have the tools to succeed. But it would be absolutely insidious to let ongoing discrimination prevent potential talent from developing.[29]

It's telling to bring the focus back to college admissions, and one instance in which "affirmative action" worked for white men, and no one complained. Brandeis University in Massachusetts first opened its doors in 1948; the graduating class four years later was 52 percent male, 48 percent female. But when admissions officers analyzed the student pool before admitting any students to the brand-new school, they found something shocking—if they made admissions based on test scores and aptitude tests alone, the school would have been 70 percent female. They chose to make gender—in this case, the male gender—a positive criterion for admission. Duster writes, "Yet, at no time did we hear the anguished cries from [conservatives] Nathan Glazer and Irving Kristol that less qualified Jewish males were getting into Brandeis unfairly bumping more qualified females."[30]

Today's equivalent of Brandeis's male affirmative action is the system of "legacy" admission, which offers a crystal-clear advantage to the children of alumni, most from privileged backgrounds. In 1992, a group of Asian Americans asked the U.S. Department of Education to see if they were being rejected for less qualified whites. Investigators found that the children of alumni, as well as athletes, consistently received what they termed a "special preference" over other applicants at elite schools, including Harvard, Yale, and Stanford. Harvard's legacies were more than twice as likely to be admitted to the school than other applicants— even though their average SAT score was 35 points lower than the average admit. The most damning evidence came from the notes of admissions officers. In one case, a Harvard admissions officer posted this note in a folder: "Without lineage, there would be little case. With it, we will keep looking . . ." There's no evidence that Harvard follows a quota system for legacies colleges ("quotas" being the evil affirmative action foes protest the hardest)—but Notre Dame, for example, has a quota decreeing that 25 percent of each class be children of alumni.[31] Legacy status, regional diversity, disability, and socioeconomics are all routinely considered when it comes to evaluating who's admitted to schools. None of them speak to the questions of who has the highest SAT scores or grades—to the (already unattainable) idea of a pure meritocracy—but all of them are part of the process of picking and choosing who it is in the school's, and perhaps society's, best interest to have attend. All, that is, except race.

Out of Academic Exile

So what happened to LaShunda? A friend helped her find her job at a technology firm. She worked through the entire 1994–1995 school year, something that helped her rebuild her shattered confidence. "I was the valedictorian at Castlemont, and here I was starting to think I had a learning disability." But she wasn't on easy street. LaShunda found herself having to fight the same battles in the workplace that she did when she was searching for a lab partner back in class. "You have to prove yourself because you are a young black woman. Like, my manager is not going to give me some of the hard tasks. I am going to have to ask him or beg him. I was working with one group, and I kept saying, 'I want something more technical.' So they told me to fix the scanner. So I went to another group, and a black guy happened to be a manager, and I got to do network engineering."

After developing a strong track record on the job, LaShunda fought her way back into school. "My self-esteem was, I am in electrical engineering at UC Berkeley. It was so important. It was almost like I was worshipping it. I guess God had to take it away from me, in order for me to appreciate it." Before she got in, she says she battled the opposition of her dean, who thought she couldn't handle the work. "When I came in to see him I had my grandmother's obituary, I had a note that my utilities were cut off, papers from the courts, a police record for when my brother got shot, and all that documentation." They finally let her in, sending her a letter saying they were glad *they'd* found a way to let her return to school. At first she posted it on the wall, a reminder she was back in the school's good graces. But now she resents what she sees as their paternalism. "*He* didn't do this. *I* did this. I don't need to look at it and get all misty-eyed."

LaShunda Prescott, soon to be a Berkeley graduate in electrical engineering, is not content to be one of the few that makes it out of the 'hood. She wants to be the exception that *becomes* the rule. "Affirmative action is a double-edged sword. It is like, OK, here is your chance to be with them [privileged white students] but only a few of you, not all of you," she says. "It is just crazy. Since we are going to be the majority, blacks and Mexicans, why are we sitting there begging for crumbs?"

One night, LaShunda goes with me to a book reading I'm doing at the law school, Boalt Hall. Earlier that year, during Black History Month, fifteen nonwhite students at the law school found flyers that read: "Rejoice, you crybaby niggers. It's affirmative action month. When I see you in class it bugs the hell out of me because you're taking the seat of someone qualified."[32] The crowd at Boalt is attentive but thin—test time is upon them—so the platters of food they've ordered for the posttalk reception are largely untouched. "Let's take them to People's Park," LaShunda says.

We load the breads, meats, and cheeses into my car and drive to the park, shrouded in darkness now. Homeless men and women sit and stand together at the edge, shooting the shit and sharing a smoke or a bottle. LaShunda steps out of the car with a wave and a shout. "We've got food," she says. Most of the men and women are black or brown like us. One of the guys gives me a kiss on the cheek. LaShunda laughs. Hers is not the self-aggrandizing charity that enforces a barrier between giver and receiver. She's come to the park as a friend, a member of the family. She's brought me here not because she's better than the group at People's Park, but because she sees herself as what they are—people trying to make it.

Border Blues:
Mexican Immigration and
Mexican-American Identity

El Paso, Texas

The land around El Paso, Texas, is an imposing desert scene painted in tones of ochre and red clay—stark mountains, vast sky, arid plains. It's so far west that it's the only major Texas city in the mountain, rather than the central, time zone. Atop a nearby mountain is the massive Christo Rey—an imposing figure of Jesus hewn out of tons of stone. It seems like a peaceful vista, but this land is the staging ground for a colossal clash of cultures—the meeting of Mexico and the United States at the border. The biggest clash is not between Mexico and the United States per se, but between many competing visions of what Mexican immigration means to the United States. Mexican immigration has been decried as an "illegal alien invasion," an erosion of America's job base, even the beginnings of a plot to return the Southwest to Mexican hands. And sometimes Mexican Americans themselves are perceived with suspicion, in the belief their allegiance is pledged to Mexico, not the United States.

What's the reality behind these perceptions? And what's life on the border like? Compared to many of the other issues I've covered in this book, I came to the border as a complete outsider. I've spent virtually my whole life living on the East Coast, where the Latino communities are dominated by Puerto Ricans, Dominicans, Cubans. I groove to Latin hip-hop and Afro-Cuban sounds, but I hadn't heard much Mexican-American music like ranchero and Tejano. I know a good plate of *pernil* when I eat one, but I couldn't tell you from *tortas*. And I've heard more opinions over whether Puerto Rico should become independent than I've heard firsthand accounts of life on the border. In other words, when I came to El Paso I was starting at ground zero. Why did I choose El Paso? Well, first, this border city has been the site of a well-publicized crackdown on illegal immigration. Second, it's been deeply impacted by government policies like NAFTA. But third, and most important to me, El Paso is not majority Anglo but 70 percent Latino and Mexican American, a place where there are bound to be differences of opinion between members of the Latino community.

I head for El Paso in the summer of 1996, a time when the federal government is debating whether to bar the children of undocumented immigrants from going to schools and whether to tighten limits on even legal immigration. The measures are championed by Senator and presidential candidate Bob Dole. A bill that would have clamped down on legal immigration also withered on the vine. It is the continuation of a vigorous ongoing national debate over immigration. Three years before, the newly installed Clinton administration had pushed for and ultimately passed the hotly contested North American Free Trade Agreement. Proponents said NAFTA would stimulate U.S.-Mexican trade, putting dollars into America's economy. Opponents argued it would cost thousands of U.S. jobs when plants relocated to take advantage of Mexican workers who earn as little as five dollars per day. Then, in November of 1994, California voters passed Proposition 187, a referendum designed to deny all public services—health care, welfare, even elementary and secondary education—to illegal immigrants. Sixty-three percent of white Californians voted for Proposition 187, while 69 percent of Latinos voted against it.[1] Before 187 could be implemented, opponents challenged its constitutionality and sent the issue to the courts.

Like California, Texas is just under 30 percent Latino.[2] But the state's governor and senators, all of them Republicans, didn't follow California's lead and try to impose new laws on illegal immigration. Instead, they voiced objections to anti-immigrant legislation.[3] Public opinion, culture, and commerce all played a role. Polls show that most Texas residents still view immigration as a boon, not a burden, while the opposite is true in California. Texas draws identity from the Mexican border, whether it's the heritage of many of its citizens, historical events like the Alamo, or the hallmarks of everyday life, like food. (The term "Tex-Mex" says it all.) And an analysis by *The Economist* points to more tangible commodities. In 1995, Texas exported $24 billion in goods to Mexico, its leading trading partner. Mexico was only California's fourth trading partner, with $7 billion in goods.[4]

But while trade with Mexico has been good for Texas in general, the NAFTA free trade treaty has hit El Paso's economy hard. The city already has an unemployment rate double the national average. Now plants that used to pay workers five dollars an hour in El Paso can pay them five dollars a day just across the border in Juarez—and not pay duty on the goods shipped back to the United States. Among the issues I want to explore here in El Paso are not just questions of Mexican-American identity—how they see themselves—but also how they see their (real or distant) cousins across the border. Do the residents of El Paso look upon the Mexicans as brothers, economic competitors—or a bit of both?

One of the first people I meet in El Paso gives me a hint of the differences in opinion about border issues. Nora is chic, almost out of place in the grungy alternative bar we're both sitting in, with high cheekbones, light skin, and curly black hair cut in a bob. "I hate to say it, but I agree with him," she says. "They need to learn English." The "him" Nora is talking about is a black city councilman who chewed out a citizen who addressed a town hall meeting in Spanish. The "they"—an implicit "they"—are recent Mexican immigrants. Nora, who used to model in New York and now works in the local clothing industry, takes the councilman's side. But some local cartoonists lampooned the politician's outrage, and many residents wrote letters of protest to the newspaper.

Many El Paso residents are from first- or second-generation immigrant families, people who remember life in Mexico and have direct family ties across the border. But it's a mistake to think that they encompass all of El Paso's Latinos. A large proportion of El Paso families, like Nora's, are *Tejano*, a term which means that her forebears have lived in Texas for generations—i.e., even before it was part of the United States. (As many Tejanos like to say, "We didn't cross the border. The border crossed us.") The unique Tex-Mex culture of the Tejanos gave rise to one of the biggest Latina singing sensations, Selena, whose premature death in 1995 woke America up to the size of the Latino community. And one lesson America has yet to learn about the Latino community is how many different cultural and political perspectives there are—even within a single group, like Mexican Americans.

Those different perspectives come into direct conflict when it comes to an issue as controversial as the border. I focused on two groups of people familiar with El Paso: the enforcers who try to keep people out, and the border crossers desperate to stay in America.

The Enforcers

Melissa Lucio gets the radio call at noon on a scorching summer day. An electric sensor just inside the U.S. border's been tripped; agents are looking around but they haven't found anybody yet. She heads for the sensor's coordinates and pulls up alongside a couple of agents. They're beating the bushes around a splotch of water halfway between a pond and a puddle. After a minute, a guy about thirty-five years old steps out of a thicket with a resigned look on his face and a satchel slung over his shoulder. A Mexican worker who's crossed illegally into the States, he also happens to be wearing an OFFICIAL U.S. TAXPAYER baseball cap.

When I laughingly point this out to Melissa, she goes me one better. "We had a guy who walked in with a Border Patrol hat the other day. We asked him where he got it and he said he found it on the bank of the river. The officer's name was still written on the inside—he'd lost it over a year ago."

Melissa's just one of the thousands of U.S. Border Patrol agents charged with the thankless (and some would say, impossible) task of keeping illegal immigrants out of America and catching them once they come in. A Mexican-American El Paso native, she's also the wife of another Mexican-American Border Patrol agent. Just thirty years old, she's also the mother of five sons. With her thick black hair pulled back in a neat French braid, her brown uniform replete with two-way radio and gun, Melissa rides the Texas–Mexico–New Mexico border tracking and detaining border crossers. Sometimes she gets help from the electronic signals of hidden sensors, but much of the time she relies on her own eyes, scanning the horizon and bending toward the earth to interpret "signs"—the scant marks and footprints in the dry earth which she reads for vital clues of time and direction. The day is hot and clear. Recent rains have made it easier to track signs—and have also put desert flowers into bloom. Melissa's comments as she navigates the covered-cab truck around bumps and gullies are punctuated with interjections about the wildlife—"Beautiful bird!" "Really cool lizard!" "Check out that jackrabbit!" But her ear is always tuned to the radio, and she's tough when she has to be. If her truck gets stuck, she breaks off branches and digs it out; if a suspect in a vehicle takes off into a residential area, she pursues and radios the local police. As we traverse highways, dirt roads, and long stretches of pristine desert, we don't run into any other female agents out in the field.

The man Melissa has just picked up doesn't protest when she puts him in the covered back area of the truck. In fact, he reaches into his satchel, pulls out a newspaper, and starts to read. At my request, she asks him where he was going and what he was going to do.

"*¿Para dónde vas?*" she asks.

"*Para Coronado,*" he answers.

Coronado is an affluent area, replete with a country club, where he was headed to cut yards. "He was actually closer to the east side of Juarez," Melissa translates, "and I asked him why he didn't cross over there. And he said there's a lot of *cholos* [bandits] stealing and robbing in that area. He says it's easier to cross over here. He says he doesn't come often, but every once in a while when he needs money."

One stereotype of illegal immigrants is that they're a bunch of welfare cheats. But this crosser, and most of the ones the Melissa picks up, are coming in strictly to work—sometimes to stay for the day and go back that night. The economics are clear cut. The starting wage in the *maquiladoras,* or twin plants—so named because they're owned by U.S. corporations who maintain both Mexican factories and their "twins" across the border—is about five dollars a day. The wages for yard work are far, far higher. "If they have their own tools, they could make sixty bucks a day," Melissa says. "If not, it could be thirty or forty." In other words, one day per week of work in the United States earns more than an entire week's labor in Mexico. Of course, there'd be no point crossing the border if U.S. employers weren't willing, even eager, to give undocumented workers jobs. If a border crosser makes it in every day, the payoff is good even relative to U.S. workers. "If you think about minimum wage, four sixty per hour with taxes taken out, [the border crossers] are going to make more," she says. "Even the Mexican police officers, some of them make four hundred dollars per month if they're lucky."

I ask Melissa if the people she picks up ever give her flack for being Mexican American and picking up Mexicans. "I've only had one person say, 'Don't you think you're being mean?' " she says. "And I say, if you had a job, you would do it to the best of your ability, right? They say 'Yeah.' "—she draws the word out to give it a dubious inflection. "And I say that's just what I'm doing. I've got five children. I want to maintain my household. And they understand."

"Like this education issue," she continues. "Let's say you educate them, and then what? They're illegal in the United States so they can't obtain work. Or let's say they become legal, then they're going to be competing against my children or me for a job that could have very well been mine." She's no fan of NAFTA, which she believes has knocked the wind out of an already weakened local economy. "Not a month goes by that you don't hear about a local company that's up and relocating to Mexico," she says. "It may be a good law, but not for the people who live paycheck to paycheck."

We drop our passenger off at the Paso Del Norte processing station, a short-term holding area that seems appropriately located in the middle of nowhere. Inside the plain building is a bullpen of officers at their desks, surrounded by large cells where individuals are sorted by gender, age, and area of origin. Locals—people from Juarez and nearby border areas—are the easiest to process and return. People from the interior of Mexico, farther south, are interviewed by Mexican officials and given bus fare home. And last of all are detainees from Central America, some of whom have traveled hundreds upon hundreds of miles from Honduras and points south, only to be caught on the final leg of their journey. There are men and women, old and young—really young. One of the kids in the pen, who flashes me an impish grin when I check him out, looks about twelve.

"Oh, we get kids who are eight, nine, ten. I ask them, 'Your Mom, doesn't she worry about you?' And some of their parents do, but they really run wild. If they know a lady at a bakery [in the United States] will give them sweetbreads, stuff like that, they'll come. Some of them have friends they come to goof off with. This is what they do. This is recreation."

By the time they're sixteen—which is the age of the next border crosser we pick up—they're usually crossing to work. The teenager has tan skin and hair bleached nearly blond by the sun; he's carrying yard tools.

"*¿Con qué te posito entro los Estados Unidos?*" Melissa asks.

"Trabajo."

"¿Qué clase trabajo?"

"En yardas," he answers. He was headed to Coronado as well.

An Economic Judgment

Melissa Lucio is not only a Border Patrol agent, but a mother and a taxpayer as well. She believes the influx of illegal immigrants could curtail her children's chances at prosperity. "When people talk about immigration issues as being racial," she says, "you have Hispanics as well as Anglos as well as other ethnic groups that will say the same thing: 'We need to be strong on immigration issues.' Why should my tax dollars and my anything be funding someone else?"

Melissa's family immigrated from Mexico a couple of generations ago. "My grandma jokes that I'm going to send her back over the border," Melissa says. She had what she describes as a typical, happy coming of age in El Paso. She met her first love, Rick, who's also Mexican American, in high school, and married him right after she graduated. Like several members of both of their families, Rick went into law enforcement, joining the Border Patrol. Melissa dreamed about the same thing for ten years before she decided to take the plunge. "I had thought about going to college and to the FBI behavioral science department, to pursue some forensics. But the more and more children I started having, I just started to see that dream being pushed further and further away," she says.

Melissa found out the Border Patrol was hiring when Rick told her about a career day he was coordinating—but he tried to discourage her from trying out. It was an arduous process. First she had to take a written test to get admitted to the academy. Then she had to get in shape. After seven years of bearing and raising five sons (Daniel, David, Derek, Dario, and Andrew—"we ran out of Ds," she says), she was two hundred and twenty pounds. She quit her job and lost forty before going into the academy, and another ten once she was there. When it came time for the induction ceremony, she received her badge from an officer who'd specially requested the honor—her husband. "As he's pinning me he whispers in my ear, 'Oh, Melissa, I never thought you would make it. You've never made me so proud.' " She beams. "It was absolutely great. It was amazing."

Now Melissa works just past the El Paso line in the Christo Rey area of New Mexico. Standing atop the hill that supports the huge statue of Christ, you can see Mexico, New Mexico, and Texas in panorama. You can also see the latest attempts to keep the border clamped down. Along the length of the border, construction crews are putting up an immense fence designed to eventually cover the entire U.S.-Mexico line. But Melissa for one is skeptical it will stop the crossings. "They'll just have to walk a little further," she says, to where mesas break the fence line.

Her division, which contains forty to sixty agents per day depending on scheduling, picks up about a hundred and fifty people per day, a thousand per week. It's labor-intensive work, particularly given the nature of the terrain. The El Paso Border Patrol region gained prominence in 1991 when Silvestre Reyes, the chief at the time, implemented a policy he called Operation Hold the Line. Instead of chasing border crossers after they walked over train tracks or through the Rio Grande (at the Juarez-El Paso border, the river is little more than a trickle in a concrete culvert), Reyes posted agents in vehicles along large stretches of the border. Their presence dropped the number of crossers at that juncture from eight thousand a day to virtually zero. But that meant more Mexicans who wanted to come to Texas chose to go through the New Mexico mountains. "You can't do that here. You'd have to have a ton of agents to watch every side of every hill. We have to be mobile," Melissa says.

It seems like an awful lot of work for each agent on an eight-hour shift to pick up the equivalent of three border jumpers a day. But the political stakes are far higher than those numbers would suggest. Tensions about immigration characterize the turn of this century as deeply as they marked the turn of the last one. But instead of the Italians, Irish, and Jews who received a lukewarm welcome disembarking at Ellis Island in the late 1800s and early 1900s, Mexican Americans crossing into the border for points as far flung as New York and the Midwest are the immigrants under scrutiny today. According to the Immigration and Naturalization Service, in 1995 eighty-six thousand Mexicans emigrated to the United States legally, to work, study, or join their families. They were the largest single group of U.S. immigrants, and joined approximately 6 million Mexican immigrants living legally in the United States. (All told, there are over 30 million Latinos living in the United States.) U.S. officials estimate there are more than 5 million illegal immigrants in the United States, 54 percent of them Mexicans, most of whom also came to work or go to school.[5] While some agents are used as human scarecrows, keeping would-be border crossers out, Melissa's job is mainly to track and capture the people who do make it through.

The pickups don't always go smoothly. Some of the border crossers have passed out and nearly died from heat stroke or dehydration as they're being taken in; other times agents just find the bodies. (One agent tells me a gruesome, perhaps apocryphal tale of finding a body whose eyes had literally popped out of the scorched head.) Sometimes people resist or carry weapons. The agents also have to watch out for *cholos*— gang members who can come from either side of the border, and who often prey on those crossing the border to work. In a Wild West twist, some of the *cholos* rob trains passing through the region. "A bandit will board the trains out West and pilfer through first, and say, 'The Nike tennis shoes are here.' Then they have their buddies, twenty or thirty or forty guys, shunt the track so the little computer tells the train to stop. As soon as it stops, these guys start throwing the stuff down. They don't care if the nine hundred ninety-nine dollar television cracks open because the good ones will land somewhere and they will grab it and sell it. Or on the other hand, in the next two weeks you'll arrest a bunch of people that are all wearing brand new Nike tennis shoes."

Sometimes they prey on the individuals working along the border fence line. As our day together draws to a close, Melissa gets a radio call from one of the men erecting the new fence. He's worried because four men are approaching and he's alone. "Ten-four. Horse patrol and myself will thirteen over there and check it out," Melissa radios back. As we approach, two men on powerful horses gallop parallel, about twenty yards away. "I'm on the list for horseback," Melissa says. "I think it's so cool." She surveys the situation as we approach. "These guys are definitely up to no good." I ask how she can tell. "They don't have any bags, which means they're not crossing. They don't have any water and they're just hanging around with no attempt to go north." They might have wanted to get their hands on some of the construction supplies, she figures.

Every eight weeks Melissa and the other agents change shift—days, evenings, overnights (which start at midnight). Now she's working days and her husband is working evenings, making it easy for him to take the kids to and from school. They try to avoid both doing the evening shift, "because we've noticed that our kids' grades drop."

To help out, Rick and Melissa have hired a live-in housekeeper, which is a drama in and of itself. "I advertised for a housekeeper two years ago, [and] the first thing off the bat was, "Are you a U.S. citizen or a legal resident? If not, I work for immigration and I can't hire you." And half the people would hang up. A quarter of the people would say, 'I'm a border crosser,' but they were not permitted to work. The lady we hired, she's late forties, great with the kids, teaching the kids Spanish, and she's a legal resident, so it worked out really really well."

"So what's funny, a neighbor came up and said, 'Do you realize your house is under surveillance?' I was like, 'Excuse me?' " One day, when both husband and wife were gone, an agent came to the home and asked their housekeeper for documents. Neighbors came out to watch, and she waved right back at them to say "I'm still here because I'm legal," Melissa says. The couple learned why the Immigration and Naturalization Service suspected them when they talked the matter over with their chief. A neighbor had phoned in with an elaborate tale how the housekeeper, supposedly illegal, had begged up and down the street for work and found it with the Lucios. "It's just someone being vindictive. I thought, that is really terrible," Melissa says. "At the time we lived in the Coronado Country Club area. They were really unhappy about Hold the Line because their maids couldn't come in illegally." As we head back into the station, I think again about the economics of the illegal immigration debate. The reality is that for every undocumented immigrant who finds low-wage work in America, there is somebody willing to hire that person. And some of the same people benefiting from below-market labor loudly decry illegal immigration at the same time.

The Politics of the Border

America likes to think its immigration laws are tough. And while they're arguably harsh on people who cross the border, most penalties on the businesses that hire illegal immigrants are modest. And people like the border crossers Melissa Lucio picked up often don't work for "businesses" at all, but everyday U.S. citizens who usually suspect the person they've hired to cut their lawn or babysit their kids doesn't hold a green card. America decries the waves of illegal immigration. But some Americans on the border and throughout the United States profit from the cheap labor these immigrants provide.

The economics of the border are full of conflict and duplicity, people who profit, people who lose, and people who lie about which camp they're in. Most important, the economics are deeply intertwined. Downtown El Paso, an unremarkable collection of modest office buildings and low-priced shops, is tethered by a bridge to downtown Juarez, Mexico. The Mexicans who cross the bridge come to work, visit, and shop. The Anglos going the other way often buy cheap groceries and pharmaceuticals (you can purchase Valium and Prozac without a prescription there), and college students hit the bars, where the words "drinking age" are meaningless. What happens when the Border Patrol cracks down on illegal crossings? Many downtown El Paso businessmen say their shops suffer, deprived of the day workers that used to buy clothes and consumer goods.[6]

Many Mexican residents of Juarez aren't happy about the increasingly fortified border, either. El Paso and Juarez are separated by an unimpressive trickle of water that, amazingly enough, is part of the mighty Rio Grande river. A cement aqueduct, fenced on both sides, contains the water and separates the people. Painted on the concrete are signs decrying the border fortification:

One reads OJO MIGRA (eyes are painted into the o's) ¡¡YA BASTA!!

Another says: POR CADA ILEGAL QUE NOS MALTRATEN EN LOS ESTADOS UNIDOS DE N.A. VAMOS A MALTRATAR UN VISITANTE GAVACHO. BIENVENIDOS LOS PAISANOS.

Their translations: "Look, Immigration—enough already!" and "For every illegal they mistreat in the United States, we are going to mistreat a visiting gringo. Welcome, countrymen."

It sounds like a bit of useless bravado, the "welcome, countrymen" sign. But the history of the Southwest is the history of what Mexico founded and America fought to win—not particularly fairly, either. Writes biographer Hugh Pearson:

In 1845, hewing to the strictures of Manifest Destiny we annexed the Republic of Texas, which had been part of Mexico. Its American settlers decided to introduce slavery into the territory, which was illegal in Mexico. Then, as gratitude for the Mexican government's inviting them to settle the territory and because they wanted to keep their slaves, they fought for independence. As former President and Gen. Ulysees S. Grant wrote in his memoirs, "The occupation, separation and annexation were, from the inception of the movement to its final consummation, a conspiracy to acquire territory out of which slave states might be formed for the American union."

After accepting the Texas republic's petition to be annexed by the United States, a dispute between the United States and Mexico ensued, regarding where the exact boundary of Texas lay. Mexican and U.S. patrols clashed somewhere along the disputed territory and the United States declared war on Mexico. In the process of fighting the war, U.S. troops captured from Mexico what is now New Mexico and what the Mexicans called Upper California. As conditions for surrender, Mexico was forced to cede all of the captured territory north of the Rio Grande River, and an agreed upon jagged imaginary line that now separates California, Arizona and New Mexico from Mexico. So today, Mexicans crossing into U.S. California are treated as illegal aliens if they don't go through the proper channels for entering territory that was originally theirs.[7]

I didn't learn any of this in high school, and I'd wager that many Americans don't know it today. What happened doesn't change the fact that America has the right to control its borders, but it does cast into sharper relief the interconnectedness of these two nations. Texas was birthed from Mexico. But—defying the stereotypes that pervade much of the news coverage about the border—many Mexican Americans are now the ones guarding the border.

Silvestre Reyes headed the Border Patrol for the entire El Paso region. After gaining recognition for starting Operation Hold the Line, Reyes resigned in November 1995 in order to run for a seat in the U.S. Congress, hoping the "sleeping giant" of Mexican-American political clout will work in his favor. (In November 1996, he won that seat.)

I meet the solid, handsome fifty-year-old in the offices where he's running his campaign with the help of his twenty-five-year-old daughter. Even in his civilian clothes, he's got the demeanor of a law enforcement officer. Reyes grew up in a small farming town where his high school graduating class was made up of just twenty-six students. When he was a child, he served as a lookout against *la migra*—the Border Patrol—

in the fields where Mexicans worked. He served in Vietnam, then worked as a Border Patrol agent for over twenty-five years. He believes that people's opinions about the border don't have anything to do with ethnic loyalty, but quality of life. "Hispanics, like every ethnic group in the country, have an expectation to be safe and secure in their neighborhoods," he says. "A Hispanic no more than anybody else appreciates undocumented people flowing through their backyards, creating a chaotic situation."

Still, Reyes says he'd like to find a way to benefit both Mexicans and Americans at the same time. "Mexican citizens don't want to come up here," he says. "They would rather stay home. But they stay home, they starve. We've got forces down in Mexico that want jobs, and people up here that want them to come up here. But the whole problem is, let's find a system that does it legally."

Despite its adverse effect on the El Paso economy, Reyes supports NAFTA as a way of increasing employment opportunities in Mexico. If things don't get better there, he reasons, illegal immigration will never stop. "Mexico has a surplus of manpower. I think 60 percent of Mexican citizens are under the age of twenty, if I remember my statistics right," he says. The problem with NAFTA in the short term is that it's relied on minimum-wage jobs, jobs that are the first to be transferred to the other side of the border. "In El Paso, we have a minimum-wage mentality. When they graduate, kids want to go someplace else. They don't want to stay here and work for four thirty-five or five fifteen or whatever the [minimum] wage finally ends up to be when they can go to Dallas, L.A., Denver, Chicago and participate in high-paying, high-tech kinds of jobs. Anybody with any kind of ambition knows that in order to make it, you've got to leave here."

One policy he doesn't support is California's Proposition 187, which voters passed in 1994 in an effort, among other things, to prevent illegal immigrants from receiving government medical care or public education. Reyes calls the measure "illegal and unconstitutional," and rejects the calls of national politicians like former Senator Bob Dole to replicate it.

"Should we amend the Constitution in order to deny children born in this country their citizenships? I think we're crazy," he says. "What's gonna keep someone from going back retroactively and saying, 'You know, your father was born to illegal parents back in 1924. Therefore he was illegal, therefore you're illegal.' " (Such logic recalls a joke by Mexican-American comedian Paul Rodriguez, who says he supports making deportations for illegal immigration retroactive and shipping the Anglos back home.) The idea of barring education to undocumented children is "insanity running amok. The way that people enslave whole segments of our society is by keeping them ignorant. . . . To me it doesn't matter whether it's blacks or Hispanics or Chinese or whites or who it is. I think it's just wrong for any country to guarantee a subculture of ignorance. And that's what you're doing when you don't educate the kids."

The wording of California's Proposition 187 was also openly militaristic, reading:

WE CAN STOP ILLEGAL ALIENS. If the citizens and the tax-payers of our state wait for the politicians in Washington and Sacramento to stop the incredible flow of ILLEGAL ALIENS, California will be in economic and social bankruptcy. We have to act and ACT NOW! On our ballot, Proposition 187 will be the first giant stride in ultimately ending the ILLEGAL ALIEN invasion.

Some advocates say the border has already become militarized, infringing upon the rights of citizens and legal immigrants. El Paso's Border Rights Coalition says that in 1995, half of the individuals who complained to their group about mistreatment by the Border Patrol, Immigration and Naturalization Service, and U.S. Customs were U.S. citizens, not legal or illegal immigrants.[8] The group helped students at El Paso's Bowie High School file a class action suit. They alleged that

Border Patrol agents were routinely harassing individuals on and near campus—in one case, arresting a group of students, U.S. citizens, who were driving to school. Today, the Border Patrol is operating under a settlement that requires they meet higher standards before detaining individuals, and limits searches at schools and churches.

Of course, the ultimate military-style solution would be to create a physical wall between Mexico and the United States. Reyes strongly disagrees with such a plan. "That's impractical, you know. The Berlin wall didn't seal, and that was using mines and barbed wire and guards and concrete, and all of that, and still people got out of there," he says. Yet as Reyes and I talk, construction on just such a wall is happening along the border near El Paso. While I'm out with Melissa Lucio, she shows me the early stages of the construction site. It's impossible to cover the whole border, of course. But by 1998, several miles of what Reyes calls the "impractical" solution stand completed.

The Border Crossers

A Family Full of Contradictions

Gilberto, an eighteen-year-old undocumented immigrant from Chihuahua, has few marketable skills but one strong advantage on his side. He has family legally in the United States who are willing to help him. Gilberto is the brother-in-law of a naturalized U.S. citizen who emigrated from Hong Kong. Chiu, who went to college in the United States, met his wife, Lorena, in a Juarez nightclub. Now they have two children, baby Jenny Anna and Andy, who turned three the day after I spoke with them. Both attend the University of Texas at El Paso, and they earn a living by running a home care facility for the elderly.

Gilberto helps out with the home care, meaning he's guaranteed a job as well as a place to stay far from the eyes of the Border Patrol. Like virtually all illegal immigrants, he's an unskilled laborer. Like many Mexicans, he finished the "secondario" level of schooling at fifteen and then started working. His first job was in a junkyard—hot, heavy work for very little money. Still, like a teenager, he used the remaining money he had to party rather than save. Asked if he's worried *la migra* will find him—something they did once before, as he was out and about—he shakes his head confidently, "No."

Chiu and Lorena's generous brick house is nestled in a pristine, upper-middle-class enclave undergoing rapid development. Bold and self-assured, Chiu strongly opposes illegal immigration, a position it's hard not to think deeply about when you see Gilberto sitting sheepishly on the other side of the table. "My brother-in-law, he's an illegal alien. He come and go whenever he wants. When you're talking about Hold the Line, it's only to make the government look good," Chiu scolds. "Washington, D.C., will furnish a lot of money for this project because it's very successful—you catch ten billion illegal aliens. Oh great job!" he sneers. "Now they have this Hold the Line thing, OK, and then they say, 'Nobody coming across.' But in the reality it's not true. In Mexico, if the people over there are making three to five dollars a day and if they cannot support their kids, do you think they would just sit there and die?"

Gilberto isn't in the dire straits many border crossers are. In fact, he originally entered not to stay but to fulfill teenage longings. "All the boys, they have the same dream: you know, they wanted to come and get some money and buy a truck, a nice truck," his sister Lorena translates, "and then go back to Mexico and spend one or two months or whatever on the money they saved up. Then after that, they come back to the United States again and work and get some more money. That's the way they think." Now Gilberto's changed his mind. He wants to stay in the United States and become a nurse. "It's very important to learn to speak English, otherwise there's no way to find a job—well, maybe in El Paso a very low job. But I want to go further," he says. He's enrolled in a local high school, where his legal status proved no problem. "As a matter of fact, they are not allowed to ask you whether you have papers or not, or whether you have a Social Security number or not, because if they do that they have violated federal law," Chiu says. "So they have to let him register although he's an illegal alien." In a clear example of how self-interest overrides politics, Chiu says that he's happy his brother-in-law can be enrolled, but that he is opposed to educating undocumented children. "When they do that they are inviting illegal immigrants to come to school here, you see. I would say no illegal immigrants to go to school in this country for free."

Neither Mexican nor American

A pensive seventeen-year-old named Diana finds herself in the opposite situation from Gilberto: with her near-perfect English and years of schooling in the United States, she seems culturally American, but this undocumented immigrant has no one to advocate for her or protect her. She's been caught between two worlds most of her life. Four years ago, Diana crossed into the United States at the Juarez–El Paso bridge that symbolizes the border so well. Now she's a senior at Fremont High School in Oakland, California (the subject of Chapter 6 of this book). Before crossing the Rio Grande, she spent her junior high school years near Durango, Mexico. And before that, from the ages of two until nine, she lived in the United States—attending American schools, playing with American toys, speaking both English and Spanish. Without a green card or citizenship, but with a keen understanding of American culture and her precarious position in it, she is neither fully American nor fully Mexican.

Diana remembers the day her family crossed over from Juarez to El Paso. "We used a raft to get across. It was really sunny that day. People were on the bridge watching us. They were like, 'Oh, look!' " she says. "I remember I saw this man with a little boy in his arms pointing at us." Once they got to El Paso, her family tried to blend in with the rest of the crowds in the downtown shopping area. "We crossed the street right in front of a Border Patrol car," Diana remembers. "The car stopped so we could cross the street! My Mom was praying and I was like, 'Mom, they're not going to do anything to us now.' They didn't."

While her experience in crossing the Rio Grande was a common one until recently, Diana's reasons for going back and forth between the United States and Mexico are personal and complex. Like most families who cross over from Mexico, Diana's came to work and make a better life for their children. Her father has a green card, so he was able to live and work legally; but he brought Diana, her mother, and Diana's older brother into the country without papers. Diana's father began drinking too much, and after living in the United States for several years, he decided to move the family back to Mexico and pull himself together. But there's little work near Durango, so he ended up going back to the United States to earn a living (taking Diana's teenage brother along with him) and sending money to the family back home. It was only once her father had stopped drinking that he decided to reunite the family, arranging for a "coyote"—or someone who smuggles people across the border—to bring Diana and the rest of the family north through Mexico, on a raft over the Rio Grande, and by truck out of Texas.

Diana was too young to remember the first time she crossed the border. She was only two years old, and friends of the family who had papers for their own toddler smuggled her in as their child. "People told me I kept saying, 'I want my mother.' They needed me to be quiet," she says. From two on, Diana lived in Chico, California, as a normal Mexican-American kid—almost. When I ask her if she knew she was an "illegal immigrant," she says, "That question really bothered me and came into my head in, I think, the second grade. Most of my friends would go to Mexico on their summer vacations to see their grandparents, and I would ask, 'Why aren't we going to Mexico?' My mother would say, 'We can't.' Then," she continues, "one time in school I said, 'Um, I'm illegal.' And my teacher said, 'Honey, don't say that out loud. You could get your parents in a lot of trouble.' That's when I started feeling a little inferior to other kids."

Sometimes she still does. "Not because of who I am but because of what I can't do," she says, quietly breaking into tears. One thing she can't do is apply to college, even though she's a solid student. Without legal residence papers, she has little hope of attending school or getting anything but the most menial of jobs. Her older brother tried enrolling in college, but after they repeatedly asked him for a Social Security number, he simply left. Now he plays in a band. "I want to get a green card so I can work, so I can go to school, so I don't need to worry about getting deported and everything. But we have to pay a lawyer seven hundred dollars for each person applying for the green card," money her struggling family doesn't have. After she gets a green card, she wants to become a citizen "because I would like to be heard in this country. I would like to vote and be part of the process."

The most wrenching part of her experience is that Diana knows she could have been a legal resident by now. In 1987, she says, "we could have gotten our papers through the National Amnesty Program," a one-shot chance for illegal immigrants to declare themselves to officials in exchange for a green card. "My mother applied for us, but my Dad [who was drinking] felt that if we went back to Mexico, everything would be for the best." She remembers the day they left the United States. "I had to leave all my friends and the things I had. We left everything: the furniture, my toys, my Barbies. I had to practically leave my life there."

Yet Diana credits the time she spent in Mexico with helping her reconnect with her heritage. She became close with her grandmother, was in the Mexican equivalent of junior ROTC, and won dramatic speaking contests, reciting poetry. "In Mexico, I always wanted to be the one with the best grades—always wanted to be the center of attention," she says. "Maybe because I believed in myself and what I did," she says. That sense of confidence is lacking in Diana today. But if she had stayed in Mexico, it would have been difficult for her to continue her education considering how little money her family had. Most of the girls Diana knew stopped going to school at fourteen or fifteen, got married to a farmer or laborer, and started a family.

So, in one sense, Diana feels she was lucky to return to the United States. But when she first arrived, she had a difficult time readjusting. She returned in time for ninth grade, which in Oakland at the time was still a part of junior high school. Teachers put her in an English as a second language program, probably because her shyness inhibited her from talking much. "It wasn't very helpful," she says. Luckily, as soon as one of her teachers found out how good Diana's English really was, Diana was moved into the regular track.

But Diana was dealing not only with educational displacement but ethnic culture shock. "In the ninth grade, there was only my Mexican friends . . . and we felt a little inferior to the rest." In her opinion, the Mexican kids broke down into two cliques: the "Mexican Mexicans," or hard-working immigrants, and the "little gangsters," or tough, Americanized teens. She hung out with the former—until tenth grade, when she went to Fremont and joined the Media Academy. There she made friends of several races. "When I got to Fremont there was African Americans, Asians, and Mexicans and everybody hangs out together and it was cool," she says.

What is heartbreaking to Diana today is that, though she loves school, she has little hope of continuing her education. She remembers a time that her teacher was leading them through an exercise in filling out college applications. "Everybody was like: 'Oh, I want to go to this place and I wanna go such and such and oh, my grades are good and everything.' My teacher was like, 'Aren't you going to fill out your applications?' And I was like, 'What for?'" Another girl in the class asked the question Diana was desperate to, but just couldn't. "What if you're not a legal resident?" Her teacher said to leave the Social Security number slot blank, but Diana says, dejected, "I didn't want to continue it."

The passage of Proposition 187 during Diana's junior year made the issues seem even more overwhelming. "I felt, Oh God, here goes another barrier. I'm trying to get over these little things and now here comes this big one." She's already experienced difficulty getting services. When she had a bad tooth, she went to the local clinic. They told her they could no longer help her if she didn't have a Social Security number. "My mom was like, 'We'll pay,' but no, she's like, 'We're sorry and everything is frozen until we get more orders.' "

As we drive through Oakland, she points out the tiny auto repair shop her father runs, nestled in an alley off of the East Fourteenth Street corridor. Her house, on a block of modest but well-kept homes with front and backyards, is filled with worn-out used furniture. Her mother, a warm, friendly woman who speaks little English, sits in the kitchen feeding an infant she babysits for extra cash. Her three younger siblings— adorable mischievous imps—run in and out of the house with their friends. Her youngest brother, who's five, doesn't have legal status, but her two middle siblings, both in elementary school, are U.S. citizens because they were born while her family was living in Chico. In California alone there are hundreds of thousands of families with mixed legal status (where some family members have green cards or citizenship and others have neither). Diana tries not to, but sometimes she resents the freedom that her two siblings have for being citizens. To her, their futures seem open, boundless; her own seems closed.

Still, "Regardless of all the barriers that are put between you and other people, America *is* the Land of Opportunity," says Diana. "No matter where you go, you will never find another place where even when you're not legal you can still get a job that pays you. There's no other place like it. In Mexico you can't even get a job. You depend on the crops on your land and live on what grows. There's nowhere for you to go, no McDonald's for you to hang out at. To me, it's better in America."

Mexicanizing America?

The unspoken fear that underlies much of our policy about the border is that an influx of immigrants will "Mexicanize" America. But my journey through El Paso illustrates the complex culture of Mexican Americans, and just how unfounded the fears about "Mexicanization" are. Those living on the U.S.-Mexican border face some difficult political and economic questions: whether Americans can compete with the low-wage workers in Mexico; whether Washington lawmakers can truly understand the issues facing Americans on the border; and, for Mexican Americans in particular, whether they should feel some connection to the problems facing Mexicans, or simply focus on their own issues. The influence of Mexican culture on America's should be seen as part of a continuum. Just as every immigration wave has shaped this country, so will the rise of the Latino population. In a best-case scenario, border towns like El Paso would help foster a rich appreciation for Mexican culture as *part* of American-style diversity. Silvestre Reyes describes his hopes for the next generation as quite literally out of this world. "You hope that someday you get to the point where *Star Trek* is today," he says. "That someday it doesn't matter who you are or what you look like or what your name is, but the important thing is that you're working in harmony."

IV

Predictions

and

Prescriptions

Toward a More Perfect Union: Ideas, Projections, and Solutions

While writing this book, I've been asked one question over and over: "Well, how is it? Are things getting better or worse?"

I've been to countless states, cities, and counties; interviewed hundreds of teens, twentysomethings, teachers, politicians, and experts. Of all the questions about race I have a reasonable chance of answering, "better or worse?" isn't on the list. We in America have an obsession with quantifying intangibles, giving every big issue a simple thumbs-up or a thumbs-down. You can measure aspects of race by standards ranging from high school graduation rates to hate crimes to infant mortality. You might be able to say that each category has gotten better or worse, but it's virtually impossible to put a blanket label on race in American life.

Race Is What We Make It

What we can do—and, I argue, what we should do—is look for ways to improve racial equality in America. It's a lot more useful to ask "How can I make things better?" than "Why are things so bad?"

In the past thirty years, we have gotten used to thinking of racial problems as insurmountable. After the hard-won victories of the Civil Rights movement, America entered a stage of confusion and complacency. Some Americans thought we had done all we needed to correct racial inequalities. Others saw the need for more changes but didn't know how to proceed. Yet others continued to fight against integration and racial equality, using new legal and social tactics. So now, at the turn of the millennium, many of us assume that racial problems are entrenched and impossible to fix. That's true only if we believe it.

Among the things we need to develop are new strategies for dealing with race and a renewed commitment to addressing our problems. The Civil Rights movement was the right solution at the right time. Now we need to find the right solutions for our time. I say solutions, because as the country has become more diverse, so has the range of issues we face. But none of these challenges is insurmountable, from educating children who don't speak English to combating the anti-"minority" prejudice in many homes and communities. The Southern Poverty Law Center in Montgomery, Alabama, runs a program called Teaching Tolerance. They distribute free materials to schools across the country, helping teachers lead constructive discussions on race and prejudice. In addition to the bilingual education programs in America that *don't* work, some are working wonderfully. And programs like the Fremont Media Academy in Oakland (Chapter 7) show how it's possible to have a high-level academic program that succeeds with at-risk urban kids.

We're so used to hearing about the failures of race in America—and there are many—that perhaps we need to reacquaint ourselves with some of the hard work that produces success. In the course of writing this book, I visited several programs across the country that are dealing with the issues of race and youth directly. All of them offer us different perspectives on ways to improve race relations for the next generation.

The Newcomer School

When New York City's Department of Education was planning its Newcomer School—one designed to educate immigrants and integrate them into American life—the chancellor realized his plans were ambitious. A 1995 *New York Times* article said: "Most other such programs offer a mix of classes in English and classes in a student's native language. . . . [Schools chancellor] Mr. [Rudy] Cortines proposes to offer, in addition to English language instruction, bilingual education in all major subjects—math, science, and social studies—in as many as 10 languages. He did, however, acknowledge in an interview that it would be difficult to find, say, a Bengali-speaking science teacher, and that he might have to scale back his ambitions."[1]

Less than a year later, in a neatly arranged classroom in Long Island City, Queens, I meet Mohammed Ali. He is a Bengali-speaking science teacher who is tutoring some of his dedicated students the week before winter break. A dignified, slightly stiff fortysomething gentleman attired in a suit, Ali teaches math and science to South Asian students. He speaks English, Bengali, Hindi, Urdu, and Punjabi. In New York City, when it comes to the breadth and diversity of the immigrant community, no expectation can be too grand.

Ali appreciates the fledgling Newcomer School for going beyond the typical boundaries of bilingual education—which tends to be focused on Spanish speakers. "I have to give my lecture in English and then their native languages. They have more progress . . . [when] I can use the native language and they can correlate that with English," he says. He says his students are "happy" to have found a place where their limited English proficiency is not mistaken for low academic ability. In addition to making sure his ninth- to eleventh-grade students learn their biology and math lessons, he also advises the Bengali Club.

Queens, the borough where the school is located, has a minority white population and high numbers of immigrants from virtually every continent of the world. Nationwide, there are over 3 million students with limited English proficiency, and the number of school-aged immigrants could double in the next twenty years. Despite the obvious need for some kind of educational strategy for dealing with education, the plan was controversial. In the past decade "newcomer schools" have come under attack for segregating immigrant children from the native-born population. The oldest such school is San Francisco's, founded in 1979; now there are schools in Dallas, Los Angeles, and Miami as well as New York. San Francisco puts a one-year limit on attending a "newcomer school"; New York's plan was contested because there's no limit on how long students can attend.[2]

Bilingual education itself is also a hotly contested strategy. For example, during the 1996 presidential race, Republican Senator Bob Dole proposed a federal "English only" law (twenty-two states already have one) to eliminate support for most bilingual education programs. Though President Bill Clinton has supported bilingual education, as governor of Arkansas he signed into effect an "English only" bill.[3] Says Ali, "I think bilingual education is good. There are students, they have a good [educational] background but they don't get a good grade because they're slowed down. It helps when they speak their own language. . . . We are to prepare them to go into the mainstream of the American society." He agrees with the goal of integrating the immigrant students into society, but says that "separate learning by language" is a necessary means of getting kids up to speed. And beyond that, the Newcomer School is integrated simply because it includes students from so many different cultures. "This is a community of world peace," he says. "If they [students of different backgrounds] know other, they get a good sense of each other."

The full spectrum of the Newcomer School's student body is represented in another classroom where English as a second language is being taught. The teacher calls everyone "Mr." or "Ms.," and though most of the students appear to be Spanish-speaking, others are East and South

Asian. "Ms. Kim, Ms. Sultana, Mr. Nawas!" the teacher calls on students in turn. Some of the kids carry little pocket Spanish-English electronic translators.

"Anybody here ever had a job besides Mr. Morillo? No?" he says. "You guys are lucky. After school, during the summer, you will have to have a job." Outside, snow swirls and eddies around the windows. Today's lesson is on the English you need to job hunt. "Where do you look for a job?"

"Payless," says one student.

"Payless?" asks another.

"A store," a third person says. The walls are covered with posters, most of them pertaining to classwork. One reads: BIAS. PREJUDICE. DISCRIMINATION. REPORT IT.

Another ESL class led by teacher Judy Sun includes students who speak Spanish, Chinese, Korean, Polish, and Albanian. Today the students have brought in pictures from home and have to describe in English the events behind the pictures. In yet another class, Miguel Pineda teaches math in Spanish; Claudia Fernandez, a round-faced girl with curly hair, asks me if I'm a new student. No, I say, adding that I don't speak Spanish but I'd like to learn. She smiles. "It's easy to learn Spanish." Today's lesson is on division, and the lowest common denominator (abbreviated MCD in Spanish). The two dozen students are animated, engaged. They laugh with Mr. Pineda—not at him—though because I can't speak Spanish I can't understand his jokes.

After checking out the classes, I go check out the cafeteria, always the nexis of social interaction. It's physically nondescript and a little dark; filled with the typical processed-food smells of any high school cafeteria. As in most city schools, many of the students have red books of tickets for free or reduced lunch. But the words that fill the room come from dozens of languages, and students mix across ethnic lines to a surprising degree, given that many have difficulty speaking to each other.

South Asians—Indians, Sri Lankans, Pakistanis—are a rapidly growing group in the nation, in New York City, and in Queens in particular. Three of the new South Asian immigrants are siblings Amna, Ali, and Rabab Tariq. Sixteen, fourteen, and seventeen years old respectively, they arrived in New York in July, just in time to get ready for the school year, and all speak English well. Amna is beautiful, slim, and soft-spoken—and just a bit too friendly to be seen as shy. "The teachers are wonderful. I like it," she says. Most of the students in her higher-level English classes are Hindi or Spanish speakers. It's the week before Christmas, and the ground is covered with the remnants of a massive snowfall. Her only complaint about America? "Here it's too cold," she says.

Ali is a popular, outgoing boy on the cusp of manhood; dark-skinned and wavy-haired, he speaks even better English than his sisters. He says he gleefully participated in a snowball fight—his first—and wants to become a doctor when he grows up. "I want to learn Spanish," he says. "A lot of my friend are Spanish and Chinese. They're a lot of fun to play with. And [knowing people from other countries] is the best way to learn English—we can't speak anything else." When I ask what he likes about the United States, he says: "I like that people have rights." He also appreciates the fact that his school is relatively free from strife. "One thing I like in this school is that they don't know anything about guns and weapons. In other schools they have metal detectors. It's sad and it's scary," he says.

Rabab, the oldest sibling, radiates a quiet self-confidence. She recently spoke at a conference titled "Struggle and Success: Celebrating Immigrant Women." "I want to be a professor," she says. "I want to do a lot of things. I want to be a reporter, a writer, go into higher education. Women are equal to men. . . . Our religion says you should always keep learning. I want to take statistics, math, economics in college." She sees success in America as a combination of "luck and opportunity. You have to learn English. If you come to America and don't learn English you can only do a job in stores. It's not a life." Here, the teachers make sure that the students have the best opportunity they can to become English-proficient. "If you speak the wrong English, they understand. It's very easy to understand the cultures and the ideas."

Today, Rabab and Amna are dressed in traditional outfits for a schoolwide holiday celebration. As one might expect, it's a richly multiethnic affair. Students from different countries have signed up to sing, dance, and even model traditional outfits—something Rabab does. A group of the Chinese students files up to the front. One steps forward to introduce their performance: "We are going to sing three Chinese songs today. The first song is called 'My Chinese Heart.'" It goes: "No matter where we go/We will forever remember/The great wall, the Yangtze, the Yellow River/We will still have China in our heart." Two girls in baggy jeans, T-shirts, and bare feet do a Punjabi dance, one that looks like it might have picked up some hip-hop flava here in New York City. A teen models a Mexican cowboy outfit, and a group of Korean students follow, two of them dressed in the delicate, high-waisted, pastel traditional dresses.

This is precisely the kind of exchange that makes Lourdes Burrows, the principal of the Newcomer School, proud. "The mission of the school is to provide an environment to allow them to transition into this new culture. . . . This may be the first time a student comes in contact with other cultures. We really want to give them an opportunity to fall in love with America. It's not appropriate to say, 'This is America—take it or leave it.'" Burrows is herself a bilingual, immigrant Cuban American. She is proud of and committed to her chosen country and to bringing new immigrants into the fold. "From the beginning, we have infused activities that introduce them to the United States. We do the pledge of allegiance," she says. Her students' favorite subject? "English—the only language that they can use in common with each other."

Each week, the school gets twenty to twenty-five new immigrants. At the end of each year, the faculty will identify which students can and should be mainstreamed into the borough's other high schools. "I can't change the world but I can change a little bit of it," she says, though she sometimes worries about the anti-immigrant sentiment sweeping through the nation. "It comes down to economics," she says. "People are afraid economically that we can't absorb these people. I don't want to think that people don't want to accept new cultures. . . . What does it take to be a good American?" she asks. "You have to have an employable skill. You have to be a good worker from an economic point of view. You must have social skills, to know how to get along with each other and resolve conflicts in a positive way. There's no place like the United States. But we're attacking each other instead of promoting unity."

Diversity in Service

Unity is precisely what the public service program City Year promotes, a program I was so impressed by that I joined their board. One of the organizations the federal service program Americorps was modeled after, City Year was founded in 1988 by Michael Brown and Alan Khazei, who attended Harvard Law School together. It began as a purely privately funded enterprise, garnering support from local businesses. Its mission? To give rich and poor, suburban and urban teens and twentysomethings a chance to live and work together while doing service, like helping as classroom aides in public schools or renovating housing. City Year has also benefited from establishing partnerships with major corporations, including BankBoston and Timberland (which supplies them with clothes as well as cash). It's part of a trend called "cause-related marketing," where corporations bask in the glow of doing good—which sometimes pulls customers into the stores and increases their bottom line.[4] The participants received a modest (even skimpy) $100 a week as a living allowance and a $5,000 scholarship upon completion. Today, though the allowance has gone up to $135 per week, most participants have a second job or live with their parents, or both in order to make ends meet.

Elizabeth, a blond-haired Bostonian from a well-off suburban family, works as a cashier at a liquor store in order to stay afloat—and her parents still help her out with the rent on her apartment. A prep-school and college grad, she's hoping to enter medical school in the fall. For the past year, she's been working side by side, day after day, with everyone from high-school dropouts to other college grads. Today, City Year is in nine cities and has over seven hundred participants.

I meet Elizabeth at City Year's 1997 annual conference in Providence, Rhode Island, one at which First Lady Hillary Rodham Clinton spoke. One hallmark of the program is not simply pulling in participants from all walks of life but also giving young adults responsibility for administering the program. One of the organization's board members is former participant Marilyn Concepcion. Born in Puerto Rico, Concepcion was a high school dropout who joined City Year, where she earned her GED, and established such a strong track record that she was later accepted as a student at Brown University.[5] And City Year Providence's executive director of two years, Matthew Brown, is just twenty-seven years old. In an interview with the local paper, Brown said: "You know, Americans don't hesitate . . . to send eighteen-year-olds to die and fight in war to protect the country. That's a very serious responsibility to give them. It's their lives, their friends' lives. It's the future of the country. But for some reason, we haven't given them the responsibility or challenged them to take care of their own community, to be on the front lines in our cities in America. And City Year is taking them seriously like the military does, and saying, 'You're seventeen, eighteen, nineteen years old. You're serious people. You've got serious solutions. And you're the unique group to lead in this country.' And we simply give them the tools to do it. We put them on teams. We're giving them experienced leadership. We're connecting them with good solid community partners. . . . And then they go in and lead . . . and get this work done." He continued, "The number one thing we do is to tutor or mentor children, in their academics—reading, we do a lot of work with ESL kids, because every City Year team has three or four languages spoken. . . . There's a real need there in terms of diversity. We often hear from teachers that not just the ethnic diversity, but the fact that half of every team is men . . . to have male mentors is extraordinary for these kids. They're showing by example you can make a difference, you can work on a team."[6]

I went to the 1996 annual conference as well and got a firsthand look at how City Year corps members interact. Ludmia (Luddie) St. Jean is a gleeful Haitian immigrant with a gap-toothed smile and hair pulled into a ponytail high on her head. She dropped out of high school and then heard about City Year; her boyfriend, Heath, whom she met in the program, is twenty-four years old and white. Like many of the other participants, Heath has a second job—hauling around kegs of beer at a liquor warehouse. "It's good because it's brainless," he says. Most days, Heath works until five-thirty for City Year and then from six to ten at the liquor store. "I don't know how he does it," Luddie says. Though City Year has a good track record of encouraging racial dialogue, Luddie says she's gotten a lot of shit for dating Heath. "When people found out, half of them stopped talking to me. Especially the Haitian guys. We used to hang out all the time," she says.

The troops arrayed for the national conference include teens with disabilities (one with foreshortened arms; another in a motorized wheelchair) and kids for whom this conference is the first time they've ever been out of state. One of the latter is Kristy, a white teen wearing rainbow gay-pride freedom rings entwined around her neck like a choker. Born and raised in Columbus, Ohio, where she's a corps member, she's psyched to take her first trip out of Ohio, though she's not a big fan of her first airplane flight. "It's unnatural," she scowls. What I see as merely a well-run event—with the corps members parading through Boston's downtown, then massing on the steps of the state house—is a life-changing experience for some of the participants.

The day following the rally, I go with a team of corps members and speakers to a service project in Charlestown, traditionally a bastion of white poor and working-class antiblack sentiment. Nowadays, young professionals are moving in and rehabbing the old townhouses. One of the spiffy rehabs even flies the gay rights rainbow flag. We pull up in front of a school near the Bunker Hill housing project, the biggest in the city. The low-rise housing projects are integrated—thus, so is the school, which has blacks, whites, and Asians seemingly getting along just fine. Corps members help tutor kids in the school, and today they're rebuilding a playground for the elementary school students.

The program, which generally has a good record of private fundraising, has hit some bumps along the way: it had to repay a quarter of a million dollars in federal funds slated for scholarships after not being able to account for the money properly, and though all high school dropouts in the program are supposed to get a GED (high-school equivalency) certificate, one report says two-thirds have not.[7] But it works hard to make sure that their mission of achievement and diversity continue. One of the team leaders tells me that 80 percent of the applicants are suburban white females. To get a mixed demographic, they work hard to recruit nonwhites and low-income participants—and to deal with the issues corps members walk through the door with, be that single parenthood or drug abuse. One of the proudest moments of the 1997 ceremony was when the year's GED recipients got up on stage to receive a token of appreciation for the work they'd done in continuing their education. Charlie Rose, a City Year coordinator who received a GED himself, passes out the certificates. And as the corps members clap ceaselessly, some of them standing, others shouting, a group of over thirty former high school dropouts—male and female, black, white, and Latino—stand and take a bow.

From Gang to GED

Many of the participants in the Community Build/Youth Fair Chance program in South Central Los Angeles are trying to get their GEDs as well. They are trying to overcome drug use, gang membership, shootings, and lack of education and opportunity. The force behind the program is Maxine Waters, the dedicated congresswoman serving South Central L.A. Waters spent fourteen years in the California State Assembly, where she helped divest state pension funds from apartheid-era South African businesses, before being elected to Congress in 1990. After the Rodney King verdict and the ensuing violence, she got the Clinton administration to help allocate $50 million for the Youth Fair Chance program, which offers educational assistance and job training for fourteen- to thirty-year-olds.[8]

South Central's Youth Fair Chance program occupies a couple of renovated buildings on an otherwise bleak stretch of Vermont Street. Classes are held in a room called the Maxine Waters Gallery. It has eight masks and sculptures and three elaborate wall hangings in a conference room; in back are over a dozen computers. The building's hardly ornate, but there aren't many well-tended offices with blue industrial carpet in South Central. The signs on the store across the street say it all. One of the walls of the deli catercorner advertises drive-in liquor; a billboard on the same face asks, PREGNANT?

Rochelle's been through three pregnancies and she's only eighteen years old. An attractive, neatly dressed, curvaceous black woman with thick blond braid extensions, she has an infant of four months, a son who's four years old and a two-year-old nestled in between. She usually brings one or more of them to class with her. Her boyfriend is in his thirties; his oldest child is her age. Though she has a remarkable presence, even warmth, about her, she's used to being disappointed. I ask for her phone number so I can call and do a follow-up interview. "You gonna call?" she asks. "Because a lot of people say they're gonna call and they don't." By the time I do call, her phone number has been disconnected.

Daily lessons at Youth Fair Chance may include everything from tips on applying for a job to how to deal with interpersonal conflict, particularly between blacks and Latinos. South Central and Watts are two historically black Los Angeles areas that have become heavily Latino over the past two decades. Though there is political and interpersonal tension between blacks and Latinos in South Central, all of the participants in Youth Fair Chance (and all of them are either black or Latino) get along. Some of the black students consider "African" to be a better signifier for them than "black"; Wendy, a pregnant Salvadoran immigrant, considers herself a Chicana. None of them professes any discomfort with the fact that South Central is now at a racial crossroads, with half the business placards in English and half in Spanish, and the population split along roughly the same line. "I like the things you do," says Denzel, a stocky but baby-faced black man, to Wendy. "All of you [i.e., Latinos] are staying in one apartment [to save money]. They should be able to come over here free, just like we go over there. I don't think there should be a border." Wendy expresses her doubts about life in the United States: "I'm going to get my money together and go back to my country. White people blame us all on us"—that is, anytime a Latino does something wrong, everyone of the same ethnicity is suspect. "We'll work for two dollars an hour on the border. If we wasn't working, we wouldn't be here."

The classroom is filled not only with teens and twentysomethings but with their children. Most of the participants in Youth Fair Chance have sons or daughters, whether they have custody or not. One of the days I attend, the room has eleven adults and four of their children. Brother Torre, the class leader, turns the topic to violence, asking how many people in the room have been shot at or actually shot. Five of the men in the room raise their hands. One of them, Damon, says, "Hit. Hit."

"It don't change nothin'," says Denzel. "You just keep going. . . . Ain't no police safe," he says. Not even black police. He does trust one policeman: "Officer Lockett. I was on a drill team. He gets to know you, plays ball with you, gets on a first-name basis." But in the next sentence he recounts an encounter he and his friends had at the mall. A girl he was with was mad at someone and yelled at them—but when the police heard, "They pushed her up against the wall and broke her arm. I don't trust no police," Denzel says. "I don't trust nobody."

Jonathan, a heavily muscled handsome man with a shaved head who carries a box of candy around to sell for pocket change, says, "If you gonna wait for somebody to solve your problems, you gonna be waiting a long time."

Denzel replies, "I'm not waiting for anybody. I'm about to uplift myself. If he [Clinton is] some kinda president, why is he cutting welfare and the programs to lift people out? Clinton—he's cute"—that is, facile. Says Damon, "It doesn't matter if he is black, white, Korean, Indian. Him being in the political system, he is corrupt." The talk moves to rap music. "Even though they cuss a lot sometimes if you listen sometimes they be telling you the truth," says Denzel. Jonathan disagrees. "I'm twenty-seven but what about the kids. They'll listen [to rap's messages]. If I get out there to gang banging again, I'm making a difference. If I go up there and buy a bunch of rap records, I'm not any better than the people who are singing it."

I come back on Friday of that week for a potluck lunch that accompanies their "graduation" from the life skills course at Youth Fair Chance. Everyone brings in soda or napkins or a homemade dish—chicken, rice and beans, dessert. Today is "job interview" day, where another of their instructors, Carlos Rendon who's worn a suit for the occasion, runs them through the paces of applying for a job. Use "I'm between jobs" instead of "I'm unemployed," he advises. If you're nervous, "Wiggle your toes, wiggle your fingers, but don't let the employer see you," he says. "Should we do that homeboy [hand] shake?" he asks, meaning the elaborate hand-gymnastics used as greeting in the 'hood.

"No," everyone says in chorus.

After one of the classes, I go sit out on a curbside with Jonathan, a.k.a. Bubbe Dog of the Mad Swans, part of the Bloods gang. The twenty-seven-year-old no longer belongs to the Bloods, one of the most dangerous and influential gangs in Los Angeles, but his membership from the age of thirteen has shaped—some might say destroyed—his entire life. Now he's trying to turn it around.

He describes his neighborhood on Eighty-fourth as one where kids were routinely expected to join the gang life. All three of his older brothers were in the life, and the "homies"—his brother's gang brothers—

expected him to sign up as soon as he had facial hair. So I'm surprised by his firm answer when I ask him if he had a choice in the path he pursued. "You always have a choice. . . . When I was coming up . . . some of my homies, some of them would tell me to go to school. I was fifteen, sixteen, seventeen. Some of them, they was almost in their thirties. It was always my own stubbornness in being stupid and go on my own way. . . . I thought it was more like the mafia. I thought it was cool. I thought there was honor in there. But it wasn't," he says. "It's changed a great deal basically because of the drugs. It's more money in it . . . [and] it's no more honor in it. It's no loyalty."

Back in the day, Bubbe Dog (his sister called him "Bubbe" back when she couldn't pronounce "brother") used to pull robberies and break into houses. The dope flooded the gang scene; Jonathan dealt and began to use himself. "Only drugs I haven't had was heroin and pills. I sniffed, and I freebased, and I drunk alcohol like water. And a lot of it has to do with why I got shot and why I done a lot of the things I done. But I had a conscious choice in everything I done. . . . I had four brothers. One of them's dead. Two of 'ems in the pen." Jonathan first went to the state penitentiary in 1988, just after he'd turned eighteen. "I started seeing a lot of things change. You done did so much for the neighborhood and then you call back, your family ain't got much money, so you call back and ask your homies for some money [for your family]. You don't ask for much. Twenty dollars. Fifty dollars. But they don't want to send you nothing. You know, so it's like, man, I thought we was homies. So I get out. I'm not tripping."

Jonathan last got out of jail two months ago, after a parole violation. He describes it as a place without opportunities to take any educational classes, a place where forced sex was common and drugs were easily available. "Sodom and Gomorrah," he says. Now he claims he's not only out of jail but out of the gang life. "I'm like, forget it. It's not worth it. I've seen too many homies die. One of my brothers is dead. Folks like, brains splattered all over the ground. I got a plate in my hip, and eight pins and buckshot wounds and other wounds. And it ain't gonna get you nowhere but life in prison or dead in the grave. And end up in hell, if you ain't right with God." He went into the penitentiary four times. "The first time I went to the pen was for robbery. The second time I went was for a violation. I didn't report [to my parole officer] and I started using drugs. And I had a stolen card. The third time was arson. I did three and a half years on that one." Most recently he did five months for not reporting to his parole officer. In between his periods of incarceration, which have eaten up his manhood, the nearly ten years between his first incarceration and the present day, he fathered two children by two different women: both sons, one five, one a year old. Though he wants to stay out of the life for good and be a solid father to his children, it's hard making ends meet. "I sell candy and they give me fifty dollars a week for my school supplies.

"I get impatient sometimes. I've been in the pen four times. I got two felony convictions—robbery and arson. I'm an ex-gang member. And I'm black. So I mean, who wants to hire me? Though everything I've done I've done for a reason. I'm going to get my GED, that will look good on my record. I'm trying to get a job, get some skills somewhere.

"I know what it is to be addicted to dope. I know what it is to gang bang. I know what it is to be shot. I know what it is to be locked up mentally, physically, and spiritually. And I wouldn't want nobody else to go that. The person that killed my brother, I wouldn't even want that for them. You know, people look at me like I'm crazy . . . when I say I would sit down and eat with that person. What I'm going to do, kill him or something? What I'm gonna get out of that? My brother not going to come back and kick it with me. He dead! He got it. Now I lie to go to hell if I get killed. It's just a waste of time. It's just a waste of time." He repeats that final phrase, again and again and again.

A Few Predictions

Groups like City Year, the Newcomer School, and Youth Fair Chance are doing the hard work of dealing with race and inequality. The success of efforts like these, as well as the efforts we each make in our own lives, will have a huge impact on how America changes in the coming centuries.

None of us knows exactly where we'll be ten or twenty or fifty years from now, despite the census's impressive demographic predictions. The economic downturn in countries around the globe during 1998 could make it more or less likely for some groups of people to immigrate. The birthrates of different groups are always subject to change, as are the laws and categories we use to define and shape race.

Still, I see a few trends worth noting. As Americans continue to intermarry, the size and influence of the multiracial community will grow. Over time, the decisions they make about how to classify themselves will reshape the racial landscape. Black Americans will start to develop a sense of ethnicity, as the number and variety of immigrants grow. At some point in the future, we will no longer assume that a black man or woman in this country has ancestors who were slaves. Some will have parents who came voluntarily from Ghana, or Cuba, or England. Asian and Latino Americans will cease to be foreigners in the eyes of many whites. As these communities grow, the sense of race as a black and white issue will diminish.

What about whites, or, as some put it, "whiteness"? Articles in publications including *The New York Times Magazine* have explored a discipline called Whiteness Studies. (There's even a Center for the Study of White American Culture in Roselle, New Jersey.) This discipline's practitioners try to examine what constitutes being "white" in America—advantages, disadvantages, and culture. The academic discipline may never become widespread, but the ideas are important. Looking at whiteness is a profound change from the way Americans usually look at race. Race is something that "minorities" have. Whiteness, in many Americans' minds, is the absence of race. As America becomes more multiracial, "whiteness" will become more of an issue. On the one hand, many white teens admire the cultural solidarity of other races. On the other, many feel they're being attacked because of their "skin privilege" or the transgressions of white Americans in the past. They will have to figure out how they feel about America's racial history and how they will position themselves on all the ongoing racial debates. This country will no longer permit any race to be seen as the absence of race, and young white Americans will seek to redefine their culture and their place in the society.

The redefinition of whiteness is a necessary part of the redefinition of race in America. Even though we have to do some collective soul searching in order to move forward, that could actually produce less racial self-consciousness. If we as a society move closer to providing equality of opportunity, we will have less reason to constantly compare and contrast the differences between the races. Some people advocate "color blindness" as a solution to our problems. I advocate "color equality." I can't forget I'm black—nor should I be encouraged to. I don't want others to forget it either. What I do want America to forget is the cultural stereotypes that are assigned to blackness. And what this country needs to learn is how to provide opportunity for all its citizens. If we can foster equality, the question of achieving "color blindness" will solve itself. There's no need to be color blind if we are not denoting some races as inferior.

We do not obey the laws of race. We make them. Now is the time for us to choose wisely what we will preserve about our racial and cultural history, and what destructive divisions we need to leave behind.

Afterword

Ten Ways to Deal with Diversity

Schools and organizations won't solve America's racial problems on their own. We all need to commit to doing our part in our own lives. In some ways, the greatest challenge we face in our fifty-year countdown to a "majority-minority" America is fear, and the greatest weapon we have is knowledge. Some suggestions on how to face our future:

1. Know the Facts About America's Diversity

It's always a hot topic of debate, but how much do we as a society really know about racial issues? According to an array of surveys, white Americans—who at this moment in time make up over three-quarters of the adult population—have an inaccurate view of how nonwhites fare in employment and education. Those misperceptions then contribute to their views on issues like the need for the government to address racial inequality. For example, a 1995 survey found most whites think blacks are doing as well or better than they are. In reality, the average white family earns 60 percent more than the average black family and is far more likely to have health insurance and be college educated. (Hispanics and Asian Americans were closer to the mark when estimating the black-white socioeconomic gap.) Those who thought blacks and whites were socioeconomic peers were most likely to reject the need for programs dealing with racial discrimination. In addition, all Americans, regardless of race, have a hard time accurately pinpointing the nation's racial demographics. A 1990 Gallup poll found: "[T]he average American thinks that America is 32 percent black, 21 percent Hispanic, and 18 percent Jewish—although the actual figures are 12 percent black, 8 percent Hispanic, and less than 3 percent Jewish." Another poll taken in 1995 found similar results. Most important, those who thought the nonwhite population was the biggest were the most adamant that we should try to restrict the growth of these ethnic groups.[1]

2. Demand Better Media Coverage of Race

Much of the coverage of race is shallow and sensationalistic, driven only by racial incidents and flashpoints, not by the need for a greater understanding of where we're headed as a nation. My first book, *Don't Believe the Hype: Fighting Cultural Misinformation About African Americans,* explored the ways in which the media portrayed blacks specifically. One of the most shocking measures of news bias came from a study that tracked a year's worth of network news coverage. Fully 60 percent of the coverage about blacks was negative, portraying victims, welfare dependents, and criminals.[2] The news and even the entertainment we read, listen to, and watch has a tremendous influence on our perception of societal problems. (Witness the link between overestimating the nonwhite population and political attitudes in the example above). It's essential to stay abreast of the political and social issues of the day, but we shouldn't be afraid of critiquing what we see. We need to demand more from the media's portrayals of race—and pay attention when journalists produce thoughtful work on the subject.

3. Foster Coalitions Among Nonwhite Groups

Particularly in urban areas, it's becoming increasingly likely that various nonwhite groups will share the same community. For example, South Asians and Latinos live next to each other in parts of Queens, New York, and Blacks, Latinos, and Asians share the same neighborhood in Oakland, California. But even though blacks, Latinos, Asians, and Native Americans often share common issues—whether it's the need to find creative ways of gaining political power for their constituency or to improve community housing—they don't have a good track record of joining together. (In New York, for example, black Americans and Caribbean immigrants have a tenuous alliance at best, as do Puerto Ricans and Dominicans.) Every city has groups trying to make a difference. A group of L.A. residents formed the MultiCultural Collaborative in response to the destruction following the Rodney King verdict—some of it specifically targeting Korean merchants. The steering committee includes members of the Korean, Latino, and black communities, and they've consistently critiqued mere "cosmetic rebuilding" after racial flareups. "There has not been a similar attempt to deal with the issues that lie under the surface of civil discord: racial disparity, poverty, neglect, police misconduct, and a failing public education system," the steering committee wrote in an open letter to the *Los Angeles Times*. Their suggestions include creating permanent infrastructures in the police department and other government divisions for dealing with racial issues, and using the schools to teach about race relations. They also applaud community groups that are able to bring together local residents of different races.[3] As America's nonwhite groups increasingly come together in common neighborhoods, it makes sense for them to develop a dialogue and political agenda that can only strengthen their collective power.

4. Foster Coalitions Between Whites and Nonwhites

Even more important than forming coalitions among different nonwhite groups is changing the often antagonistic politics between the racial majority (whites) and racial "minorities." At the highest echelons, American politics is still disproportionately white. For example, only one of the one hundred U.S. senators is black, and only one is Native American. (Only nine are female, even though women make up just over half of the U.S. population.) Politics is about coalition building, as when a Democrat or Republican sponsor of a bill pulls people from the other side to support a measure. But when it come to issues involving race, the small number of nonwhites in power finds it difficult to build large enough coalitions to influence policy. The same issues that play out on a national scale also factor into local and community interactions. In several states in the South, including Georgia, white suburban voters have rejected bond measures that would have funded the mostly black city schools. Of course, in the long run, education is the best way we have of fostering racial equality—something that will ultimately impact the white families as well as black. If America is to find a middle ground between ignoring diversity and panicking at its inexorable approach, America's racial and ethnic groups will have to learn to work together.

5. Don't Stop Dialogue Before It Starts

On an individual level, it's very easy for people of different races to have even a minor misunderstanding—and then conclude that they should just write off everyone of that race. Sometimes people unfamiliar with the customs or culture of another community can ask questions that seem rude—but are essentially well-intentioned. A woman I met at a conference recounted how she met one of her best friends: during a tense discussion about race. The woman, who is white, told a South Asian woman she thought Asians were beautiful and "exotic." The South Asian woman found the term "exotic" pejorative, as it's often been part of a sexual stereotype of seductive nonwhite women. But because the South Asian woman discussed her feelings rather than writing the other person off as small-minded, they were able to develop a close friendship. We certainly shouldn't tolerate outright bigotry, but when we get a negative impression of someone's racial understanding, we should find out if it's really bias or simply naïveté.

6. Follow Others' Lead in Defining Their Own Race and Community

Some Latinos hate the term "Hispanic," which they see as outdated and conservative; some Mexican Americans hate the term "Chicano," which they see as outdated and liberal. Some individuals of black and white parentage call themselves black; others biracial; and yet others refuse to label themselves at all. As time goes by, how we discuss race and ethnicity is bound to change, and will likely become more complex. As we negotiate what racial terms mean, it's essential to pay attention to the people with the most at stake—members of the individual communities.

7. Demand "Color Equality" Before "Color Blindness"

Segregation is still a pervasive problem in American society, most of all for blacks but also for virtually every other race. But does that mean we should attempt to overcome segregation and bias by demanding a "color blind" society—one where we talk less, think less, and certainly act without regard to race? The term "color blind" has become increasingly popular, but it avoids a couple of fundamental truths. If racial inequality is a problem, it's terribly difficult to deal with the problem by simply declaring we're all the same. As the first example in this section illustrates, those who perceive us as "the same"—regardless of the socio-economic realities—have less desire to change the status quo. Moreover, do we want to be the same, or equal? Who, for example, could envision New York without a Chinatown and a Little Italy? Many critics of multiculturalism see racial solidarity as isolating, even incompatible with racial equality. But it was precisely the racial solidarity shown, for example, by blacks during the Civil Rights movement that fostered the advances in racial equality we've seen thus far. If we do become a "color blind" society, let it be because we've conquered the problems of race—and not because we're blind to the facts.

8. Re-desegregate the School System

While there's no reason to fear constructive, voluntary ethnic solidarity, there's still great reason to fear involuntary segregation. America's neighborhoods are still segregated. A third of blacks live in racial "ghettos," with Latinos and Asians experiencing lesser degrees of segregation.[4] When it comes to teaching the next generation about race, schools play a crucial role—especially when the learning comes naturally, as a result of kids of different races being educated together. But that's always been a difficult proposition, and today it seems as if we've lost even our political will to try. Four decades after the *Brown v. Board of Education* ruling, over 60 percent of black students still attend segregated schools. In many municipalities, the statistics are getting worse, not better. The Supreme Court has consistently ruled in the past decade that even strategies like creating magnet programs in majority-minority schools could not be used as a desegregation strategy. It would be nothing less than a tragedy if at the precise moment we are becoming a more diverse country, we are steering children and teens into increasingly segregated schools.[5]

9. Reward Programs That Make Diversity a Part of Work and Learning

We tend to deal with race relations only in times of crisis: after the riots in the 1960s; after the Rodney King verdict, after corporate fiascos like the Denny's and Texaco discrimination suits. Dealing with the crisis (for example, when Texaco paid over $100 million to settle the suit with black employees) is costly, and not always very efficient. We need to begin to reward programs—in schools, in workplaces, in politics—that avoid the crisis mentality and deal consistently with issues of race. Some of the best examples are youth-oriented programs like City Year, which teach interracial relations as job and life skills, just as corporate managers learn to deal with interpersonal relationships as a part of their management training. Rather than putting out the fires of racial conflict, we'd do a lot better using training to "fireproof."

10. Anticipate the Unexpected

In my travels across the country for this book, I've met a teen who looks Asian and says he's black, blacks in integrated neighborhoods in Colorado who want to move back to more heavily black areas, and Latinos who favor clamping down on the border while whites crusade for greater tolerance of undocumented immigrants. I've never been disappointed when looking for new experiences or perspectives on America's racial diversity. I couldn't have predicted some of the things I'd find, but I tried to understand them.

The changes the next millennium brings will at the very least surpass and quite possibly shatter our current understanding of race, ethnicity, culture, and community. The real test of our strength will be how willing we are to go beyond the narrowness of our expectations, seek knowledge about the lives of those around us—and move forward with eagerness, not fear.

Notes

Chapter One: Race Right Now

1. Bureau of the Census, *Census of Population: 1950*, Vol. II, Pt. 1, U.S. Summary, Table 38, pp. 90–91, and Table 61, pp. 109–11, and *U.S. Census of Population: 1950*, Special Reports, "Nonwhite Population by Race," Table 2, p. 16; Table 3, p. 17; Table 4, p. 18; and Table 5, p. 19.

2. Bureau of the Census, *Statistical Abstract of the United States 1997*, Table 22, pp. 22–23.

3. Kristen A. Hansen and Carol S. Faber, "The Foreign-Born Population: 1996" (P-20-494) (Washington, D.C.: Bureau of the Census Public Information Office, 1997); CB95-155, Bureau of the Census, "Foreign Born Residents Highest Percentage of U.S. Population Since World War II," 29 August 1995. (Immigration accounted for 30 percent of U.S. population growth in 1994. However, only Asian Americans had a higher rate of international immigration than "natural increase," or births in the United States.)

4. *Post-Intelligencer* Staff News Services, "Clinton Hails Locke as a National Symbol," *Seattle Post-Intelligencer*, 5 February 1997.

5. Bureau of the Census, Current Population Reports, "National Population Projections Resident Population of the United States: Middle Series Projections, 2001–2005, by Sex, Race, and Hispanic Origin, with Median Age"; "Hispanic Population on Rise," *News & Observer* (Raleigh, N.C.), 7 August 1998, p. A-10.

6. Bureau of the Census, Current Population Reports, "National Population Projections Resident Population of the United States: Middle Series Projections, 2035–2050, by Sex, Race, and Hispanic Origin, with Median Age" (Washington, D.C., 1996).

7. Special Report, "Minorities in Congress," *Congressional Quarterly*, 4 January 1997, p. 28.

8. PR Newswire, "BBDO's 13th Annual Report on Black TV Viewing Finds Greater Disparity Between Viewing Preferences of Black and Total Households," 26 March 1998.

9. Clara E. Rodriguez, "Where Are Latinos? They're a Sizable U.S. Minority, but on TV They're Mostly Invisible," *Boston Globe*, 30 November 1997, p. D-4.

10. Robert Entman, "Representation and Reality in the Portrayal of Blacks on Network Television News," *Journalism Quarterly* 71, no. 3 (Autumn 1994): 509–20.

11. Farai Chideya, *Don't Believe the Hype* (New York: Plume/Penguin, 1995), pp. 9–10, 193, 211.

12. Bureau of the Census, *Statistical Abstract of the United States 1997*, Table 22, pp. 22–23.

13. Nick Charles et al., "Rap Inc.: A Hip Hop Connection from the Bronx to the World," *New York Daily News*, 1 April 1997, p. 6; People for the American Way, *Democracy's Next Generation II: A Study of American Youth on Race* (Washington, D.C.: People for the American Way, 1992).

14. *Merriam-Webster's Collegiate Dictionary,* 10th ed. (Springfield, Mass.: Merriam-Webster Inc., 1993), p. 398.

15. Nick Charles et al., "Rap Inc.: A Hip Hop Connection from the Bronx to the World," *New York Daily News*, 1 April 1997, p. 6.

16. Scott Shepard (Cox News Service), "The Black and White Thing Still Dominates," *Wisconsin State Journal*, 3 September 1997, p. 1–A.

17. Ibid.

18. Tom W. Smith, *Ethnic Images* (Chicago: National Opinion Research Center, University of Chicago, 1990).

19. Brian E. Albrecht, "Welfare Cuts Take Toll on Refugees: Reform Restricts Assistance Legal Immigrants Can Get," *Cleveland Plain Dealer*, 1 March 1998.

20. Sue Anne Pressley, "Texas Students, Faculty Protest Racial Remarks," *Washington Post*, 17 September 1997, p. A-3.

21. Patricia Williams, "Postcard from Heathrow," *The Nation*, 5 May 1997, p. 8.

22. Chideya, pp. 198–99.

23. David Gates, "White Male Paranoia," *Newsweek*, 29 March 1993, p. 48.

24. Dinesh D'Souza, *The End of Racism* (New York: The Free Press, 1995).

25. Peter Brimelow, *Alien Nation: Common Sense About America's Immigration Disaster* (New York: Random House, 1995).

26. Bob Peterson, "Teacher of the Year Gives Vouchers a Failing Grade," *The Progressive,* April 1997, p. 20.

27. John Leo, "A Generation Worse than Skinheads: Multiculturalism Creates a Culture Without Any Judgment," *Charleston Daily Mail,* 16 July 1997, p. 4A.

28. Peter T. Kilborn, "For Many in Work Force, 'Glass Ceiling' Still Exists,' *New York Times,* 16 March 1995, p. A22.

29. Gates, p. 48.

30. Bureau of the Census, "No. 49, Social and Economic Characteristics of the White and Black Populations: 1980 to 1995," p. 48; "No. 50, Social and Economic Characteristics of the Asian and Pacific Islander Population: 1990 and 1995," p. 49; "No. 52, Social and Economic Characteristics of the American Indian Population: 1990," p. 50; "No. 53, Social and Economic Characteristics of the Hispanic Population: 1995," p. 51; *The Statistical Abstract of the United States: 1996,* online ed. (Washington, D.C., 1997).

31. Frank A. Aukofer, "Urban League Data Point to Poverty," *Milwaukee Journal Sentinel,* 23 November 1996, p. 6.

32. Richard Morin, "A Distorted Image of Minorities," *Washington Post,* 8 October, 1995, p. A1.

33. Drew Jubera, "Twentysomething: No Image in the Mirror," *Atlanta Journal and Constitution,* 10 June 1991, p. E1.

34. Cara Tanamachi, "Teens' Freedoms Dwindling Under New Laws," *Austin American-Statesman,* 24 May 1997, p. A1.

35. Richard Herrnstein and Charles Murray, *The Bell Curve* (New York: The Free Press, 1994), pp. 472–73.

36. William G. Bowen and Derek Bok, *The Shape of the River* (Princeton, N.J.: Princeton University Press, 1998).

37. John Iwasaki (*Seattle Post-Intelligencer*), "Study Says Whites Benefit from Affirmative Action," *Oregonian,* 28 January 1996.

38. Eugene Marino, "Media Coverage of Generation X Too Negative, Survey Says," *Rochester Democrat and Chronicle* and *Times-Union,* 28 November 1994.

39. Robert H. Bork, *Slouching Towards Gomorrah: Modern Liberalism and American Decline* (New York: ReganBooks/HarperCollins, 1996), p. 21.

40. Susan Mitchell, "The Next Baby Boom," *American Demographics*, October 1995, p. 22.

41. Jonathan Tilove, "True Colors," *Minneapolis Star Tribune*, 3 May 1992, p. 1E.

42. Steven A. Holmes (*New York Times*), "Census Bureau Grapples with Racial Categories," *Orange County Register*, 30 June 1998.

Chapter Two: "Other"

1. Stephen Jay Gould, *The Mismeasure of Man* (New York: Norton, 1996).

2. Nancy M. Gordon, "Prepared Statement of Nancy M. Gordon, Associate Director for Demographic Programs, U.S. Bureau of the Census, Before the House Committee on Government Reform and Oversight," Federal News Service, 23 April 1997; Haya El Nasser, "Measuring Race," *USA Today*, 8 May 1997, p. 1A.

3. Seth Schiesel and Robert L. Turner, "Is Race Obsolete?" *Boston Globe Magazine*, 22 September 1996, p. 13; Jonathan Tilove, "True Colors," *Minneapolis Star Tribune*, 3 May 1992, p. 1E.

4. Dinitia Smith and Nicolas Wade, "DNA Test Finds Evidence of Jefferson Child by Slave," *New York Times*, 1 November 1998.

5. Antonio McDaniel, "The Dynamic Racial Composition of the United States," *Daedalus* 124, no. 1 (January 1995): 179.

6. Gabrielle Sandor (*American Demographics*), "Mixed Heritage Still Brings Problems," *Dallas Morning News*, 8 August 1994, p. 7C.

7. Nancy M. Gordon, "Prepared Statement of Nancy M. Gordon, Associate Director for Demographic Programs, U.S. Bureau of the Census, Before the House Committee on Government Reform and Oversight," Federal News Service, 23 April 1997.

8. Angela Ards, "The Multiracial Movement Raises Questions About Political Black Identity," *Village Voice*, 11 February 1997, p. 36.

9. Jonathan Tilove, "True Colors," *Minneapolis Star Tribune*, 3 May 1992, p. 1E.

10. Mike Nichols, "Firm's Minority Status Questioned," *Milwaukee Journal Sentinel*, 31 March 1997, p. 1.

11. Reuters, "De Klerk Tries to Close Chapter on Apartheid Rule," Reuters North American Wire, 21 August 1996.

12. Associated Press, "Clinton Touches Down in Africa," 23 March 1998; Caryle Murphy, "From Birth to Grave, South Africans Live with Race Label," *Washington Post*, 10 September 1978, p. A31; Robert Price, *Race and Reconciliation in the New South Africa* (Stoneham, England: Politics & Society, 1997).

13. Murphy, p. A31.

Chapter Three: Back to Antebellum

1. Klanwatch, "Intelligence Report," Special Year-End Edition 1992, 1993, 1994, 1995, and 1996 (Montgomery, Ala.: Southern Poverty Law Center, 1993, 1994, 1995, 1996, 1997).

2. Tom W. Smith, *Ethnic Images* (Chicago: National Opinion Research Center, University of Chicago, 1990).

Chapter Four: Hip-hop in the Heartland

1. Bureau of the Census, "1990 STF3 Extract Report: U.S. Counties," Delphi, Indiana, Chamber of Commerce.

2. Richard Roeper, "Nothing's Changed at N. Newton High," *Chicago Sun-Times,* 3 April 1994, p. 11; E. Jean Carroll, "The Return of the White Negro: Race Relations in Morocco, Indiana," *Esquire,* June 1994, p. 100.

3. Niki Cervantes, "4 Students Charged in Beating," *Buffalo News,* 16 January 1997, p. 4B.

4. Robin D. Givhan, "Soul Exchange: White Kids Who Want to Be Black See Fashion as a Way into African-American Culture," *Chicago Tribune,* 21 July 1993, p. 17.

5. Bureau of the Census, "1990 STF3 Extract Report: U.S. Counties," Delphi, Indiana, Chamber of Commerce.

6. Nick Charles et al., "Rap Inc.: A Hip Hop Connection from the Bronx to the World," *New York Daily News,* 1 April 1997, p. 6.

7. D. James Romero, "Column One: Influence of Hip-hop Resonates Worldwide," *Los Angeles Times,* 14 March 1997, p. A1.

8. Jannette L. Dates and William Barlow, eds., *Split Image: African-Americans in the Mass Media,* 2nd ed. (Washington, D.C.: Howard University Press, 1993), pp. 103–20.

9. John Leland, "Rap and Race," *Newsweek,* 29 June 1992, pp. 47–52.

10. David Samuels, "The Rap on Rap: The 'Black Music' That Isn't Either," *New Republic,* 11 November 1991, p. 24.

11. John Castellucci, "A Conversation With: Rap Music Authority Renea Henry," *Providence Journal-Bulletin,* 1 April 1996, p. 1C

12. Charles et al., p. 6.

13. Johnnie L. Roberts, "The World of Puff Daddy," *Newsweek,* 17 August 1998, p. 58.

14. Andrew Hacker, *Two Nations: Black and White, Separate, Hostile, Unequal* (New York: Scribners, 1992).

Chapter Five: A Nation Within a Nation

1. Kathy Lewis, "Tribal Leaders Share Race Concerns with Clinton," *Dallas Morning News*, 14 January 1998, p. 3-A.

2. Chris Carroll, "Indian Leaders: Most State Tribes Not Getting Rich," *Wausau* (WI) *Daily Herald*, 3 March 1998.

3. Kirsten A. Conover, "Tribal Colleges: Gains for 'Underfunded Miracles,' " *Christian Science Monitor*, 21 May 1997, p. 12.

4. Mary Beth Marklein, "Tribal Colleges Threatened: Recent Welfare Reform Jeopardizes Progress," *USA Today*, 21 May 1997, p. 3-D.

5. *The Bulletin's Frontrunner*, "Indians Oppose Burns' Plan on Tribal Jurisdiction," Bulletin's Broadfaxing Network, 29 January 1998.

Chapter Six: "Perfect" Diversity in an Imperfect World

1. James Kitfield, "Preference Prejudice," *Government Executive*, June 1995.

2. Census Public Information Office, "Table 6: Race and Hispanic Origin: 1990," *Colorado: General Population Characteristics* (Washington, D.C., 1992), pp. 21–22.

3. Paul R. Campbell, "Table 3: Projections of Population by Sex, Race and Hispanic Origin for Regions, Divisions and States: 1995 to 2025," *Population Projections for States by Age, Sex, Race, and Hispanic Origin: 1995 to 2025* (Washington, D.C.: Population Division, U.S. Bureau of the Census, 1996), p. 60, and overview on p. 1; Bureau of the Census: Claudette E. Bennett, *The Black Population in the United States: March 1992* (Washington, D.C., 1993).

4. Ann Scott Tyson, "How One Illinois Community Is Fighting 'White Flight,' " *Christian Science Monitor*, 21 July 1995, p. 1.

5. Douglas S. Massey and Nancy A. Denton, *American Apartheid* (Cambridge, Mass.: Harvard University Press, 1993), pp. 48, 57, 60–67, 76–77.

6. Alan Snel, "In the Spotlight: Local Principal Best in the U.S.," *Denver Post*, 18 January 1996, p. A-1.

7. Renate Robey, "Minorities Take Creek to Task: District Biased, Some Parents Say," *Denver Post*, 3 June 1996, p. A-1.

8. Stacie Oulton, "Feds to Probe Aurora's Minority-Suspension Rate," *Denver Post*, 9 April 1997, p. B-1.

9. Bill Vogrin, "The Dobson Effect," *Orange County Register*, 17 April 1997, p. E-1.

10. Mark Shaffer, "Colorado Grapples with Fallout from Anti-gay Ordinance," *Houston Chronicle*, 3 January 1993, p. A16.

11. "MCI Denies Regrets About Moving to Springs; *Wall St. Journal Story* Irks City, Firm," *Denver Post*, 30 June 1996, p. C-05.

12. Massey and Denton, pp. 80–93.

13. Ibid., p. 87.

14. The Committee on Policy for Racial Justice, *The Inclusive University* (Washington, D.C.: Joint Center for Political and Economic Studies, 1994), p. 42.

Chapter Seven: Good Kids and Bad Schools

1. Johnathan Tilove, "Minorities Fighting Each Other for Power," *New Orleans Times-Picayune*, 8 December 1996, p. A20.

2. *Location and Population Characteristics of the Oakland Unified School District*, Oakland Unified School District, Board of Education, 1997, p. 1.

3. Ibid.

4. Richard Herrnstein and Charles Murray, *The Bell Curve* (New York: The Free Press, 1994).

5. Peter Applebome, "War of Words," *New York Times*, 1 March 1997, p. 10; Chrisena Coleman, "Ebonics Foe to Join Board," *New York Daily News*, 2 January 1997.

6. Applebome, p. 10.

7. Judy Packer-Tursman, "Rescuing Urban Schools," *Pittsburgh Post–Gazette*, 18 March 1997, p. A9.

8. T. M. Smith et al., *The Condition of Education 1994*, Report NCES 94–149 (Washington, D.C.: U.S. Department of Education, 1994); and Bureau of the Census, "Social and Economic Characteristics—United States (1990 CP-2-1)," 1990 Census of Population (Washington, D.C.: U.S. Government Printing Office, 1993), cited in Carol J. De Vita and Kelvin M. Pollars, "Increasing Diversity of the U.S. Population," *Statistical Bulletin—Metropolitan Life Insurance Company*, 18 July 1996, p. 12.

9. Don Terry, "Latino Community Remains Divided over Future of Bilingual Education," New York Times News Service, 5 June 1998; Don Terry, "Bilingual Education Lives After All," *New York Times*, 3 October 1998. Both from online edition.

10. Judy Ronnigen, "U.S. Assails Oakland Schools," *San Francisco Chronicle*, 5 November 1993, p. A22.

Chapter Eight: The End of Affirmative Action

1. "Cal Today," University of California at Berkeley, recruiting brochure, 1995.

2. Troy Duster, "Individual Fairness, Group Preferences and the California Strategy," *Representations* 55 (Summer 1996): 41–58.

3. Ibid.

4. Bureau of the Census, "No. 49, Social and Economic Characteristics of the White and Black Populations: 1980 to 1995," p. 48; "No. 50, Social and Economic Characteristics of the Asian and Pacific Islander Population: 1990 and 1995," p. 49; *The Statistical Abstract of the United States: 1996*; online ed. (Washington, D.C., 1997).

5. Amy Wallace, "Thousands Rally at UC Campuses for Affirmative Action," *Los Angeles Times*, 13 October 1995, p. A1.

6. William Claiborne, "California Ban on Affirmative Action Cleared; State's Voter Initiative Goes into Effect Today," *Washington Post*, 28 August 1997, p. A-1.

7. Lance Williams, "Regents' Historic Vote," *San Francisco Examiner*, 21 July 1995, p. A1.

8. The Potomac Institute, *Affirmative Action: The Unrealized Goal* (Washington, D.C., 1973), 1; cited in The Committee on Policy for Racial Justice, *The Inclusive University* (Washington, D.C.: Joint Center for Political and Economic Studies Press, 1993), p. 15.

9. Bureau of the Census: Claudette E. Bennett, *The Black Population in the United States: March 1992* (Washington, D.C., 1993), p. 10.

10. Richard Herrnstein and Charles Murray, *The Bell Curve* (New York: The Free Press, 1994), pp. 317–40.

11. Associated Press, "Reverse Discrimination Complaints Rare, Labor Study Reports," *New York Times*, 31 March 1995, p. A23.

12. Donna St. George, "Rejecting Preference, Embracing Fairness?" *Philadelphia Inquirer*, 18 June 1995, p. E1.

13. William G. Bowen and Derek Bok, *The Shape of the River* (Princeton: Princeton University Press, 1998).

14. John Iwasaki (*Seattle Post-Intelligencer*), "Study Says Whites Benefit from Affirmative Action," *The Oregonian*, 28 January 1996.

15. Chang Lin Tien, "Update on Affirmative Action: A Message from Chancellor Tien," *The Berkeleyan*, 30 August–5 September 1995, p. 1AA.

16. Jesus Mena, "Update on Affirmative Action: Impact on Admissions," *The Berkeleyan*, 30 August–5 September 1995, p. 2AA.

17. "Universities Heading Back to Segregation, Researchers Warn," *Columbus Dispatch*, 13 April 1997, p. 3D.

18. Ralph Frammolino and Mark Gladstone, "UCLA Chief Admits Possible Favoritism," *Los Angeles Times*, 17 March 1996, p. A3.

19. Sharon Waxman, "Admissions Allegations Rock California," *Washington Post,* 11 April 1996, p. A3.

20. Suzanne Espinosa Solis, "Affirmative Action Critic Used His Minority Status," *San Francisco Chronicle,* 8 May 1995, p. A1.

21. George Will, "Court Ruling Could Change Everything," *Atlanta Constitution,* 28 March 1996, p. 22A.

22. Steven A. Holmes, "Programs Based on Race and Sex Are Challenged," *New York Times,* 16 March 1995, p. A1.

23. Peter T. Kilborn, "For Many in Work Force, 'Glass Ceiling' Still Exists," *New York Times,* 16 March 1995, p. A22.

24. Ibid.

25. Department of Health and Human Services, *Characteristics and Circumstances of AFDC Recipients: Fiscal Year 1991* (Washington D.C., 1993).

26. Dorothy Gilliam, "Damaging, Destructive Doublespeak," *Washington Post,* 17 June 1995, p. H1.

27. Donna St. George, "Rejecting Preference, Embracing Fairness?" *Philadelphia Inquirer,* 18 June 1995, p. E1.

28. Herrnstein and Murray, chapter 19.

29. Duster, pp. 41–58.

30. Ibid.

31. Connie Leslie with Pat Wingert and Farai Chideya, "A Rich Legacy of Preference," *Newsweek,* 24 June 1991, p. 59.

32. B. Drummond Ayres, Jr., "Conservatives Forge New Strategy to Challenge Affirmative Action," *New York Times,* 16 February 1995, p. A1.

Chapter Nine: Border Blues

1. Economist Newspaper Ltd., "Immigration: A Tale of Two Very Different States" *El Paso Herald-Post,* 15 July 1996, p. A-1.

2. Paul R. Campbell, "Population Projections for States by Age, Sex, Race, and Hispanic Origin: 1995 to 2025," Table 3, *Projections of the Population by Race and Hispanic Origin, for Regions, Divisions and States* (Washington, D.C.: Population Projections Branch, U.S. Bureau of the Census, 1996), p. 349.

3. Economist Newspaper Ltd., 1996.

4. Ibid.

5. Frank del Olmo, "Immigration Issue Is Too Complex for Simple Solutions," *Dallas Morning News*, 2 March 1997, p. 5J.

6. Joel Brinkley, "A Rare Success at the Border Brought Scant Official Praise," *New York Times*, 14 September 1994, p. A1.

7. Hugh Pearson, "Immigration and American Amnesia," *New York Newsday*, 8 August 1996, p. A42.

8. Border Rights Coalition, "Statistical Report of Abuse Complaints Made to BRC from El Paso Sector: January–December, 1995" (El Paso, Tex., 1996).

Chapter Ten: Toward a More Perfect Union

1. Pam Belluck, "Newcomer Schools Raise Old Questions," *New York Times*, 26 March 1995, p. 39.

2. Thomas Huang, "Schools for Immigrants Spread," *Dallas Morning News*, 12 January 1997, p. N05; Pam Belluck, "New to the U.S., Back in School," *New York Times*, 18 February 1996, p. 27.

3. Joyce Price, "English-Only Advocates Sense Momentum," *Washington Times*, 7 September 1995, p. A2; "Campaign English from Senator Dole," 10 September 1995; Margot Hornblower, "Putting Tongues in Cheek: Should Bilingual Education Be Silenced?" *Time*, 9 October 1995, p. 40.

4. Victoria Griffith, "All in a Good Cause—and Profitable," *Financial Times*, 12 May 1997, p. 12.

5. Scott MacKay, "Brown Student to Tell of Success," *Providence Journal-Bulletin*, 26 August 1996, p. 1A.

6. Ken Mingis, "A Conversation With: Matthew Brown of City Year," *Providence Journal-Bulletin*, 20 May 1997, p. 4C.

7. Kate Zernike and Adrian Walker, "City Year Slips as it Rushes to Grow," *Boston Globe* 18 August 1996, p. A1.

8. Pamela Johnson, "Toyota Salutes Congresswoman Maxine Waters," *Essence*, May 1996, p. 64; Paul Feldman, "Waters Lobbying Nets a $3-Million Windfall," *Los Angeles Times*, 12 September 1994, p. B1.

Afterword: Ten Ways to Deal with Diversity

1. Richard Morin, "A Distorted Image of Minorities," *Washington Post*, 8 October 1995, p. A1; George Gallup, Jr., and Dr. Frank Newport, "Americans Ignorant of Basic Census Facts," *The Gallup Poll Monthly*, March 1990, p. 2.

2. Robert Entman, "Representation and Reality in the Portrayal of Blacks on Network Television News," *Journalism Quarterly*, forthcoming.

3. Joe R. Hicks, Stewart Kwoh, and Frank Acosta, "Where's the Leadership on Race Relations?" *Los Angeles Times*, 29 March 1996, p. B9.

4. Douglas S. Massey and Nancy A. Denton, *American Apartheid* (Cambridge, Mass.: Harvard University Press, 1993), pp. 76–77.

5. James S. Kunen, "The End of Integration," *Time*, 29 April 1996, p. 38.

NEW HANOVER COUNTY PUBLIC LIB.

3 4200 00505 9924

DISCARDED
from
New Hanover County Public Library

NEW HANOVER COUNTY PUBLIC LIBRARY
201 Chestnut Street
Wilmington, N.C. 28401

GAYLORD S